Ruth

Ruth

A Somewhat Different Commentary

Edgar Stubbersfield

RESOURCE *Publications* • Eugene, Oregon

RUTH
A Somewhat Different Commentary

Copyright © 2021 Rachel Stubbersfield. All rights reserved. Except for brief quotations in critical publications or reviews, no part of this book may be reproduced in any manner without prior written permission from the publisher. Write: Permissions, Wipf and Stock Publishers, 199 W. 8th Ave., Suite 3, Eugene, OR 97401.

Resource Publications
An Imprint of Wipf and Stock Publishers
199 W. 8th Ave., Suite 3
Eugene, OR 97401

www.wipfandstock.com

PAPERBACK ISBN: 978-1-6667-1631-3
HARDCOVER ISBN: 978-1-6667-1632-0
EBOOK ISBN: 978-1-6667-1633-7

10/22/21

Scripture quotations taken from the (NASB®) New American Standard Bible®, Copyright © 1960, 1971, 1977, 1995, 2020 by The Lockman Foundation. Used by permission. All rights reserved.www.lockman.org

This commentary on the Book of Ruth is dedicated to Barry Garmeister, a farmer's farmer, a man who is acquainted with the providences of life and the weather. It is also dedicated to his wife, Leone, his equal in the gospel.

Contents

Abbreviations | ix
Introduction | xi

Chapter One | 1
Chapter Two | 40
Chapter Three | 80
Chapter Four | 112
Application | 148
Technical Matters | 151

Bibliography | 177

Abbreviations

AV	Authorized Version
GNB	Good News Bible
HCSB	Holman Christian Standard Bible
LXX	Septuagint
MT	Masoretic Text
NASB	New American Standard Bible
NEB	New English Bible
NIV	New International Version
NRSV	New Revised Standard Version
RSV	Revised Standard Version
RV	Revised Version
TWOT	*Theological Wordbook of the Old Testament.* 2 vols. Edited by by Gleason L Archer, Bruce K Waltke R. Lloyd Harris, Chicago: Moody, 1980.

Introduction

RUTH IS MY FAVORITE book in the Bible. I know it probably should be the Gospels as they talk of Jesus or perhaps a book with deep theology like Romans but, for all of that, it remains Ruth. I love it because there are no miracle workers, no triumphant generals and no kings' palaces. Instead, there are just simple country people with a real faith that allows them to do better than cope with all that God and nature can hurl at them. Granted, there are some major bumps along the way but in the end, they shine.

This is the life I know. I have lived my life in a small country town in the Lockyer Valley, a farming community in Queensland, Australia. I am a member of a Baptist church situated in the middle of a potato field. Despite the debilitating effects of drought continuing to be a constant shadow over the lives of friends, they live faithful lives. They testify to the same faithful God who was served in the little town of Bethlehem so many years ago, despite his face likewise often being hidden.

What then is the value of such a book when it doesn't deal with majestic themes? To quote a Rabbi of old, "This scroll [of Ruth] tells us nothing either of cleanliness or of uncleanliness, either of prohibition or permission. For what purpose then was it written? To teach how great is the reward of those who do deeds of kindness."[1] Kindness and ḥesed (a term that will be explained and illustrated as we progress through this book) can be given even by the poor. The book shows the power of blessing to "transform futility into fertility and despair into hope."[2]

---

1. Ruth Rabbah: 2:14.
2. Eskenazi and Frymer-Kensky, *Ruth*, L.

Introduction

It is universal practice to start a commentary with technical matters as an introduction which then colors our reading of the comments. In this case however, I suggest that you immerse yourself in this wonderful story first. There is a technical section at the end of the book which you may wish to turn to now, but why be a creature of habit? This commentary uses the Open English Bible but, where no translation of other books exist in this version, I have used the NASB.

The subtitle of this book is *A Somewhat Different Commentary*, so how is it different? This book was written with my small drought ravished community in mind and whenever possible I have tried to tie the lessons of Ruth back to the issues I see in my own community. It also is one with foreign farm workers, successful landholders, older godly women who no longer work but have influence and the issue of "who gets the farm".

Edgar (Ted) Stubbersfield

Note that the transliteration of the Hebrew in the body of the commentary is intentionally simplified.

Chapter One

¹In the time when the judges ruled, there was once a famine in the land. A man from Bethlehem in Judah took his wife and two sons to live in the territory of Moab.

IN CHAPTER 4 OF Ruth, we are presented with "perfect justice" where no good deed is left unrewarded, and all loose ends are tidied up. Yet justice was a commodity in short supply during the time of the Judges. The Book of Judges, with its lawlessness and sexual immorality, is more reminiscent of the Canaanites than descendants of Abraham! Instead of simply saying "in the time of the Judges," the writer deliberately uses the word twice which points us to more than the historical setting or the time of the story. The most vulnerable in society, women and children, were treated deplorably at that time. Despite that, or more likely, because of that, the double emphasis in the beginning sentence points us to a story which has as its concern, *mishpat* or "justice" which derives from the word to "judge" or "rule."[1]

The double reference can also be read as the judging of the judges,[2] pointing to a time when Israel rejected their rule either because they were rebellious, or the judges simply were not worthy of it.[3] This sentiment is very relevant in our society where respect for our elected and spiritual leaders has greatly diminished for similar reasons. In a postmodern age, a society that does not accept absolutes could likewise be compared with the people who did what was right in their own eyes (Judg 17:6; 18:1; 19:1; 21:25).

The Book of Judges pointed to the sad consequence of the power vacuum that arose from a time when there was no king. Four times the

---

1. Moore, *Joshua*, 309.
2. Ziegler, *Ruth*, 13.
3. Babylonian Talmud: B. Bat. 15b

lack of a king is mentioned (Judg 17:6; 18:1; 19:1; 21:25) and for the writer of Judges, this is the primary reason for Israel's poor state. The tribes are simply too weak on their own.[4] The deliberately vague timing of the book is in keeping "with the objective of the book itself, which presents Ruth as the solution to the entire era."[5] The book starts with that same power and moral vacuum where everybody did what was right in their own eyes and ends with the birth of the ancestor of Israel's greatest king. Despite that, it does challenge the belief that the lack of a king is the root of all their woes. Michael Moore summarizes the situation saying:

> In Judges 17–21, the major characters balk in the face of challenge. In Ruth, they persevere. In Judges, most of priests, landowners, husbands, wives, and warriors simply abandon their responsibilities. In Ruth, people usually shoulder their responsibilities, however burdensome. In Judges, men treat women insensitively, shamefully, even violently. In Ruth, men treat women like partners on a common mission. And there is no king here.[6]

In Judges, we see the direct hand of God in correcting his people, of violent premature death and raising up powerful deliverers. In our book, yes people die, but it is not through violence and injustice but apparently through natural means. God's hand in Ruth is seen in his control of the weather to judge and bless but also as, "he works quietly through the lives of ordinary people."[7] What will distinguish this book from Judges also is the prevalence of blessings.[8] Judges begins with blessings, continues with blessings and curses and deteriorates into mainly curses towards the end. By contrast, the Book of Ruth "turns a cursed society into one filled with blessing."[9]

While set in the time of the Judges, the Book of Ruth ties the patriarchal period with its unconditional covenant with Abraham to the time of the kings, with the later unconditional covenant with David. So, what are we to make of the intervening time when the conditional covenant with Moses was at the forefront? The Promised Land was not like other lands, as Israel was warned it would be more sensitive to the spiritual condition of the people (Lev 26; Deut 28). Daniel Block sees that through the establishment

4. Moore, *Ruth*, 295.
5. Ziegler, *Ruth*, 91.
6. Moore, *Ruth*, 295.
7. Block, *Ruth*, 50.
8. Block, *Ruth*, 50–51.
9. Ziegler, *Ruth*, 451.

of Israel as his covenant people and giving them Canaan, "YHWH sought to create a microcosm of the original creation order; so that the peoples of the world could see the transforming effects of divine grace and the replacement of the curse with divine blessing."[10] Unfortunately, instead of blessing, Judges shows a land in spiritual decline and often under the Lord's judgement. There was a famine in the land but "the Hebrew word . . . signifies far more than the absence of food; it can also signify a lack of morality and a widespread disobedience to God's will which leads to famine as a punishment."[11] That this extended meaning is intended, is inferred from verse six when Yahweh remembered his people. Like my own valley, there were no large watercourses like the Nile or the Euphrates so the population was dependent on the rain which should have seen a dependance on God who sent it, not a turning from him.

The Book of Ruth completes what has been called the "Bethlehem trilogy" and for those acquainted with the Book of Judges, the two mentions there of Bethlehem of Judah would immediately suggest a story that is not going to end well. Despite that, the story of Judah in the promised land started well. When the Patriarch Jacob blessed his children, the pre-eminence was given to Judah (Gen 49:8–12). In the history of the conquest, following Joshua's death, the Lord chose Judah as the first tribe to face the Canaanites (Judg 1:2). They were successful in capturing the hill country but not the plain. As for the rest of the tribes, there was far less success (Judg 1:21–36). Across the land as a whole, after the successes of the conquest, a second generation grew up who did not know the Lord or what he had done. They became a generation who did evil and worshipped Baals (Judg 2:10). Nowhere could the effects of this about-turn be seen more clearly than in the two mentions of Bethlehem in Judges.

Israel's spiritual life was in freefall. Chapters 2 to 16 of Judges describe a cycle of descending into apostasy. The Lord then punishes his people through oppression by their neighbors and then, when his people cry out to him, the Lord sends a deliverer. The people return to the Lord, at least for a while. The last five chapters climax with the tribes of Dan and Benjamin almost being eliminated and, in this, Bethlehem of Judah has a leading role in the story. Notably also, both stories involve Levites who should be setting the example but, here in Ruth, moral leadership will come from an old farmer and a widow from a cursed nation.

10. Block, *Ruth*, 107.
11. Weinstein, *Naomi's mission*, 46.

Dan moved into the far north of the land, establishing its own religion with a Levite from Bethlehem as its priest (Judg 17–18) and so entered into spiritual oblivion. A certain Levite, the husband of the concubine from Bethlehem, who had returned to her family home, started to take her back to his home at Mount Ephraim. He avoided staying in Jerusalem, at that time a Jebusite city, by pushing on to find refuge in a city of his own people (Judg 19:11–15). Following the murder of the concubine in that town, all Israel rose against the tribe. Again, the LORD chose Judah to lead the attack on Benjamin (Judg 20:18).

What the Levite found in Gibeah of Benjamin was not kindred souls but a wickedness so vile that it sealed them for destruction as it had for Sodom and Gomorrah (Judg 19–21). The similarities in both events and words are too striking for the accounts to be passed over as coincidental. All the prerequisites for God's judgement upon Israel and their eviction from the land, as they were warned in Deuteronomy 29 and 30, seem already to be in place. There was no way to provide for the continuation of the relationship broken by such sin. So, the question is, why, when the sins of "'Sodom and Gomorrah' are a catchphrase referring to a place of absolute evil that warrants their annihilation;"[12] is this national trauma yet hundreds of years off?

The Book of Ruth holds a mirror to the story of the Levite and his concubine and gives the background to a very different covenant not based on obedience. These similarities are examined further in my comments on chapter 2. In contrast to the conditional covenant with Israel and the conditional kingship of Saul, there was to come the promise of a permanent and unconditional dynasty (2 Sam 7:15; 1 Chr 17:13). There would be human punishment with rod and stripes, but not the divine punishment of the withdrawal of God's *hesed*.[13] This is one of the most important words in the Old Testament and as Daniel Block says:

> Its meaning cannot be captured with a single English word, because it incorporates an entire cluster of ethical and spiritual concepts: love, mercy, grace, kindness, goodness, benevolence, loyalty, and covenant faithfulness.[14]

---

12. Ziegler, *Ruth*, 45. Refer Isa 1:9–10; Jer 23:14; Amos 4:11; Zeph 2:9; Lam 4:6.
13. There is a detailed examination of this word in the chapter, *Technical Matters*.
14. Block, *Ruth*, 146.

When the kingdom was divided due to Solomon turning away from the Lord, the tribe of Benjamin stayed with Judah. Jerusalem, the capital, remained because of David's obedience to God (1 Kgs 11:34–36). Samaria, the capital of the northern kingdom, fell in 722 BC and the reason given was that, "They rejected His statutes and His covenant which He made with their fathers and His warnings with which He warned them. And they followed vanity and became vain, and went after the nations which surrounded them, concerning which the Lord had commanded them not to do like them" (2 Kgs 17:15 [NASB]). Yet even when the land of Judah was in a state of apostasy, it was not swept away because of David's sake (1 Kgs 15:4).

Katherine Sakenfeld observed this paradox saying, "The tradition of a covenant which insists that the people will lose the land for apostasy is held in tension with the historical and theological fact that the dynasty has survived despite its mixture of relatively good and bad kings." *Hesed* to David, "for the sake of David."[15] But if Divine *hesed* looks back to the obedience of David, surely, with a God who lives outside of time, it also looks forward to that same obedience. We see in Ruth the day-to-day ordering of the circumstances of and provision for the lives of David's ancestors and also the root of the character that would set him apart. It is even stronger than that. The Book of Ruth will depict his appearance as being orchestrated with the same providential care as was taken with the patriarchs, making it clear that he, not Saul, was Yahweh's choice.[16]

David cannot be seen as someone who catches the Lord's eye as he emerges by chance out of the fog of history, but rather as someone chosen and cultivated for this role over generations. Yet, if we are honest, the obedience of David falls far short of ideal obedience to deserve this unconditional *hesed*. He was a man of blood, and that blood was not just of his enemies but of his trusted servant, killed so he could have his wife. For someone totally worthy, we will have to wait for David's greatest son.

David's sin takes the Scriptures into uncharted territory. The law only provided for forgiveness for sins of ignorance, not acts of deliberate and extreme sin (Num 15:22–31). David's actions fell well outside of sin for which there was a sacrifice. His deep sorrow and repentance showed there was a way back from a broken relationship not given through Moses.

---

15. Sakenfeld, *Meaning*, 143–44.

16. Hubbard lists eleven similarities between Ruth and the Patriarchs/Matriarchs and Judah in particular, *Ruth*, 40, 42.

Ruth

Of course, the covenant with David was not the first unconditional covenant. The promise to Adam and Eve of a redeemer was unconditional and likewise that given to Abraham. In Ruth, we see the continuance of grace over judgement in the lives of simple people, whose past and future generations were given promises to their descendants of unconditional blessing. However, Elimelech was not aware of what was going on in a cosmic scale. He was faced with the predicament of famine throughout the land. It was not just in his locality, and with that, there was hunger and the real prospect of starvation.

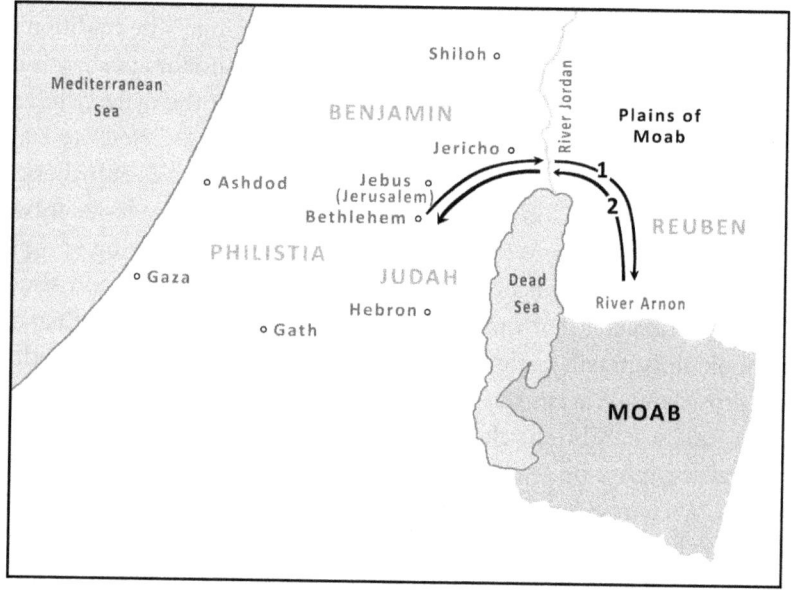

Moab in relation to Bethlehem

²His name was Elimelech and his wife's was Naomi, and his two sons were Mahlon and Chilion. They were Ephrathites from Bethlehem in Judah.

In verse one, there is simply a man, his wife and two sons, people without names. The location was more important than who they were but in verse two they are given names. Yael Ziegler comments, "The opening verses of the Book of Ruth draw our attention to the manner in which this family hovers between names and namelessness, offering the reader an insight into a major theme of the narrative."[17] The word *shem* (name) occurs five times in this introduction, twice in chapter 2 in relation to Boaz and then is carefully mirrored seven times in chapter 4.[18]

Elimelech is introduced without a genealogy, indicative of his minor role in the book and perhaps his role in the community. What should have been his genealogy is given in the conclusion (4:18–22) and again he is not mentioned. Was he just a farmer like all the others or was he a leader[19] whose presence was needed? While it is tempting to see him as unworthy of producing a king, we are not given enough information, just ambiguity. The meaning of *Ephrathites* is also very uncertain. The word refers to a place which is equated with Bethlehem (Gen 35:16, 19; 48:7). Its use here and in 1 Samuel 17:12 where David is introduced as the son of Jesse is more in keeping with the word referring to a district or a more likely a clan within Judah who would live in a number of towns.[20]

The wife of Caleb was Ephrat (1 Chron 2:19, 50) who became the mother of a major line in Judah and Ephrathah, is also the place Rachel is buried (Gen 35:19). Instead of just saying Bethlehem, the mention of Ephrathah introduces into the story shadows of strong women. Rachel emerges from the background and is mentioned directly in 4:11. The setting, despite its uncertain meaning, would be so ingrained into Israel's consciousness that Micah would say the Messiah would be born in "Bethlehem of Ephrath" (Micah 5:2).[21]

Some years ago, I made a lifelong friendship with a young man from Addis Ababa University who came to the agricultural university in my hometown to complete his PhD. During all this time our valley was in drought. Now, the farmers who live in the Lockyer Valley region like to talk about its rich soil as being the most fertile in the world, but Wikipedia says it is only among the top ten. It readily gives a harvest when there is rain. My friend's eyes were opened. When the rains fail in Ethiopia, people starve. In

---

17. Ziegler, *Ruth*, 109. *Sham*, "there" a word with the same consonants also appears twice in the introduction (1:2, 4).

18. Ziegler, *Ruth*, 110.

19. Midrash Tanhuma: *Behar* 3. He can also be depicted, without evidence, as a stingy man who went to Moab to protect his wealth rather than support those who came to him for help, Zohar Hadash: Ruth:35a.

20. Campbell, *Ruth*, 55. That and the mention of Judah differentiates this town from one with the same name in Zebulun (Josh 19:15).

21. Eskenazi and Frymer-Kensky, *Ruth*, 6.

our glorious valley, we start the pumps and irrigate from a large aquifer. As long as the aquifer holds, farming continues. Under all of this is a very generous social welfare safety net sustained by the overall national prosperity. The reality Elimelech faced was that of Ethiopia, not prosperous Australia.

We can fail to appreciate how primitive farming was for the Israelites during the time of the Judges and the resulting consequence from the smaller crops when the rains failed. Iron was introduced to Canaan by the Philistines in the middle of the twelfth century BC, and they had a monopoly on it till the time of David (1 Sam 13:20–21). A plough shear could be turned into a sword and used against them. This prevented the widespread adoption of iron tipped ploughs and even the sickles were made from bronze. Ploughs were likely simply made of wood, or at most, with a bronze tip and they only made a shallow open furrow as opposed to turning the soil. This meant that there was little agricultural surplus to carry over during the times of drought and storage facilities were very limited as there was not too much to store. That changed during the Iron Age.[22]

So, when the Good LORD described the Promised Land as, "a land flowing with milk and honey"; "a down payment on paradise restored;"[23] it was in a period of wooden ploughs. Those who live in my fertile valley can be forgiven for thinking that he had a sense of humor. To us, the land seems marginal at best and begrudging of all it yielded. Apart from the normal short-lived droughts, the land failed Abraham badly and he fled to Egypt (Gen 12:10). We are not told he sinned by doing this, though his conduct in that country was not becoming of the great man. His son, Isaac also experienced another severe drought and considered going to Egypt. The LORD himself appeared to the Patriarch and told him not to leave Canaan (Gen 26:2). The LORD did his part and provided a harvest that we are meant to see as miraculous. Not just Jacob but the whole lineage is seen as being preserved by their move from Canaan to Egypt (Gen 42:2). There is no question that we are meant to see the provision of food and safety in Egypt as a miraculous provision. The LORD again appeared and assured Jacob that he should not be afraid of going to Egypt because he would go with him there and bless him (Gen 46:3–4).

The language of the first verse mirrors that of Abraham's famine and departure to Egypt (Gen 12:10) and Isaac's later dire situation when he was given a miraculous harvest (Gen 26:1). The storyteller at the beginning

---

22. Borowski, *Agriculture*, 11.
23. Ulrich, *From famine*, 107.

gives the book a patriarchal setting and we will see in chapter 2 a favorable comparison between Ruth and Abraham. As for Jacob, for all the safety and provision his family received, he knew that Egypt was not his home and, on his deathbed, ensured that his body would be returned to Canaan (Gen 48:29–31). Joseph also knew that Egypt was not his home or the home of his descendants and gave orders that when the time came to leave Egypt, that his body would go with them (Gen 50:24–26). In this patriarchal tone, the departure was only meant to be temporary, *lagur*, translated here as "to live," would be better understood as "reside temporarily."[24]

With hunger in their belly, or at least its pressing danger, good ancestral precedents and without the benefit of a theophany and a miraculous harvest, the family moved to Moab. It was a country visible from Bethlehem across the Dead Sea. There is no word of guidance anywhere in the book nor is there any word of censure or criticism. Had they taken the northern route skirting around the top of the Dead Sea, this was probably a journey of at least 90 km. When the Patriarchs left Canaan, they chose Egypt where the Nile constantly watered the land. Whereas, the climate of Moab could be similar to that of Israel. Combined with the Moabites lack of generosity, the choice is surprising.[25] Israel's relationship with Moab varied from open warfare (Num 25:1–16; Deut 2:16; 1 Sam 14:47; 2 Sam 8) to times of relative friendship, to the extent that David would later send his parents there for protection (1 Sam 22:3). At least the language and culture of Moab were similar, and we have no idea of the border situation with Egypt. It may not have been an option.

Some commentators are very judgmental and see this departure as, "living in unbelief and disobedience and . . . not enjoying the blessings of God."[26] After all, they were leaving Bethlehem, the "house of bread" for Moab, a land whose name is associated with Lot's incest with his daughters, a people who had refused to give bread and water during the exodus (Deut 23:3–5). The famines the Patriarchs experienced when living in Canaan among idol worshipers were not given a theological significance. After the conquest, however, we are meant to see the drought as a consequence of sin. But this is national sin, the consequence of which envelopes the righteous and the unrighteous alike. Were they a family of sinners? A righteous family that was collateral damage is more likely to be correct. I agree with

---

24. Stigers, Gûr in *TWOT*, 155–56.
25. Ziegler, *Ruth*, 99. This destination is used to suggest he was wealthy.
26. Wiersbe, *Be Committed*, 18.

commentators that this departure is a "compromising picture"[27] but so is the scene in the threshing floor of chapter 3. Despite that, it does not raise the disapproval of the LORD or Boaz. Despite their departure, they did not sell the farm! They lived or rather, as mentioned, "sojourned" in Moab which meant to live as someone without the rights of a resident.[28] However, their home was in Bethlehem. Instead of using the expected *eretz* for "land" the narrator uses *sadeh* or "field" which contrasts the barren fields of Bethlehem and sets the stage for the field of Boaz in 2:2 and finally the redemption of Naomi's field (4:3, 4).

An unavoidable reality may have, and most likely did, give them little choice but to leave. We are given the picture of small family subsistence farms such as that of Elimelech existing alongside that of larger holdings with many employees, like that of Boaz. These small farmers would have very little reserve to see themselves through a time of famine. When the LORD did return a harvest to the community, there appears to be little attempt by the community to assist with the returnee's needs. The closest male relatives were nowhere to be seen, so how much less than when the famine was starting to bite.

Moab was the land which the LORD cursed and warned Israel to avoid (Deut 23:3–6) making their journey a reversal of Joshua's glorious entry into the land, which now in turn appeared cursed. This journey may well have been one into being godforsaken. The return will be even more so. The question must have been asked, "Will God be faithful to his covenant?" This path is one already trodden by the Patriarchs and by many saints since.

> **3** *After they had been living in Moab for some time, Elimelech died, and Naomi was left with her two sons,* **4** *who married Moabite women named Orpah and Ruth. After they had lived there about ten years,* **5** *Mahlon and Chilion both died, and Naomi was left alone, without husband or sons.*

The men exit the story with stark brevity and in five verses we have a famine, emigration, three deaths, two marriages and at least ten years of life. No comment good or bad is made. The text is ambiguous. It could be a total of ten years in Moab or the sons' marriage could have lasted ten years. The storyteller did not want us to focus on the famine and any potential

---

27. Block, *Ruth*, 51.
28. Stigers, Gûr in *TWOT*, 155–56.

judgement of sin; *hesed* rather than cursing is his theme. This is only exceeded in its brevity by 4:13 where we have the marriage, its consummation and the subsequent birth all in one verse. The unfolding tragedy is told in a strict chiasm:[29]

   A The death of Elimelech and its effect on Naomi 3a–b
      B The actions of Naomi's sons 4a
         C The names of Naomi's daughters-in-law 4b–c
      B' The actions of Naomi's sons 4d
   A' The death of Naomi's sons and its effect on the women 5 a–b[30]

In verse two, Naomi was mentioned as the wife of Elimelech, but now he is called the husband of Naomi indicating a shift in the story to focus on the women and particularly Naomi. The two sons are treated as one unit. *The names of his two sons were Mahlon and Chilion* and we are not told who married whom. It only comes up when the inheritance is mentioned.[31] As part of the focus switching to the women, they are given individual identities—*The name of the one was Orpah, and the name of the other was Ruth*. The double mention of "alone" (*tisha'er*) in verses three and five but with the sense of "survived" (*sha'ar*) in verse five reflects that the death of all the men, was in a sense the wives own death also. They had to grieve due to the extreme deprivation that follows as a consequence. In her grief, Naomi even loses her own name. She is just "the woman" and will soon abandon the hopes her parents had for her when they named her "Pleasant" to take on another, "Bitter."

The use of *yeled* to describe her married sons is surprising as it is normally used for young children and, in the Joseph story, it is used of teenagers (Gen 37:30; 42:22; 44:20). Its use here is intentional as it balances the story when in 4:16 Naomi takes a new *yeled* to her bosom.[32] In verse three, she left "with" her sons and in verse five she left "from" her sons, i.e., "without". They are mentioned before her husband to emphasize her fresh sorrow.

It has been argued Naomi brought her sorrow upon herself, firstly by not trusting the God of Israel and leaving a starving land and then, by

---

29. Chiasms were a common feature of ancient Near Eastern writing. They involve a crosswise structure where the idea is stated and then repeated in reverse order.
30. Block, *Ruth*, 71.
31. Ziegler, *Ruth*, 118.
32. Campbell, *Ruth*, 56.

allowing her sons to intermarry. This view turns Ruth into a story of sin with its resultant punishment and then *hesed* with its associated reward. It is assumed because they stayed longer in Moab than was necessary, Mahlon and Chilion ultimately intermarried. The happy ending of Ruth, what I have called "perfect justice," may be intended to contrast the sin/judgment of the family in leaving Canaan with reward for the *hesed* displayed by Boaz, Naomi, and Ruth. Ange Hayyim noted, "Does the text itself yield a sin/punishment conclusion? It remains possible; but no more compelling than a non-sin/punishment reading. This uncertainty encapsulates our difficulty in pinpointing any one specific interpretation of the ephemeral characters in the opening verses of the Book of Ruth."[33] The story does not dwell on the famine and the deaths which discourages us from reading too much into these unfortunate events. Instead it uses them as a setting for a very plausible story.

Another interpretation is to find in the Book of Ruth and particularly with Naomi, parallels and contrasts to the Book of Job, (c.f., Job 27:2; Ruth 1:20). Like Job, Naomi complained about the way that the Lord had treated her and like Job, her joy and lineage was restored despite there being no likelihood of this happening. As a contrast, at the beginning of Job the activity of God and the evil one is made clear, but not in Ruth. Even if a link to Job is intended, the nature of the link is uncertain, "with the characters in Ruth held more responsible for their original suffering and given more credit for their eventual happiness."[34]

If there is intended to be a parallel to Job, then the deaths are meant to be seen as theologically important but there is no explanation of why. I have argued that the family may have had little choice when they left Canaan during a famine and nothing sinful occurred. We can legitimately reject scrutinizing these verses for judgement on sin and see them as no more than background to the story of Naomi, Ruth, and Boaz. The sin/judgement interpretation of the intermarriage as a direct cause of their deaths[35] seems unreasonable as there was up to a ten-year gap between the marriage and the death of her sons. Their deaths may have been theologically significant, or they may have just died in a time when life was short and hard. We will be returning to the theme of uncertainty as we explore Ruth further.

33. Angel, "*Midrashic,*" para. 17.
34. Angel, "*Midrashic,*" para. 17.
35. Angel, "*Midrashic,*" para. 15.

Possibly the true similarity of Ruth to Job can be the attitude of his miserable counsellors, being often repeated in this book's interpreters. Eliphaz, Bildad, and Zophar were adamant and would not relent, that because Job was suffering, he must have sinned. Elihu put the argument differently, because God is righteous, if you are suffering you must have sinned. As Job was denied his integrity, so they would deny Naomi and her family theirs. She was not the first nor far from the last to complain bitterly against the "frowning providence" of God. You do not have to be a Christian for long to realize that divine providence is a two-way street. If not, there would be no need for books like "Why do the Righteous Suffer?" Edward Campbell observes that "As in Job, there will be a resolution of calamities, but not a final answer to the question why."[36]

But did the sons sin in intermarrying in Moab? In Deuteronomy 23:2–6 we read:

> ²No one of illegitimate birth shall enter the assembly of the Lord; none of his *descendants*, even to the tenth generation, shall enter the assembly of the Lord. ³No Ammonite or Moabite shall enter the assembly of the Lord; none of their *descendants*, even to the tenth generation, shall ever enter the assembly of the Lord, ⁴because they did not meet you with food and water on the way when you came out of Egypt, and because they hired against you Balaam the son of Beor from Pethor of Mesopotamia, to curse you. ⁵Nevertheless, the Lord your God was not willing to listen to Balaam, but the Lord your God turned the curse into a blessing for you because the Lord your God loves you. ⁶You shall never seek their peace or their prosperity all your days (NASB).

It has been argued in Judaism that the restriction about marrying into Moab was limited to a Jewish woman marrying a Moabite man. Rabbi Hillel ben David put it this way, "The Talmud[37] explicitly states that a Moabitess

---

36. Campbell, *Ruth*, 59.

37. Babylonian Talmud: Yebam. 76b. "An Ammonite and a Moabite are forbidden and their prohibition is forever. Their women, however, are permitted at once. An Egyptian and an Edomite are forbidden only until the third generation. Whether they are males or females. R. Simeon, however, permits their women forthwith. Said R. Simeon: this law might be inferred a minori ad majus: [from the smaller to the larger] if where the males are forbidden for all time the females are permitted forthwith, how much more should the females be permitted forthwith where the males are forbidden until the third generation only. They replied: if this is an *halachah* [Jewish law based on the Talmud], we shall accept it; but if it is only an inference, an objection can be pointed out. He replied: not so. [but in fact] it is an *halachah* that I am reporting."

[*mo'aviah*] is permitted and a Moabite [*mo'avi*] is not permitted. Therefore, King David and Yeshua HaMashiach depend on the legitimacy of the Torah Shebalpeh [oral law] for their authority to even be a part of the congregation of Israel."[38] The role of Moab in hindering Israel's passage to the land through hiring Balaam and denying them food was done by the men. This very lack of concern for others and a miserly nature of the men precluded them from the nation of Israel.[39]

Countering this is the judgement of the writer of I Kings who condemns Solomon's marriage to foreign women. We read in chapter 11:

> [1]Now King Solomon loved many foreign women along with the daughter of Pharaoh: Moabite, Ammonite, Edomite, Sidonian, and Hittite women, [2]from the nations concerning which the LORD had said to the sons of Israel, "You shall not associate with them, nor shall they associate with you, *for* they will surely turn your heart away after their gods." Solomon held fast to these in love (NASB).

The issue is not black and white but gray. Solomon's marriage to Pharaoh's daughter is mentioned without censure (1 Kgs 3:1) and Rahab, a Canaanite is listed as a hero of the faith (Heb 11:31). Factored into this must be the simple necessity for the two young men and the exemplary nature of Ruth and Orpah. Later of course is Ruth's conversion. From what we know of Ruth's character and her devotion to Mahlon and his mother, this was clearly a case of being equally yoked, at least in character.

During the exodus, the men of Moab lacked that very Israelite capacity, *hesed*. By contrast to the men, Ruth and Orpah do the works of God in showing *hesed* to Naomi. It should be noted that the only person to whom *hesed* is clearly attributed is the initially pagan Ruth. She, especially "is a paradigm of kindness, consistently and selflessly giving to Naomi."[40] So central should kindness be to the Jewish nature that the famous Rabbi, Maimonides, declared that if you meet one who is cruel you should suspect his ancestry.[41] Israel's inability to fully conquer Canaan and their adoption of the practices of the inhabitants contributed to the nation not reflecting the values we see in Ruth.[42] Ruth, for her part, showed herself as someone

---

38. Hillel, "*Legitimacy*," para. 2.
39. Ziegler, *Ruth*, 20.
40. Ziegler, *Ruth*, 20.
41. Mishneh Torah: *Gifts to the Poor*, 10:2.
42. Ziegler, *Ruth*, 20.

who acted like a true Israelite despite living in Moab before she "returned" to Bethlehem.

While differentiating the gender in the Old Testament passage is a reasonable argument in the attempt to harmonize Scripture, its weakness is that the singular "Moabite" can be used as a collective noun to refer to the entire people as does "Israel." But ultimately, does Yahweh, who called the pagan King Cyrus his "messiah," have to harmonize his actions with Scripture? Jesus would teach us what loving our neighbor was through the actions of a despised Samaritan. His Father taught Israel what *hesed* was through another who was considered outside of the grace and mercy of God and of Israel. In the biblical record, it is not just wishful thinking, for there is a way into the assembly of Israel for a Moabitess despite what Deuteronomy 23 says. There always was a way when the God of Israel was acknowledged. Otherwise, what hope likewise was there for prostitute Rahab, a hero of faith? Ruth serves rather as a model for the righteous Gentile who is to be welcomed and guided.[43]

As mentioned, the text can be understood to say that the sons were married for ten years but could also have been for a much shorter time, with Mahon and Chilion going to Moab as children. The marriage of Ruth to Mahlon is likely to have been for a reasonable time for her to have developed such a strong loyalty to him and his mother. It is hard to imagine that a family who could inspire such love and dedication and ultimately great faith, could be one that was so sinful that God had to punish them with death. Still, at the end of verse five we are left with a barren land and Naomi, Ruth, and Orpah are also all "barren." Despite that as the obvious theme, the word is never mentioned and the repeated word through this chapter will be "return."

> **6** *So she set out with her daughters-in-law to return from the land of Moab, for she had heard that the* L<small>ORD</small> *had remembered his people and given them food.*

The end of the famine in Canaan is the first of only two times the storyteller acknowledges God's involvement in the events that set the scene for the birth of the great King David. The second is in regarding Ruth's pregnancy (4:13). Here knowledge of God is only learnt through hearsay,

---

43. Eskenazi and Frymer-Kensky, *Ruth*, xlvi.

not experience. In both cases, God's involvement seems incidental to the overall flow of the story and leaves the reader wondering how much the LORD was involved at all. The bread was not miraculous manna falling from heaven but was the result of the back breaking work of the residents of Israel. We are introduced to an important theme of Ruth—God's actions and those of men and women can be the same. Both Ruth and Boaz will answer the prayers they sent to Yahweh on Ruth's behalf.

While Naomi's departure from Moab was motivated by there being bread at home, there is no indication that there is a famine in the land where she came for refuge which would have reinforced the decision to leave. Elimelech had taken the initiative in taking his sons and his wife to Moab. Naomi now takes the initiative in choosing her future. It is not likely that she would urge Ruth and Orpah to stay in that land if there were famine. There was more than the need for food involved here. The people of Bethlehem are identified as "his people," "signaling the reconciliation of the two parties to the covenant relationship."[44] There is nothing in the Law governing the relationship of daughters-in-law who are without male protectors, and more so with mixed races and migration across borders.[45] What could they expect? Ultimately, for Naomi at least, she judged it better to live in the covenant land in legal uncertainty, even if under her perceived curse from God, than to live in Moab.

When discussing the word for "visit," *pakad,* Victor Hamilton noted "It has been said of this word that occurs more than three hundred times in the Old Testament "there is probably no other verb that has caused translators as much trouble as 'PQD.'"[46] It is translated by the AV as "to visit" fifty-seven times. In these cases, it indicates a change of fortune to a subordinate by someone in a superior position. This can be either for good or ill, c.f., Gen 40:13 and 19. A number of these cases are translated by the RSV as "punish" but in many of these cases the results are beneficial, e.g., Gen 50:24–25, 1 Sam 2:21 and in this verse. "Blessed" or "favorably disposed" would also be acceptable in this instance and "gracious" would be acceptable too as in the NIV of Genesis 21:1. Leon Morris says of this word, "When God visits, everything depends on the state of affairs He finds. The verb is a warning

---

44. Block, *Ruth*, 107.
45. Sakenfeld, *Ruth*, 22–23.
46. Hamilton, Pāqad in *TWOT*, 731.

against presuming on the holiness of God and a reminder that God delights to bless."[47]

Michael Moore compares the use of this word in Judges (21:3) with that of Ruth. In Judges, the tribes question why God "visited" Israel and the tribe of Benjamin which was almost destroyed and, in Ruth, it ends a period of suffering. He observes,

> Nowhere is Yahweh's mysterious sovereignty more evident than in these two passages. Yahweh's visits, in other words, come totally at Yahweh's discretion. Yahweh and Yahweh alone decides whether they are to be peaceful, beneficent or malevolent.[48]

Can a drought last for ten years? Having lived through one (and, at the time of writing, well on the way to an even worse second one) I can say, "Yes." To criticize the family for this long period away from the home is too harsh and judgmental.[49] Here we learn that the drought had been caused by the LORD withdrawing his blessing. With his blessing returning, Bethlehem was again a "house of bread." Despite hearing of the return of God's blessing, as the story develops, we see that her provision comes through human generosity. This is initially through the food Ruth brought to Naomi after gleaning (2:17–18), and when Boaz sent her a gift of grain (3:17).

Having stood in what was once Moab and looked over towards Jericho, I could not help but be struck by the realization that the road the three women were planning to take to Bethlehem was not an easy one. Nor, without male protectors, was it a safe journey. Personal safety for three women is one consideration, let alone the arduous nature of the road. Bethlehem is 775 metres above sea level, going down to 390 metres below at the Dead Sea rising to at least the same height in Moab. The capital Dhiban (biblical Divon) is 726 metres above sea level. Because it is only Ruth who will later go to glean and not both, we can reasonably assume Naomi's mobility was becoming limited.

The decision-making process behind their group departure is not given but there had to be a remarkable relationship among the three. The decision by Naomi to send the daughters-in-law back to Moab may point to her being the decision maker of the group[50] but it is only conjecture. The fate of a widow in Moab must have been grim indeed to commence this journey

---

47. Morris, *Ruth*, 252.
48. Moore, *Ruth*, 315.
49. Evans, *Ruth*, 245.
50. Evans, *Ruth*, 243.

and the return of the Lord's blessing a very strong attraction for Naomi to attempt this journey. The Law in Israel at least provided some relief through gleaning and, as we will learn in chapter 4, there was still the farm.

In verses six and seven there is a repetitive use of four different words for departure (*vatakom, vatashov, vatetze and vatelakhma*) when only one was needed. The first verb with the implication of rising from the prostrate position[51] can refer to the end of the mourning period as with Abraham mourning Sarah (Gen 23:3). This suggests Naomi's departure as soon as the mourning period is over for her sons. As an example of the ambiguity of the book, these two verses could show interagency on her behalf. Ziegler offers a paraphrase "and she got up [but then she sat down again], and she returned from the fields of Moab [but then she went back]. And she departed from the place [only to return to it]. And she went on the road."[52] It would reflect the difficulties of leaving her husband and sons' graves and returning to the town she had abandoned.

While the book starts with a departure, we are now introduced to a key word in Ruth, translated *return or restore* which occurs twelve times in just seventeen verses. Here in verse six, Naomi decides to return (singular) to Judah and in verse seven she starts to return (plural) with Ruth and Orpah. Naomi urges her daughters-in-law to return to Moab in verse eight, but they will not, as they wish to return to Naomi's people (1:10). Naomi does not let the matter rest and urges them to return again in verse eleven and verse twelve but only Orpah returns to her people (1:14). Despite pressure to follow Orpah, Ruth refuses yet on their arrival in Bethlehem, Naomi complains that Yahweh had returned her empty (1:21). Ruth would be called the "returnee" (2:6) and on Obed's birth he is called the "life returner" (4:15).

> *7As they were setting out together on the journey to Judah, 8Naomi said to her daughters-in-law, "Go, return both of you to the home of your mother. May the Lord be kind to you as you have been kind to the dead and to me. 9The Lord grant that each of you may find peace and happiness in the house of a new husband."*

Verse seven mirrors verses one and two where Elimelech, his wife and his two sons set out to Moab and now, with Naomi as the new head of

---

51. Coppes, Qûm in *TWOT*, 793.
52. Ziegler, *Ruth*, 134.

the family, she sets out for Bethlehem with only two daughters-in-law. The transformation of their fortunes is as big a contrast as can be imagined. Strictly, only Naomi is returning, not the three, but the word indicates a unity of purpose. Naomi's words to her daughters-in-law are in the form of a chiasm with the center focusing on the model of *hesed* the two Moabite daughters-in-law have shown towards her and her dead family:

A Go, return each of you to your mother's house.
  B May the LORD deal kindly with you,
    C as you have dealt with the dead and with me.
  B' May the LORD grant you that you may find a place of rest,
A' each one in the house of her husband (NASB).

Naomi, who in verse thirteen would say, "Yahweh's hand has gone out against me," does a very strange thing, despite seeing herself under his disapproval, (if not cursed), she prays a blessing upon her daughters-in-law in his name. She asks for people of a cursed land, the kind of blessing she so desperately wanted herself. This is the first of eleven blessings in this short book (1:8, 9; 2:4, 12, 20; 3:10; 4:11, 12, 14). The four prayers in this book are all prayers for blessing (1:8–9; 2:19–20; 3:10; 4:11–12, 14). We see something similar to Naomi's prayer when childless Abraham prays for Abimelech that his wives and slaves could bear children (Gen 20:17–18). Rabbi Rashi observes the mystery of God's dealings when he says of Abraham's prayer that Scripture, "places this section after the preceding one to teach you that whoever prays for mercy on behalf of another when he himself is in need of that very thing for which he prays on the other's behalf, will himself first receive a favorable response from God."[53] This will be Naomi's experience also.

A woman with nothing to give, financially and, it appears, emotionally, could still give blessings and *hesed* from Yahweh. She does not see his past actions towards her as a good prospect for future blessing so looks to her foreign daughters'-in-laws example as the pattern God should follow. As Phyllis Trible says, "They show the deity a more excellent way . . . [setting] . . . a paradigm for future kindness of the divine being."[54] (Boaz will later take up a similar theme when he meets Ruth in the barley field.) This prayer for favor will be answered first in the barley field and then on the threshing floor and finally a home at the city gates. In fact, each of the four prayers for

53. Rashi, *Commentary*, 87.
54. Trible, *Rhetoric of Sexuality*, 169–79.

blessing for others will be answered. As for herself, she asks nothing, possibly thinking that her own distress is beyond the remedy of prayer. But as Sakenfeld observes, "by the end of the story, the prayer not uttered because it could not even be imagined will nonetheless receive its answer."[55]

By invoking Yahweh in her blessing upon Ruth and Orpah, Naomi shows she had not ceased to worship him. Her two daughters-in-law are blessed with the hope that Yahweh's *hesed* will flow to them in the same way that they freely showed *hesed* to her and her dead sons. In verse eight we are first introduced to one of the most important themes of Ruth. The ever-increasing ripples of *hesed* that can be seen in later chapters started with two Gentile women. Their faithfulness and love were beyond what could be expected. There was no covenant relationship driving the *hesed* of Ruth and Orpah. The *hesed* shown by both Ruth and Orpah and later by Boaz, towards the dead is the most altruistic kindness because they cannot repay. These acts of *hesed* are presented to Yahweh as acts that he should imitate. This is similar to the Lord's Prayer where the Father is urged to imitate our forgiveness.

With her sons unable to repay the faithfulness and herself in no position, Naomi must look to Yahweh as the only one able to supply a suitable reward and, "commits their future responsibility over to God."[56] The blessing and commitment of the daughters-in-law to God's care shows her intent to free them both of any responsibility they may have felt. This was a responsibility that they were both always free to disregard as it was always voluntary on the death of their husbands.[57] It was more than a farewell but, "a final decision concerning change of primary personal relationships."[58] If departing Orpah had shown *hesed*, how much greater must Ruth's actions be viewed.[59] As the story unfolds, both Naomi and Boaz's blessings will ultimately be fulfilled by their own hands.

The blessing was bestowed on both daughters-in-law with the expectation that they would return to their homes in a land whose people were forbidden from God's assembly. As mentioned, Naomi had no problem asking for the God of Israel to work in grace and mercy amid a cursed people in a cursed land. Jay Williams observes that, "Ruth is a gentle reminder to Israel that foreigners are not all bad and that in fact the great King David

---

55. Sakenfeld, *Ruth*, 29.
56. Sakenfeld, *Meaning*, 109.
57. Sakenfeld, *Meaning*, 109.
58. Sakenfeld, *Meaning*, 109.
59. Campbell, *Ruth*, 30.

was descended from one. If so, it may well have been included in the canon to offset what might be regarded as the excessive exclusiveness of such men as Ezra and Nehemiah who forbade foreign marriages entirely."[60]

The blessing God had promised to Israel after they left the wilderness and conquered the land, in return for covenant faithfulness, was to be granted "rest." Naomi prays for this same covenant blessing to be shown to her daughters-in-law. It is not relaxation but freedom from worry.[61] It was a blessing she did not experience herself at this time and moreover, thought it unlikely to achieve. So strong is her desire that her daughters-in-law find rest with a husband that she repeats the word again in 3:1. There was a very real possibility that, as foreign women, they would end up as abused concubines in Israel.[62]

While Naomi considers it better for the widows to be with their mothers, not their mother-in-law, it could be expected that she would have said "return to their father's house." The expression is unusual and elsewhere is in the context of love and marriage (Song 3:4; 8:2; Gen 24:28) so Naomi was most likely releasing them to marry. The reference to "mother's house" does draw further attention to this book being about the interconnection of women who are now separated from men. Beyond that is the possibility of a veiled xenophobic statement. Ziegler suggests that, given the history of Lot, the founder of the nation of Moab, sending daughters to their father to solve a fertility problem might, in the eyes of an Israelite, not be the best idea.[63]

> 10 *Then she kissed them; but they began to weep aloud and said to her, "No, we will return with you to your people."* 11 *But Naomi said, "Go back, my daughters. Why should you go with me? Can I still bear sons who might become your husbands?* 12 *Go back, my daughters, go your own way, because I am too old to have a husband. Even if I should say, 'I have hope,' even if I should have a husband tonight and should bear sons,* 13 *would you wait for them until they were grown up? Would you remain single for them? No, my daughters! My heart grieves for you, for the LORD has sent me adversity."*

60. Williams, *Understanding*, 294.
61. Block, *Ruth*, 87.
62. Moore, *Ruth*, 316.
63. Ziegler, *Ruth*, ,139.

Ruth

Ambiguity is at the heart of the story of Ruth and Naomi's attitudes and motives as she urges her daughters-in-law to return to Moab which illustrates this. One view is that Naomi is not willing to compromise her religious beliefs.[64] Supporting this view is her, "observation that Orpah's return to Moab came with religious consequences as well: "So she said, 'See, your sister-in-law has returned to her people and her gods. Go follow your sister-in-law'"[65] Another view is not as kind towards Naomi as it views her seeming concern for her Moabite daughter's-in-law well-being really cloaked a desire to protect her own noble self-image in Judean society.[66] Evidence for this is seen on the stress of Ruth being called a "Moabite" seven times. Yet again, Naomi can be seen as the ideal mother-in-law. As Rabbi Hayyim Angel commented, "Bereft of her husband and sons, with only Ruth and Orpah to comfort her, Naomi was more concerned with their welfare than in tending to her own loneliness."[67] There is no mention here or in chapter 3 of the importance of restoring the male line, but rather the imperative that her daughters'-in-law marry and so have future security. Her emphasis is on the living which will not be the case as men discuss property at the gate of Bethlehem (4:9–10).

The complexity of human nature is such that it is difficult to do anything from totally pure motives. However, if Naomi was not an exceptional mother-in-law it is difficult to envision how she could have found such loyalty. Ruth and Orpah had (possibly) years to observe her and insincere care and concern would surely have been discerned. Still, there was the issue of conversion which could not be brushed aside. Chemosh, the god of the Moabites required human sacrifices (2 Kgs 3:27; 2 Kgs 23) and this was an abomination in Israel. Conversion would have been necessary to live happily and be accepted in the new land. The repeated references to Ruth as a Moabitess (1:22; 2:2, 6, 21; 4:5, 10) are important but not as suggested by Naomi wanting to protect her reputation. Block puts it this way; they "invite the hearer to interpret those events in the light of Deuteronomy 7:3–4, which prohibits Israelites from marrying pagans."[68]

The passage in verse thirteen, "for it grieves me seriously for your sakes" has different translations depending on whether one follows the MT

---

64. Ruth Rabbah: 2:16.
65. Angel, *"Midrashic,"* para. 22.
66. Angel, *"Valor,"* para. 23.
67. Angel, *"Midrashic,"* para. 26.
68. Block, *Ruth*, 46.

or other early translations. The NASB (similarly also the NIV) follows the MT and says, "it is much more bitter for me than for you" while the RSV follows the LXX and Syriac and says it is exceedingly bitter to me for your sake. Along much the same lines, Frederic Bush translates this as, "my life is much too bitter for you."[69] So, is Naomi unhappy because she is looking inward at her own situation or is her grief exacerbated by looking at the needs for security of her daughters-in-law? Both could be correct and in reality, both probably are, depending on what time of day the question was asked. A third alternative is possible, "For I am very bitter from you," suggesting her troubles have come about somehow through her daughters-in-law.[70] This is part of the sea of ambiguity of the book which, "allows and even encourages multiple explanations."[71] Naomi's bitterness (*mar*) will be taken up again in verse twenty when she asked that she no longer be called by a name that means "pleasantness" but Mara.

Naomi envisions her situation as the hand of God being against her and initially all but, "accusing God of botching up her life"[72] before stating it outright in verse thirteen. This punishment is rightly deserved, some commentators say, for leaving the land of promise and remaining an inordinate time in Moab. Perhaps, though suffering without explanation just as Job did, is equally possible and more likely. Her lament acknowledges God's sovereignty but there is no hint of affirming God's goodness. Naomi sees herself without the hope (*tiqwâ*) that comes through having a husband and sons. The root means, "to wait or to look for with eager expectation;"[73] and this attitude is a continual expression of faith in both testaments. What is true of Naomi is what has been described as, "an unguarded glimpse into the soul of someone radically succumbing to the quicksands of depression."[74]

In the face of depression, her judgement of what is happening, and her lack of hope is questionable, as unfolding events will demonstrate. Implied in her words that she is too old to be with a man is the belief that her situation is beyond remedy. If God had indeed "botched" her life, he was the only one who could remedy it. The storyteller does not disagree with or correct her, because this is God at work. Ronald Hals sees here,

69. Bush, *Ruth/Esther*, 71.
70. Ziegler, *Ruth*, 142.
71. Ziegler, *Ruth*, 142.
72. Hubbard, *Ruth*, 108.
73. Hartley, Qāwâ in *TWOT*, 791.
74. Moore, *Ruth*, 317.

"an expression of the basic Israelite belief in Yahweh's all-causality [and by accepting Yahweh's sovereignty] Israel seems to have been willing to accept the beclouding of God's goodness implicit in the attribution to him of woe as well as weal."[75] For all this acknowledgement of God, it is his hiddenness that permeates this story.

Taking Ruth and Orpah to Israel would have put them in the same situation Naomi was in in Moab, i.e., having no male providers. Her second blessing indicated that sadly, "life for a young widow in that culture would be tolerable only if she married again."[76] Naomi's comments about waiting for a levirate marriage (from the Latin for brother-in-law and a hint to the direction of the story), even if that were possible, suggests that she considers that Israelite men would not want to marry a Moabitess.[77] Boaz's blessing on Ruth on the threshing floor that you didn't follow young men, whether poor or rich (3:10) goes contrary to this. Saying things through negative questions is a characteristic of both Naomi and Boaz.

The subject of levirate marriage, when a brother of a deceased husband marries the widow, and the first male offspring will continue the line and inheritance of the deceased is introduced. The concept of a man marrying his brother's widow to continue his line and secure the status of his wife is understood by both Ruth and Orpah reflecting its widespread practice. The problem with Naomi's proposal is that it would involve, "a double application of levirate practice: she must find a relative of her husband to sire two sons who in turn would do the brother's duty for the two younger widows."[78] The kinsman redeemer (*goel*) will become the core of the book, but this dealt with property, not marriage.

> **14***Then they again wept aloud, and Orpah kissed her mother-in-law goodbye, but Ruth stayed with her.*

The responses of both Ruth and Orpah show that they are not subject to their mother-in-law but make their own choices, one to leave and one to follow. Granted that this story only has room for one heroine, but this is not a case of there being no consequence like an actress exiting stage left.

75. Hals, *Theology*, 9.
76. Evans, *Ruth*, 244.
77. Evans, *Ruth*, 244.
78. Campbell, *Ruth*, 84.

Rather, we are left pondering the fate of a compassionate and loving family member, albeit by marriage, departing to worship the false god/s of Moab (the word can be either singular or plural). Just as the storyteller does not praise Ruth, he/she has no words of censure for Orpah who acted like a true obedient daughter accepting the wise counsel of her mother.[79] Instead, just a word from Naomi would have seen her go to Bethlehem and rest under the care of the God of Israel. How different this is from the evangelistic command of Jesus to go into the world, proclaiming the good news and making disciples from all nations. By saying that Orpah was returning to her god is not a tacit recognition of the god's existence alongside Yahweh. Notably, even before Ruth's pledge of allegiance to Yahweh, Naomi refers to the gods of Moab as Orpah's only (her gods) not Ruth's (your gods). Ruth was truly standing at the crossroads.[80]

Naomi was looking to God for his *hesed* and failed to find it, yet it was staring her in the face through her two foreign daughters-in-law. Orpah would not know the conversion of Ruth, but was this pearl,[81] who so unknowingly yet freely and lovingly did the work of the God of Israel, destined for damnation? Perhaps we can take some consolation in the difference between the gospel age and that time as described by Paul in his sermon in Athens, "So having overlooked the times of ignorance, God is now proclaiming to mankind that all people everywhere are to repent" (Acts 17:30 [NASB]). Orpah's great love may well have covered a multitude of sins (1 Pet 4:8) and her actions are not presented critically.[82] Had Naomi seen the Almighty as her friend and not her adversary, she may have been more reluctant to send her daughters-in-law back to the contemptible god/s of Moab.

Ruth cleaved to Naomi. The word *davak* is not a common word, especially when used of people, yet it is used three more times when Boaz advises Ruth to stay close to the young women (2:8, 21, 23) and in Ruth it has the association of union and loyalty. It is the word used to describe marriage (Gen 2:24) where a bride leaves one family for another and also describes the relationship Israel was to have with Yahweh (Deut 10:20; 11:22).

---

79. Hubbard, *Ruth*, 114.
80. Eskenazi and Frymer-Kensky, *Ruth*, 21.
81. Weinstein, *Naomi's Mission*, 49.
82. Despite there being no evidence in the text, Orpah can be described as an immoral and promiscuous woman. Some of the depictions of her are vile, e.g., Ruth Rabbah: 2:20.

Her deep love for her mother-in-law stands as an example of how Israel should have responded to their God.[83] Ziegler says that in her choice to abandon Moab and worship Abraham's God, "Ruth becomes the paradigm of *hesed* and morality, having adopted the traits of Abraham and enabled her descendants to do the same."[84]

Translations invariably use "your sister-in-law" to refer to Ruth's relationship to Orpah but the word is more complicated. It is described as follows: "The primary meaning . . . is to assume the responsibility to marry one's widowed sister-in-law in order to raise up a male heir to the deceased brother."[85] The verbal root is only found in Genesis 38:8 where Judah encourages his son Onan to marry Tamar. It is also found in Deuteronomy 25:5–10 where the laws of levirate marriage are laid out. While Naomi will rule out the possibility of such a marriage in verses eleven to thirteen, Campbell suggests the word is used purposefully to suggest levirate marriage and, ironically, by applying it to Orpah.[86]

> 15 *"Look," said Naomi, "your sister-in-law is going back to her own people and to her own gods. Go along with her!"* 16 *But Ruth answered, "Do not urge me to leave you or to go back. I will go where you go, and I will stay wherever you stay. Your people will be my people, and your God my God;* 17 *I will die where you die, and be buried there. May the* Lord *bring a curse upon me, if anything but death separate you and me."* 18 *When Naomi saw that Ruth was determined to go with her, she ceased urging her to return.*

The Book of Ruth is read in the synagogues each year on the eve[87] of the Shavuot holiday (the Feast of Weeks), what Christians know as Pentecost. The book's setting around the barley harvest is appropriate for a festival which is also timed to the barley harvest. Shavuot is also a celebration that became associated with the giving of the Law[88] when the nation

---

83. Kalland, Dā'ēb in *TWOT*, 177–78.
84. Ziegler, *Ruth*, 71.
85. Alexander, Yābam in *TWOT*, 359–60.
86. Campbell, *Ruth*, 72–73.
87. On the second day outside of Israel.
88. Mishna Torah: *Issurei Bi'ah*, 13:1–4.

of Israel was converted and, "all Jewish people became proselytes."[89] Ruth likewise voluntarily took upon herself obedience to the Law.

While there are many examples of Israelites marrying foreign wives, the idea of conversion and its process is missing from the Old Testament and Ruth is probably the only clear example of it. The Talmud views Ruth's entreaty to Naomi as the model of a conversation that the rabbinical courts should have with a potential proselyte, including the threefold attempt to dissuade:[90]

> '[The proselyte] is not, however, to be persuaded, or dissuaded too much.' R. Eleazar said: What is the Scriptural proof?—It is written: And when she saw that she was steadfastly minded to go with her, she left off speaking unto her. 'We are forbidden,' she told her, '[to move on the Sabbath beyond the] Sabbath boundaries!'—'Whither thou goest' [the other replied] 'I will go.'
>
> 'We are forbidden private meeting between man and woman!'—'Where thou lodgest. I will lodge'
>
> 'We have been commanded six hundred and thirteen commandments!'—'Thy people shall be my people.'
>
> 'We are forbidden idolatry!'—'And thy God my God'.
>
> 'Four modes of death were entrusted to Beth din!'—'Where thou diest, will I die.'
>
> 'Two graveyards were placed at the disposal of the Beth din'!—'And there will I be buried.' Presently she saw that she was steadfastly minded etc.[91]

Conversion in Ruth will be seen to be more than an initial pledge, however well-meaning it may have been. It required affirmation, first by Boaz, the residents of Bethlehem and finally God himself.[92] She will still be called the Moabitess until the very last mention of her name in 4:13.

The Jewish and Christian Convert, a Digression

On the day of Pentecost, the day the Spirit was given to the church, the first ingathering of Christian converts saw 3000 added to their number (Acts 2:41). Some Rabbis believe that the day we now know as Pentecost, is the

---

89. Eskenazi and Frymer-Kensky, *Ruth*, xxvi.
90. Ruth Rabbha: 2:16.
91. Babylonian Talmud: Yebam. 47b.
92. Eskenazi and Frymer-Kensky, *Ruth*, xliv.

day Moses came down from Mt. Sinai with the Law, and when 3000 died (Exod 32:28).[93] This contrast is not meant to be coincidental. With Peter, conversion came as a result of urgent warning and pleading (Acts 2:40). In Ruth there is active discouragement and at Mt. Sinai an even different response with a call for the people to decide who is on the Lord's side and actively purge sin from the camp.

Paul proclaimed in Acts 17:29–31, "Therefore, since we are the descendants of God, we ought not to think that the Divine *Nature* is like gold or silver or stone, an image formed by human skill and thought. **30** So having overlooked the times of ignorance, God is now proclaiming to mankind that all people everywhere are to repent, **31** because He has set a day on which He will judge the world in righteousness through a Man whom He has appointed, having furnished proof to all people by raising Him from the dead" (NASB). The message is not to return to their former gods or the gods of their family. Is this a message then without cost?

The hearers of Peter's message were cut to the heart when they came to understand that the Author of Life, their Messiah, had been slain by evil men. Those from the reformed tradition of faith would see this as the proper work of the Law, convicting the sinner and leading them to plead for a savior. This then was not a message without cost but was initially dependent on their own precarious situation. Their understanding of their perilous situation required an end to any notion of their own goodness and resulting claim they may have felt they had on their God. For the early centuries of the church, with open persecution not too far from the surface, the cost of conversion would have been known to all. This remains a present reality in varying degrees in a number of countries.

My own Australian society now knows little of conviction of sin nor of persecution in its extremes. It could be argued that there is little cost in conversion. Any cost may seem limited to a loss of reputation as the church is no longer held in respect and honor by many if not most. Our five year long *Royal Commission into institutional responses to child sexual abuse* has exposed a church, whose sacred mission it is to protect children and redeem the world, is too often in need of salvation itself. The commissioners reported that they, "heard more allegations of child sexual abuse in relation to institutions managed by religious organizations than any other

---

93. The link is hard to make despite the popularity of this view.

management type."⁹⁴ What went wrong for there to be traitors in our midst even worse than those outside?

My own journey to faith came through the torments of knowing myself a sinner in need of a savior. I reflect at times on a young Congregational boy with a conversion that would meet with the approval of Jonathon Edwards and his sermon *Sinners in the Hands of an Angry God*. I had a denominationally orthodox conversion in the reformed tradition! However, in my old age I am convinced that the role of the church is to present and re-present the good news of a loving savior who forgives all our sins and cancelled the record of our debt that stood against us (Col 2:13–14). For the Christian, salvation is the free gift of grace (Eph 2:8) by the God/man Jesus but it was never intended to be cheap. The Christian martyr, Dietrich Bonhoeffer called out the cancer we see in the present church calling it *Cheap Grace*. He described it this way:

> Cheap grace is the preaching of forgiveness without requiring repentance, baptism without church discipline, Communion without confession. Cheap grace is grace without discipleship, grace without the cross, grace without Jesus Christ, living and incarnate.⁹⁵

The Christian church must not know the attitude of Naomi who dissuaded or of the Beth Din⁹⁶ which will neither persuade or dissuade but must remain one that urges and pleads. By lessening and in some cases totally casting aside the demands of faithful discipleship we have become heirs of the warning to the scribes and Pharisees; "Woe to you, scribes and Pharisees, hypocrites, because you travel around on sea and land to make one proselyte; and when he becomes *one*, you make him twice as much a son of hell as yourselves" (Matt 23:15 [NASB]).

Returning to the Subject in Hand

Up to this point Naomi had been giving instructions based on her authority as the family head but Ruth now asserts herself and internalizes her mother-in-law's pain. She replies in a chiasm made up of five two-line verses:

---

94. Australian Government, "*Royal Commission*," para. 4.
95. Bonhoeffer, *Cost of Discipleship*, 36.
96. A court of Jewish law.

Ruth

A Do not urge me to leave you or to go back,
  B I will go where you go, and I will stay wherever you stay.
    C Your people will be my people, and your God my God
  B' I will die where you die and be buried there.
A' May the LORD bring a curse upon me if anything but death separate you and me.

Ruth introduces opposites to describe her commitment to Naomi, when she vows to go where she goes and stay where she stays. While this could just be the trip back to Bethlehem,[97] it is more likely to refer to a lifelong commitment to her mother-in-law.[98] She even swears she will die is a similar way to Naomi and be buried with her. This is a commitment beyond death itself. Family tombs were common in Israel at that time and the bones were placed in a common store. With her family buried in Moab, which was shame enough, Naomi would have been buried alone so Ruth's pledge is rich in meaning.[99] We cannot know what Ruth understood about the nature of the God of Israel or what, if anything, she learnt from her husband. She calls God initially by the generic term, Elohim, whereas the others call him by his personal and covenant name, Yahweh. This is the only place in the book where Ruth shows a theological awareness.[100] Her words can be interpreted as a statement of her intent, but it could also and, "possibly better interpreted as a declaration of the present;"[101] meaning she had abandoned Chemosh in the land of Moab.

The oath formula used by Ruth is found twelve times in the Old Testament but, in itself, it is almost meaningless as there is no direct object nor even is it stated what God would do. Sheldon Blank describes the oath as, "neutral and evasive, as though the oath-taker is reluctant to define the curse."[102] Despite the vagueness of the words, the oath may have been accompanied by a gesture that explained the punishment. This oath formula normally uses the general name Elohim but here God's personal name, (which is only used once by Ruth and in a vow), attests to her complete acceptance of the God of Israel. The formula using Yahweh is only found here

---

97. Campbell, *Ruth*, 73–74.
98. Bush, *Ruth*, 82.
99. Ziegler, *Ruth*, 157.
100. Block, *Ruth*, 48.
101. Block, *Ruth*, 94.
102. Blank, *The Curse*, 90.

and with the covenant Jonathan made with David. In both cases, the parties were making a promise to their personal detriment. Ziegler suggests that the extreme seriousness of the oath is what prompts the use of the divine name.[103] She observes that by both continuing together on the road they are, "in essence, declaring that they believe that it is the will of the God of Israel that they should act selflessly in this situation."[104]

The allusion to a bond as strong as marriage found in verse fourteen, where Ruth cleaved to Naomi, is further reinforced as "leave" is also found in the marriage institution of Genesis 2:24. Ruth's sworn oath to Naomi could have promised her no more than a life of abject poverty. Orpah, in choosing to be a wife, had made the sensible and obedient decision; but Ruth's decision to remain a daughter seemed foolish. She had forsaken her family, nation, and god with no guarantee of acceptance in Israel and, "threw herself on the mercy and care of the God of Israel."[105] Help certainly wasn't going to come from Naomi as she did not have the resources financially, or it would seem, inwardly (1:20). Remaining faithful to Naomi would prove to involve great personal risk as the warnings and instructions in the barley field will show. So, calling for God's punishment if she should leave Naomi proved to be more than just idly spoken words.

For Naomi, the best that a woman could expect for her good deeds is marriage and a son to care for them in their old age, but she has no expectation of this being possible in Bethlehem. For her part, Ruth chose to commit herself to an old woman and not seek a husband. The radical nature of this decision cannot be understated, as one woman has chosen another woman in a society where they were dependent on men.[106] What is the source of this devotion that went beyond, "coercion by custom, culture or biblical demand?"[107] No reason is given, and her first words are loyalty to Naomi and nothing is said about her husband. The women of Bethlehem give a simple answer, "Ruth loves her" (4:15) and her devotion shows Israel what it means to love the strangers (Lev 19:33–34).

Naomi, for her part, after the strong emotion of her daughters-in-law showed no emotion and certainly no joy. The word for ceased, *hadal*, could

---

103. Ziegler, *Ruth*, 163.
104. Ziegler, *Ruth*, 164.
105. Ulrich, *Famine*, 42.
106. Eskenazi and Frymer-Kensky, *Ruth*, 22.
107. Sakenfeld, *Ruth*, 34.

be read as deliberate action,[108] more than just saying no more about the subject[109] it could even give the sense that there was "stony silence."[110] As Trible observed, "Naomi has isolated Ruth by making Orpah the acceptable model. If Naomi stands alone by the force of circumstances, Ruth stands alone by the force of decision."[111] Ruth's plea that Naomi not "harm" her by forcing her to return to Moab, is taken up again in 2:22 where Ruth finally is shown complete maternal care and acceptance through Naomi counselling her how to avoid "harm." By depicting Naomi as a fundamentally good person but with mixed motives in her actions, it is "a more illuminating and useful scenario than an idyll that strips out ordinary human emotions and conflicts."[112] Ruth's response to her mother-in-law's utter desolation is with an equal measure of determination (*ameṣ*). The word is used of Moses' encouragement to Joshua as he enters Canaan, "be strong and determined" (Deut 31:7) and involves exertion, courage and strength.[113] These are all properties Ruth will need in spades.

Perhaps it is our familiarity with the story, of knowing the happy ending, or reading it as a male or just reading it through our twenty-first century mindset that we miss the enormity of what has transpired in the last thirteen verses. The feminist writer Trible puts this into perspective:

> Ruth stands alone; she possesses nothing. No God has called her; no deity has promised her blessing; no human being has come to her aid. She lives and chooses without a support group, and she knows that the fruit of her decision may well be the emptiness of rejection, indeed of death. Consequently, not even Abraham's leap of faith surpasses this decision of Ruth's. And there is more. Not only has Ruth broken with family, country, and faith, but she has reversed sexual allegiances. A young woman has committed herself to the life of an old woman rather than to search for a husband, and she has made this commitment not 'until death us do part' but beyond death. One female has chosen another female in a world where life depends on men. There is no more radical decision in all the memories of Israel.[114]

108. Yamauchi, Ḥādal in *TWOT*, 265.
109. Bush, *Ruth*, 84.
110. Ziegler, *Ruth*, 145.
111. Trible, *Rhetoric of Sexuality*, 172.
112. Eskenazi and Frymer-Kensky, *Ruth*, 10.
113. Finberg, ʾāmēṣ in *TWOT*, 53–54.
114. Trible, *Rhetoric of Sexuality*, 173.

> **19**So they both went until they came to Bethlehem. When they had come to Bethlehem, all the city was excited about them, and they asked, "Is this Naomi?"
> **20**She said to them, "Don't call me Naomi. Call me Mara, for the Almighty has dealt very bitterly with me. **21**I went out full, and Yahweh has brought me home again empty. Why do you call me Naomi, since Yahweh has testified against me, and the Almighty has afflicted me?"

It would normally be sufficient to say something like "and they went" but the storyteller says literally, "and they went, the two of them" but the word "together" which is what you would expect if the two were of one heart, is missing.[115] It suggests that Naomi and Ruth are not of one heart and perhaps not surprisingly when Naomi saw the name she was given and the hopes for her life, *pleasantness,* now as a mockery of the fate inflicted upon her by the God of Israel. She asks, instead, that she should be called by a new name, *Mara* meaning bitter. Was it her nature or her life situation that was bitter? Either or both could be correct. Her language is similar to that of Job, but again it is ambiguous as to whether she sees herself suffering unjustly. However she did suffer without explanation. Like Job, she also will be restored when any hope of restoration seems impossible. The belief in Yahweh being a covenant keeping God, whose nature was joyously celebrated in the community by the feasts at that time of year, was completely subsumed by Naomi to the "truth" of her situation. Reg Grant puts her thoughts this way, "This bitterness is the only reality I know or that can be known."[116]

In a chiasm, Naomi, without any attempt at subtlety, lays the cause of all her troubles directly at the feet of God whom she calls by the revealed name Yahweh and the more general name *Sha-ddai* which was used also among neighboring countries.

A The Almighty has given me a bitter lot
  B I had plenty when I left, but the Lord has brought me back empty handed
  B' Why should you call me Naomi
A' Now that the Lord has afflicted me?

---

115. Eskenazi and Frymer-Kensky, *Ruth*, 25.
116. Grant, *Literary Structure*, 432.

The word translated "testified" (*anah*) can also be translated as "to afflict"[117] and this choice of a word with multiple meanings is likely intended "to convey the multidimensional depth of Naomi's pain. Thus, we feel not only her sense of legal impotence (testimony) but also her sense of theological abandonment (affliction)."[118] Ziegler suggests that "the book presents Naomi's desperate situation as a mirror of the nation's predicament" mirroring the broken despondent survivors of the civil wars at the end of Judges. If this is so, we can better understand the national character and its road to recovery.[119] It is possible that Naomi believed that her suffering was a testimony by Yahweh against her decision to flee to Moab but even so, it was coming from depression and despair so is not necessarily what is happening. The story is only in chapter 1.

Her words remind us of Job who longs to bring a legal case against God for his injustice. It has been described this way, "She portrays herself as the defendant in a legal action in which the charges and the testimony are in effect unknown to her, in which she has been deemed guilty, in which punishment has already been meted out. Worst of all, her antagonist is God."[120] All she knows is the sentence. The bitterness of her soul that she saw coming from the hand of Yahweh occurred in Moab, not Israel. Famine from God's hand caused her to flee to Moab and yet, beyond the borders of the promised land, Yahweh pursued her and there she was widowed and bereft of her sons. Nothing in her sad situation was by chance. Despite her bitterness, she had sufficient trust in the God of Israel to return to Bethlehem to submit to whatever the hand of God dealt her. Ruth also had come under the same circumstances, but we do not see the bitterness of Job or Naomi in her words or actions.

Naomi was participating in the Old Testament's "Theology of Complaint" which is not only, "tolerated by God, but it can even be the *proper* stance of someone who takes [a sovereign, just and merciful] god seriously."[121] In Job's case, he certainly was not right in concluding so quickly that God was unjust, but God showed that he was, "better pleased with honest heresy than with fraudulent piety; and although the outworks of his faith were sorely shaken, his ultimate faith in God weathered the

---

117. Coppes, 'ānâ in *TWOT*, 679–84.
118. Moore, *Ruth*, 324.
119. Ziegler, *Ruth*, 121.
120. Campbell, *Ruth*, 83.
121. Campbell, *Ruth*, 83.

storm triumphantly."[122] His doubt came not as a result of a settled attitude of rebellion and unbelief but from a despair that trembled on the brink of suicide, (7:21). Naomi's faith, like that of Job's, developed through her journey along the road of doubt.

The ambiguity of Naomi's complaint does not ultimately allow us to know if she sees herself as suffering innocently or receiving her just deserts. If being punished deservedly, the God she served was harsh and unforgiving. As a widow she could, "rightly expect gentler treatment from God, whom she accuses of afflicting her, despite her vulnerable position."[123] The name she twice uses for God is *Shaddai*, the name frequently used by Job (thirty-one times of its forty-eight occurrences) in his complaints about the justice of God or by his friends in defense. The translation of this name of God as "Almighty" goes back to the LXX but, based on the suggested origin of the word, the meaning is now considered uncertain. A possible origin more widely accepted now is, "God/El of the mountain, i.e., God's abode."[124] God, as *Shaddai*, appeared to Abraham (Gen 17:1), to Isaac (Gen 28:3) and Jacob (Gen 35:11; 43:14; 48:3) regarding the promised progeny as a reward for faithful obedience to the covenant.[125] Its usage, as opposed to origin, favors an association with God's power.[126] As part of the sea of ambiguity that surrounds Naomi and her actions, it may point to Naomi feeling outcast from the nation of Israel.

How well were Naomi and Ruth received? The word *vatehom* translated here as "excited" has many possible meanings from "excited surprise" to "being stirred up"[127] after she had "deserted" Bethlehem in its need. Again, this adds to the ambiguity of the book. Mary Evans sees it as "lukewarm"[128] and this is probably correct as we are not told of any assistance from the women. Certainly, the male close relatives did nothing. They had to have been aware of their state and need of assistance. Their exclamation, "Is this Naomi?" may well reflect how "time, grief, and deprivation had taken their

---

122. Pollock, *God and a Heretic*, 270.
123. Ziegler, *Ruth*, 173.
124. Hamilton, Šadday in *TWOT*, 907.
125. Hamilton, Šadday in *TWOT*, 907.
126. Morris lists at least a dozen different possible origins of the word but points out that knowing the origin means little, what is important is how the word is used. In Genesis each usage relates to the power and compassion of God and in the Psalms the emphasis is on power, so almighty is within the meaning of the name. Morris, *Ruth*, 266–67.
127. Weber, Hûm in *TWOT*, 212–13.
128. Evans, *Ruth*, 222.

toll on her form and visage."[129] As she is not involved in the gleaning in chapter 2, the effect of the arduous trek from Moab could be the cause. Only the women talk, and we hear no more of them until the conclusion of the story when they become supportive and bless her. When it came time for Ruth to glean, Naomi did not bother to tell Ruth to look for the field of a relative with the hope she should be better received there. The lack of assistance, by both the male relatives and women may well intend, "readers to draw conclusions as how far the community *in the days when the judges ruled* was adhering to covenant principals."[130] In all this, Ruth is ignored even by Naomi whose words about her afflictions should equally have included Ruth.

Naomi certainly did not leave Bethlehem full as she protested against God. She may have left with her husband and two sons, but she was fleeing starvation. Likewise, she did not return "empty" as she was accompanied by a daughter-in-law who was worth seven sons. Also, we will learn in chapter 4, she still owns land. The storyteller picks up on the word "empty" again in 3:17 when Boaz sends Ruth back to her with six measures of barley. The return to the land of promise isn't achieved by Naomi crossing land borders because in her home she calls herself *Mara*. Her return is complete only when she can call herself Naomi again. The hope for her redemption is alluded to in the fact that it is God who brought her back but in verse six it was her own decision.

> **22***So Naomi returned, and Ruth the Moabitess, her daughter-in-law, with her, who returned out of the country of Moab. They came to Bethlehem in the beginning of barley harvest.*

Naomi "is empty, bitter and devoid of hope [and] has a total absence of any expectations, hope or ambitions."[131] Her complaints against the Almighty are all in the past tense with no view to a change in circumstances. Ziegler suggests that she has come home to die.[132] Naomi has not returned without reason for hope. She has come with a daughter-in-law whose love and actions mirrored that of *Yahweh*. The women of Bethlehem would

129. Block, *Ruth*, 101.
130. Evans, *Ruth*, 248.
131. Ziegler, *Ruth*, 181.
132. Ziegler, *Ruth*, 181.

later remind her that Ruth was better than seven sons (4:15). The presence of Yahweh for good had never departed from her as her daughter-in-law embodies it.[133] Ruth had spoken to her in the future tense, but for all her misery, Naomi does not have the last word. It is the storyteller who introduces the two elements of hope for a resolution. She is accompanied by a daughter-in-law who loves her in a way that sets the example for Yahweh and now the famine has given way to the barley harvest. Barley may only have been thought of as animal food or the food of the poor;[134] it was food none the less. In the next scene, the storyteller introduces a third reason for hope—Naomi is not devoid of family or the possibility of aid.

While there are many ambiguities in the Book of Ruth, we do not see this ambiguity when it comes to Ruth herself. Ruth has some parallels with Abraham (Gen 12:1–2) in that she left her family, and the ruler of a great nation would come from her. The contrasts are perhaps more striking. There was no divine appearance and command. She left voluntarily. There was no safety net of Abraham's great wealth or, later, of a promise of a son. The astounding love of Ruth to Naomi and Mahlon is only seen when you consider that for all her sacrifice, she could only expect a lifetime of begging and discrimination in return.

The thrust of the first chapter is movement with "return" mentioned twelve times and "walk" ten times. What is surprising then is mention of Ruth returning from the country of Moab when she is in fact abandoning her homeland. This has been described as a closing of the loop that started when Lot separated from Abraham. Had Lot refused Abraham's request to separate (Gen 13) and cleaved to him as Ruth did to Naomi, there would have been no Moab.[135]

Having left the cold winter of Moab, the pair arrive in spring at the time of the barley harvest, towards the end of April. This leads into the story of "redemption" through the kinsman redeemer, Boaz. Grant sees the timing of their arrival from a foreign land and Ruth's subsequent work in the barley field as a veiled reference to three feasts of Israel, Passover, (14/15 Nisan), Unleavened Bread (15/22 Nisan) and First Fruits (16/17 Nisan), all of which are timed to the ripening of the barley crop. The Passover is Israel's great time of deliverance where Yahweh showed he is the "redeemer" (*goel*) of Israel. The feast of Unleavened Bread speaks of the nation cutting itself

---

133. Ulrich, *Famine*, 49.
134. Masterman, "Barley," 431.
135. Ziegler, *Ruth*, 70–72.

off from the old life in Egypt and likewise Ruth cut herself off completely from her Moabite past. In First Fruits, which involved a wave offering of a sheaf of raw barley, Israel acknowledged Yahweh as its provider. Naomi would see herself beyond the help of her God,[136] but Ruth will be the one holding the sheaf. Intentional or coincidental, this is certainly what happened in our story.

Whether through being shunned for leaving the community in its distress, the presence of a Moabitess daughter-in-law, or through simple indifference, the lack of support from the townsfolk leaves no choice but to glean as a pauper. While nothing is said here, Naomi's return must have come as a rude shock to whoever was using the family land! It is hard to imagine productive land not being used, especially when the owners may well have been dead.

Naomi and her tragedy have been the focus of chapter 1 but over the next two chapters she fades into the background, only to emerge again as the main character all along when, in chapter 4 her tragedy is resolved. With her resolution comes the resolution of Israel's tragedy with the course set for the kingdom. The role of both Ruth and Boaz in the book prove to relate back to Naomi.

Note on the Barley Harvest

The setting is likely late April. In the early stages of the Israelite settlement the most important cereal was barley . . . because of the necessity to settle fringe areas and barley's tolerance of harsh conditions.[137] Our understanding of grain harvesting (in developed countries) is now limited to broad-acre farms and combine harvesting (which only dates to 1885). Modern harvesting starts with quicker growing varieties and for the threshing process to work efficiently, the farmer has to wait till the grain drops to a moisture content of 12–13 percent. Also, if cut above this moisture content, the grain has to be further dried before it can be stored otherwise it could rot/ferment.

Before combine harvesting, traditional hand-reapers, using sickles or scythes and working as a team, usually cut a field of grain clockwise, starting from an outside edge and finishing in the middle. Scything would therefore leave a windrow of cut stems to the left of the reaper and if cut

---

136. Grant, *Structure*, 429.
137. Borowski, *Agriculture*, 7.

skillfully, leave the seed heads more or less aligned. These are then picked up and tied into sheaves by following workers using other cut stems as ties. These workers, or a following team, would then stand the sheaves up in stooks to dry. This all left room for a wastage of grain.

In biblical times, and even today where harvesting is still primitive, grain with a moisture content of 20 percent or so was harvested with a sickle and tied into a sheaf and left for further drying. This meant that harvesting could be done a couple of weeks earlier than now. This also means that the harvest period would have been over an extended time giving more opportunity for the poor to glean, a process where the very poor could pick over the remnants for food.

Chapter Two

As I read through chapter 2, I was initially troubled about how, or if it could even be possible to make the core of this chapter relevant. While the theme of seeking and finding grace is always at the heart of the Christian message, how was I to make the physical act of gleaning applicable to my own once green Lockyer Valley? Again, Wikipedia says of my home that, "the valley is referred to as 'Australia's Salad Bowl' which accurately describes the area as one of Australia's premium food bowls." There are no droughts here until the pumps suck air, not water and as I write these words in December 2019, they are finally sucking air. But there will be no starvation through a famine similar to what we saw in chapter 1 and there has been no destitute poor gleaning in the fields. To be sure, cutting grass on the roadside or collecting seconds of farm produce for stock feed is a common enough sight, but not the hungry looking for food for their own survival.

James, the brother of our Lord said, "Religion that God our Father accepts as pure and faultless is this: to look after orphans and widows in their distress and to keep oneself from being polluted by the world" (James 1:27). We see that in Boaz his religion was pure and faultless, and it has been the model set before us by the generations gone before, but what of today? Modern biosecurity requirements would prevent strangers entering farms and workplace health while safety around machinery makes members of the public on the field during harvest an impossibility. Perhaps this is all irrelevant now as our welfare state is meant to ensure that it can be possible to remain alive, though not to prosper. Gleaning is certainly in the past and an awareness of the need to find favor, either with man or God also has largely gone. We have a society that knows and demands its rights, free of the shackles of religion and patronage.

The need for the "true religion" of James has not passed, despite our government welfare. The 2020, i.e., pandemic Foodbank survey into hunger in Australia revealed that one in five Australians who are food insecure ran out of food that year and were unable to purchase more. Of these, more than four in ten went a full day without food, up from one in five pre pandemic. (Foodbank is an organization serving as a pantry to the charities). High rent, high electricity costs,[1] and unexpected bills are contributing to increased food insecurity. My own town of 8.000 has charity shops run by five organizations, four of them Christian. This chapter dealing with attitudes towards and help for the poor, destitute, and hungry is not some historical curiosity with no present relevance. Those scourges are with us still and increasing at an alarming rate. It is vital that chapter 2 finds a new expression in our largely urban and secular Australian culture. One such expression is found by some of our church members who have a packing shed and ship produce that does not meet market specification (too large, too small) to Foodbank, which, in turn, during 2019 gave food relief to over 800,000 people per month. This, they report, is not meeting the demand as in my own State of Queensland, food supplies for the hungry need to increase by a third.[2]

As I read this chapter carefully, I also recognized the same attributes in my own mother and father who were people of substance and virtue in the same tradition of Boaz and Ruth. I could see others from all levels of society who fitted this description. None of these could control the weather though their lives were such that the land should have been healed (2 Chron 7:14), but what they could control, themselves and their attitudes to the poor, they did control. While the physical act of gleaning has passed, the core spiritual activity that day was *hesed* and the need for that has not passed away. This spiritual quality is surely the beginning of awareness of the needs and for finding solutions that meet the individual circumstances of people where we live.

Perhaps the greatest takeaway from this chapter is that grace is something to be sought and found. In the chapter "Technical Matters," I show the strong chiastic structure of chapter 2 which is built on the theme of seeking

---

1. Readers may be unaware of the great concern this is in Australia. We went from having probably the cheapest power in the world to now having amongst the most expensive. It is two to three times the cost of power in the USA.
2. Foodbank, *Hunger*, 8, 11–12.

and then finding grace. It comes to the "meat in the sandwich," the center of the chiasm where Boaz grants Ruth grace and she questions "Why" (2:8–10). The balancing response will be that God is repaying your faithfulness and your faith (4:11–13). Ruth's response, as ours also should be, is to ask for even more grace. Lest we think that this grace is earned by her good works, remember she was a Moabitess, from a people whose welfare was to be no concern for Israel (Deut 23:6). Grace seeks, rather than rewards.

> ¹*Naomi had a relative of her husband's, a mighty man of wealth, of the family of Elimelech, and his name was Boaz.*

In chapter 1 we are given the impression that the family line which will produce King David is in danger of extinction. Chapter 2 is introduced with the two women still in isolation, but we learn that Naomi was not as devoid of resources as she first claimed. Now in the remaining three chapters, Boaz,[3] a near relative[4] will, after a faltering start, attempt, albeit unknowingly, to preserve it. Despite, or perhaps because of his self-giving, the line of the Messiah will be counted through a man of virtue instead. A simple but profound message anyone can take away from chapter 2 is that, "a righteous person's behavior transcends proper, but uninspired, correctness."[5] Chapter 1 has shown the remarkable love of Ruth towards Naomi and how she went beyond what could ever be expected and provided extra, much extra. Now, in this chapter, we are introduced to Boaz who also provided extra, beyond his social and religious expectations and duties. In later chapters he will start to provide much extra. How typical Bethlehem was of the nation we can't know, but at the very least there was an individual who showed what Israel should be and could be. Boaz was someone who, "represents the Israelite ideal of covenant"[6] even if he will need some prompting in the next chapter.

---

3. One of the pillars at the entrance to Solomon's temple was called Boaz but we can't know if there was a connection.

4. Hubbard prefers to follow the Ketiv (what is written) and describe Boaz as a friend through her husband while our translations follow the Qere (what is read) which see him as a relative. Hubbard, *Ruth*, 132. Friendship would describe how she knows his nature very well (3:18) but does not explain why Ruth is not directed to his field.

5. Campbell, *Ruth*, 96.

6. Block, *Ruth*, 59.

In an introductory sentence we would normally expect Boaz's name to be mentioned first, then the family relationship but verse one reverses this, stressing instead his relationship to the two widows. Boaz is introduced early so we can understand the events as they unfold on the harvest field. He was more than just a member of the same clan or subtribe as Naomi's husband. The relationship was very close. The word *moda* translated here as "relative" is derived from *yada* which means "to know intimately" as with a very close friend or even sexually. The storyteller plays with this word as the story unfolds. It is found in 2:10, 11, 3:2–4, 11, 18, and 4.4. The closeness of his relationship to Elimelech can't be known, but he certainly wasn't the closest relative.

Rather than using "relative," Campbell suggests it should be translated "covenant brother" as, in the five occurrences outside of Ruth 2:1 and 2 Kings 10:11, it indicates a very close relationship.[7] An example of this close relationship is seen in Psalm 88 where, in verse eight, all his "covenant brothers" shun the Psalmist and in verse eighteen the only one left is darkness. This makes the word very similar to *goel* or "redeemer" which will be introduced by Naomi in verse twenty. Because the root of this word is also closely tied to parties of a covenant, he suspects, "that the storyteller confronts us here with an archaic term belonging to a societal structure that reaches beyond blood ties. It adds a dimension of covenant responsibility to that of family responsibility."[8] An appropriate translation for *mimmispahat* would also be "same sub-tribe."[9]

When commenting on 1:1, I noted how the spiritual and moral tone of the nation had deteriorated to the point that, in chapter 19 of Judges, it matched the depravity of Sodom and Gomorrah. The linguistic similarities of what happened in Gibeah are very striking. Under the conditional covenant of Moses, Israel had met and probably well exceeded the requirements for being expelled from the land. Instead, we see that things are starting to turn, and, in the virtuous Moabite widow and the man of substance, we see a picture of *hesed* behavior that is pleasing to Yahweh. In Table One I show how the author has taken the story of Israel's failure with the Levite and his concubine and, through Boaz and Ruth, tells another of hope and redemption. In my comments on chapter 4, this is further expanded with two extra tables that give a comparison of Judges 20 and 21 to the Book of Ruth.

7. Campbell, *Ruth*, 89–90.
8. Campbell, *Ruth*, 90.
9. Campbell, *Ruth*, 90.

Ruth

The Raped Concubine in Judges 19	Ruth 1—3
Referred to in low status terms (maidservant)	Referred to in low status terms (stranger, maidservant, servant)
Husband referred to as her master v27	Refers to Boaz as her master 2:13
Betrays her husband	Faithful to her husband
Flees to her father's house	Leaves her father's house
After four months her husband goes to father's house to persuade her to return	Pleads to be allowed to return with Naomi
Husband speaks to her heart v3	Boaz speaks to her heart 2:13
Husband eating and drinking and being merry in father's house v6	Boaz eats, drinks and was merry in threshing floor 3:7
Husband didn't want to be treated as a stranger in a Jebusite city	Ruth is treated like a stranger
Elderly Ephramite (not a local) returning from fields offers hospitality	Elderly man, an Ephrathite, still in the fields, is the only one to show hospitality
A night scene with sexual tension with lack of safety and abuse	A night scene with sexual tension but safety and no abuse
Lying on her face dead v29	Falls on her face with gratitude 2:10
Woman dies and husband arises early 26–27	Ruth arises early 3:14
"In the morning" mentioned 3 times in quick succession 25–27	"In the morning" mentioned 3 times in quick succession 3:13–14
No mention of food given to woman	Boaz gives food to Ruth and Naomi
Concern for lodging is only for himself v18	Concern for Ruth's reputation 3:14
Woman dies	Ruth is redeemed

The Raped Concubine in Judges 19	Ruth 1—3
Woman has no name, voiceless and objectified.	Ruth has a name, speaks and is honored

Table 1 Similarities and differences to the murdered concubine of Judges 19 and the Book of Ruth[10]

This is more than a comparison of two events in Israel's history showing the nation's sin and the start of the nation's redemption. The storyteller would have also been playing on his audience's knowledge of the Davidic kingship and the one it replaced. Saul was the people's choice as king. David was God's choice. Saul was from Gibeah (1 Sam 10:26). David was from Bethlehem. Devastation was found in Gibeah. Hospitality is found in Bethlehem. Who would want a king from such a place as Gibeah![11] He/she finishes the book with the word "David" (4:17).

Micah, in Judges 17, had a "hollow religiosity" where he believed that because he has employed a Levite from Bethlehem to serve his idol, his god would bless him. With Boaz we will find "solid integrity"[12] even if he would ultimately require a push in the right direction. So many of the characters of Judges have been nameless but, Boaz is introduced not just as a man of substance and strength but also with a name. He will be shown to be, "Judge like in the respect he commands, and people obey him."[13] This solid integrity can be summarized as righteousness. Block comments that while the, "word [*tzadik/tzedakah* righteous] does not occur in Ruth, . . . the [*hesed*] the characters display accords fully with Moses' charge: 'Righteousness and only righteousness you must pursue' (Deut 16:20)."[14] Likewise, the Torah is not specifically mentioned yet its presence pervades the story and, while Boaz was, "guided by the Law, he was driven by the Spirit."[15] By the time the book has concluded, Boaz will have shown love, joy, peace, patience, all of which are fruits of the Spirit.[16]

10. Ziegler, *Ruth*, 48–53.
11. Ulrich, *Famine*, 9–12.
12. Moore, *Ruth*, 302.
13. Ziegler, *Ruth*, 48.
14. Block, *Ruth*, 40.
15. Block, *Ruth*, 154.
16. Block, *Ruth*, 154.

Chapter 1 concluded with Naomi's complaint that she was empty, and right at the beginning of this chapter we are told of a relative who was full. Boaz is introduced with the words *'ish gibor hayil* which, in the translation I have used, is rendered as "mighty man of wealth" and is a term usually associated with military men. Similar words are found in the angel's tongue in cheek[17] greeting to Gideon, "Hail you mighty man of valor" (Judg 6:12) and of David before he becomes king (1 Sam 16:18). A male hero[18] is called a *gibor* while *hayil* has, as its basic meaning, "to be firm" or "strong."[19] Because of this, the expression is often interpreted, "as a reference to his economic or political standing in the community ("prominent rich man" NRSV)."[20] The hearers would have initially taken this as its meaning but, as the story unfolded, they would quickly realize that this misses the point of this word *hayil*, which has many meanings. In this context, an *hayil* is better interpreted as seeing Ruth as his female counterpart, despite their diametrically opposed social, financial and ethnic standing as the same word is used of Ruth (3:11). This is the approach of the HCSB with, "a prominent man of noble character."

Boaz will show what it means for a man to have a noble character. In chapter 4, the man with no name, who also had the spare cash to purchase the widow's land, is not given that description. What is the source of such a nature? The true mighty man of valor in the Old Testament is God himself and the one who provides the, "true prototype of the mighty man . . . with wisdom, might, counsel and understanding" (Pss 106:8; 145:4, 11, 13).[21] By the end of the story, Boaz will show he has these divine characteristics in abundance, as well as courage to go against social norms. Boaz has been described already (and will be again) as a man who was guided by the Law and led by the Spirit in the way that he, like Enoch, walked with God. It is not surprising then that his actions mirror the true hero and redeemer of Israel.

---

17. He was threshing wheat in a winepress to hide from the Midianites.
18. Oswalt, Gābar in *TWOT*, 148–49.
19. Weber, Ḥayil in *TWOT*, 271–72.
20. Block, *Ruth*, 52.
21. Oswalt, Gābar in *TWOT*, 148–49.

> *²Ruth the Moabitess said to Naomi, "Let me now go to the field, and glean among the ears of grain after him in whose sight I find favor." She said to her, "Go, my daughter." ³She went, and came and gleaned in the field after the reapers; and she happened to come to the portion of the field belonging to Boaz, who was of the family of Elimelech.*

The frequent tears of chapter 1 are past and with it any reference to emotion, for Ruth it has now given way to reason and hard work. With no mention of food being offered by the women of Bethlehem or by their close male relatives, the situation of the returnees would have been perilous. Israel was a nation of redeemed slaves and the evils of slavery should have been in their consciousness. But slavery comes in many forms, including abject poverty with no way of purchasing food. Fortunately, the Law provided a system of relief from the circumstances that oppressed an Israelite. Part of this safety net for the Jewish widow and the alien was through giving them the right to glean, a word that will occur twelve times in this chapter. The passages that stipulate a landowner's duty are:

> Leviticus 19:9-10. ⁹Now when you reap the harvest of your land, you shall not reap to the very edges of your field, nor shall you gather the gleanings of your harvest. 10 And you shall not glean your vineyard, nor shall you gather the fallen grapes of your vineyard; you shall leave them for the needy and for the stranger. I am the Lord your God. (NASB).

> Leviticus 23:22. When you reap the harvest of your land, moreover, you shall not reap to the very edges of your field nor gather the gleaning of your harvest; you are to leave them for the needy and the stranger. I am the Lord your God. (NASB).

> Deuteronomy 24:19-21. ¹⁹When you reap your harvest in your field and forget a sheaf in the field, you are not to go back to get it; it shall belong to the stranger, the orphan, and to the widow, in order that the Lord your God may bless you in all the work of your hands. ²⁰When you beat the olives off your olive tree, you are not to search through the branches again; that shall be left for the stranger, the orphan, and for the widow.

> ²¹"When you gather the grapes of your vineyard, you are not to go over it again; that shall be left for the stranger, the orphan, and the widow. ²²And you shall remember that you were a slave in the land of Egypt; therefore I am commanding you to do this thing (NASB).

While this describes the ideal situation, in the Book of Judges there is a number of accounts where members of the house of Israel fail to provide food for one another (8:4–6, 8; 19:15). This was a continuing problem, and the prophets and Psalmists would also condemn the oppression of the defenseless (Isa 1:23; 10:1–2; Mal 3:5; Pss 94:6–7). Ziegler describes what was probably the reality, rather than the practice saying, "The nation of Israel has lost all semblance of social cohesiveness, along with a basic decency that compels people to offer food to those in need."[22] It makes no sense in a land where crops were poor by modern standards and harvesting inefficient, to make it less so. But as one writer says, "We might classify gleaning as an expression of compassion or justice, but according to Leviticus, allowing others to glean on our property is the fruit of holiness. We do it because God says, "I am the LORD your God."[23]

The words from Leviticus, "I am the LORD your God," are from the preamble to the Ten Commandments, the covenant between the LORD and Israel. Here, in these and other passages from Leviticus, they were most likely shorthand for the covenant. The farmer who did not harvest up to the boundary was saying, "I may never see God's mighty hand in this life like my forefathers, but even if not, I remember where I have come from." It was a reminder that, with a mighty hand, they were brought out of Egypt, out of the house of bondage. There was no rule about how much of the corners of the field they were not to harvest and the moment a rule was made, it ceased to be a spiritual exercise. To not harvest right up to edges of the field was an acknowledgement that God is not always busy elsewhere. The old Scottish saying which was common when I was young was, "Many a mickle makes a muckle" but this law about harvesting was saying that your prosperity does not come from frugality but from God's blessing on your generosity. In the final washup, it was the legal landowner, Yahweh himself, who was the compassionate benefactor of the poor, not the tenant.[24]

The right to glean the edges of the field was not just given by the Almighty to benefit the righteous who were "worthy" of support but to the "unworthy" as well, as it extended to the foreigner. We have an insight into a modern application for believers in a secular world. A foreigner was not to be questioned to see if he/she was a follower of Yahweh. As well, their morals may have been less than the Jewish ideal and Moabites are not pictured

---

22. Ziegler, *Ruth*, 31.
23. Theology of Work Project, *"Gleaning,"* para. 2.
24. Hubbard, *Ruth*, 136.

favorably (Num 25:1–5). Generosity was to be extended to the needy exile on the same conditions as a virtuous impoverished believer.

Despite Ruth's commitment to the God and people of Israel, she is still called the Moabitess here and in verse six and twenty-one stressing her position as an outsider. In the first of five conversations in chapter 2, Ruth has moved to being the central character, doing something about their dire situation with the decision to glean. Her words are ambiguous as they can, "express a request for permission or a firm determination."[25] Translations, e.g., NIV see her deferring to Naomi by asking permission though I suggest that with the dual meaning of her words, and the seriousness of their situation, it could be no more than a rhetorical question. Naomi and Ruth were now among the "institutionalized poor" and had hit rock bottom.[26] The old woman's two-word reply includes the first words of intimacy since Ruth defied her.

Irrespective of her status as a foreigner, Ruth is prepared to do what is necessary to survive, even if the prospect of prospering seems a remote possibility. Ruth understands that survival will require her finding "grace" or "favor" (*hen*) not *hesed*. Though we are told she will be looking for human grace, the storyteller will imply that it is Yahweh's grace she encounters. Favor here is not just being able to do what is her right but to gain special benefits as will happen. By actively seeking favor, rather than sitting at home waiting for a man to come and show it, she has done what is in her power to shape her destiny. That Ruth had to initiate this and Naomi's brief two-word response which offered no warning or hope that she will prosper, indicates that her, "return home had increased rather than helped her sense of depression and reduced her ability to think clearly."[27] It would have been helpful to know that there were close relatives with fields and to warn her of the dangers and the need to adopt behaviors that would minimize her risks. Ruth's attitude is very different. She is pictured as a woman of action with four verbs that describe a sequence of consecutive actions "and she said," "and she went," "and she came," "and she gleaned." There was no time to recover from the journey as the harvest would not last forever.

We are not told why Naomi is not gleaning. She has just made the long, arduous trek from Moab to her home which may in itself provide the answer. Her sense of depression and wretchedness that she showed a

---

25. Campbell, *Ruth*, 91.
26. Moore, *Ruth*, 328.
27. Evans, *Ruth*, 250.

few verses beforehand also provide an answer. Still, two people gleaning would have been more productive and offered some safety for Ruth. What they gleaned had to last a year! Gleaning must have involved a great loss of dignity and there is no expectation from Ruth that Naomi would join her. Her willingness to glean to provide food, not just for herself, but for her mother-in-law as well, showed that she was free of the stinginess that prevented the Moabites providing food to Israel during the exodus (Deut 23:4). This was the act that precluded Moab from any entry into Israel and those hearing the storyteller would understand this as Ruth breaking ranks with her people.[28] The reality of Ziegler's assessment of the spiritual condition of Israel is probably recognized by her mother-in-law, in not directing her to the fields of her close relatives and this questions how deep any national or local repentance was if there was one at all. The likelihood of finding such a person who will look with favor on her was probably remote, so Ruth would need "luck" on her side.

When the storyteller says that she gleaned in a field, it is likely that this refers to the end result of the day, not her initial success. The storyteller says that "She went, and came and gleaned" and the second term, "came" seems unnecessary. This succession of verbs could reflect her experience that day, going from field to field and "being promptly compelled to exit."[29] The workers on Boaz's field were aware of his genuine concern for them, providing not just a safe workplace, but providing food, water, and shade. With Boaz's actions coming from his commitment to Yahweh, it is little surprise that the workers will at least pay lip service to his observance of the covenant requirements. Knowing the landowner's adherence to his religious requirements, it is reasonable to expect the workers, "would have been hesitant to expel anyone needy without first consulting their pious landlord."[30] The Mishnah condemns the attitude Ruth probably encountered in the strongest terms saying, "One who does not allow the poor to glean, or he allows one, and not another, or he helps one, indeed, he openly steals from the poor, as it is said, 'Do not withdraw the eternal border.' (Prov 22:28)"[31]

The same word that was used for the Moab plateau is now used of the cultivated plots around Bethlehem, yet another example of the storyteller's wordplay. Ruth was hoping that in one of these fields she would find "favor,"

---

28. Block, *Ruth*, 117–18.
29. Ziegler, *Ruth*, 210.
30. Ziegler, *Ruth*, 210.
31. Babylonian Talmud: Pe'ah 5.

hen and in verse two it carries the simple meaning of the relationship of a superior to an inferior.³² She would have been very aware of her status in the field and that she would need permission, even if it was her right. In a truly spiritual society, she should not have to hope that someone would be kind to her. The next two uses of the word in verses ten and thirteen show a slightly different use as she moves from hoping for at most probably begrudging permission to finding true favor.

We know Naomi is too old to remarry and Boaz is now introduced, another older person, both senior citizens from whom we can expect wisdom. The remainder of the chapter will center around young men and women from whom, conversely, impulsive and unwise actions can be expected, and Ruth will be warned of just this.

As she set out, Ruth's "chance chanced upon" (*vayiker mikreha*) a field owned by a close relative of her dead husband. The two fold use of derivatives of *qarah* reminds us of the double use of "judge" in 1:1. The meaning of *qarah* in this case is, "the happening and/or occurring of that which is for the most part beyond human control."³³ Our translations usually remove or play down the element of "luck" involved in her random choice, e.g., "she happened to come" (NASB and RSV). We, however, might say, "As luck would have it."

God is spoken about freely in this book, so it is surprising the storyteller only once speaks of him being active in the affairs of men, as opposed to hearsay, and then it is right at the end (4:14). Was it "luck" or "providence," the question is left unanswered, but we are meant to see God's hidden and continuous providential care and sovereignty. If I have a favorite Christian doctrine, it is providence, a word that summarizes much of my personal journey of faith and my work life. I must agree with Block, who uses "sheer luck" for these two words, when he says it, "is as shocking in Hebrew as in [his] translation."³⁴ It is shocking for the Christian also.

The word *qarah* is a by-form of *qara'* which was used by the Philistines who suffered plagues while the Ark was in their possession. Their plan was to test whether their calamities were just coincidental to their housing the Ark in the temple of their god or actually from Yahweh (1 Sam 6:9). Ruth, for her part would have been more familiar with the idea of "luck" (and her luck hadn't been that good) than a loving and caring God who will soon be described, quite possibly, as a mother hen protecting her chicks under her

---

32. Yamauchi, Ḥēn in *TWOT*, 303.
33. Coppes, Qārâ in *TWOT*, 814.
34. Block, *Ruth*, 119.

wings. Her "luck" was not just in arriving at Boaz's field but also by being there when he arrived.

This is not the beginning of "chance" in the story of Ruth. Boaz's own prosperity was the result of chance. God has blessed Boaz with a productive farm, and he was fully aware of God's role in his labor, because he repeatedly invoked the Lord's blessing (2:4; 3:10). But Boaz's possession of this land was not his through astute business practices or better farming. It came to his father by casting of a lot, the throw of a dice, after the conquest. Another Judean we see in Joshua 15 complained that she had been allocated desert and asked for a spring. Again, this "ambiguity runs through all of Ruth, as the reader often cannot tell where human initiative stops, and God's intervention begins."[35]

> **4**_Behold, Boaz came from Bethlehem, and said to the reapers, "May Yahweh be with you." They answered him, "May Yahweh bless you."_

The fact that Boaz arrived on the scene would have meant nothing to Ruth, but the storyteller wants the readers to be surprised (_hinneh_). Boaz has already been introduced as someone with the right family connections and the right bank balance. Ruth had hoped to find someone who would act with kindness towards her, and who should turn up at the right time and the right place, none other than Boaz yet Ruth remains oblivious to its significance for the whole day. Bush believes the delight the readers are meant to see in this term can be translated "Of course!" or "Wouldn't you know it!"[36] The storyteller reveals the piety of Boaz through having his first word spoken being the name of God. His workers also will use God's name despite Boaz and Naomi not fully trusting them to act appropriately. By invoking the covenant name of God, the greeting, which is also a blessing, is covenantal with the implication of all the blessings that come from obedience to it. Boaz's greeting to his workers is the start of the Priestly Blessing (Num 6:24–26) and appropriately he will, "bear the divine name with integrity"[37] as every word we hear from Boaz over the next three chapters is gracious. His greeting echoes the often-repeated words of Yahweh, "I am with you."

---

35. Angel, "_Midrashic_," para. 41.
36. Bush, _Ruth_, 112.
37. Block, _Ruth_, 126.

Shalom, the "peace" that is the outworking of the covenant is alluded to in verse twelve when Boaz asks Yahweh to repay Ruth for her *hesed* to Naomi. Where Boaz will differ from his workers is that he takes personal responsibility to ensure the laws relating to poor in the field and redemption are obeyed. His, "religious integrity is a necessary prerequisite for the founder of monarchy that is intended to restore piety to this errant society."[38] From Judges 17 through to the end of the Book of Ruth, he is the only male who is consistent with his integrity and compassion.

Despite Boaz being a wealthy man and prominent in the Bethlehem community, his relationship with his employees is wholesome. The Law did not have a great deal to say about employer/employee relationships which could be started and ended on a whim, unlike a slave. So, different from the laws for gleaning, how he managed this relationship came from within him, as a man of integrity. That Boaz had a healthy relationship with his workers is shown when he first greeted them in Yahweh's name, instead of going directly to his overseer. It is not just a greeting, it is a blessing. While it is too much to say, "This was a peaceable community in which the temptation for those in authority to LORD it over those in their charge was restrained, a community in which men sought the interest of women, and the weak and marginalized were invited to full participation."[39] It certainly was the case in this field.

By linking the name of God in a greeting, the theological and social are merged. The greeting of Boaz, "emphasizes that God cares about social interactions of human beings. God is ultimately responsible for, as well as being intimately woven into the fabric of correct social interaction."[40] His greeting, "May Yahweh be with you" could also be interpreted as a question, "Is Yahweh with you" and refer to their keeping of God's law. Their reply, which can also be interpreted as, "God shall bless you," would support this. Blessing was a promised result of allowing the poor to glean (Lev 25:19).[41] This would see his, "coming to his field during the harvest not as mercenary but religious. Boaz himself attends to the proper observance of the biblical precepts regarding the poor."[42]

The meaning of *barak* (bless) is wide and can be, "either the verbal enduement with good things or a collective expression of the good things

---

38. Ziegler, *Ruth*, 47–48.
39. Block, *Ruth*, 53.
40. Ziegler, *Ruth*, 204.
41. Ziegler, *Ruth*, 197–98.
42. Ziegler, *Ruth*, 198.

themselves."⁴³ Its source is the "active outgoing of the Divine goodwill and grace."⁴⁴ The benefits of God's blessing were not immediately evident as they were normally futuristic. The person receiving the blessing could be viewed as possessing the power for an abundant life. God's blessing therefore should be seen, not as a magical incantation, but requiring the active and continuing faith of the recipient. Abraham's continued faith in the promise of an heir is a good example of this.

When *barak* is addressed to men it is a prayer for God's favorable intervention on behalf of someone. Block explains the need to seek God's blessing saying:

> The entire book and the notion of blessing itself assumes that by default people are under some sort of curse, and the favorable intervention of God is required for the curse to be lifted and replaced with concrete evidence of divine favor.⁴⁵

The name of God has a pervasive presence throughout this book, in the blessings that people bestow on each other or when people bless or bemoan their fate (1:20–21). The readers will have to wait till the end (4:13) for God's blessing to go from hearsay (1:6) to wishful thinking here, to it becoming something tangible. And then only once is God acknowledged as acting favorably.

> *5 Then Boaz said to his servant who was set over the reapers, "Whose young lady is this?"*
> *6 The servant who was set over the reapers answered, "It is the Moabite lady who came back with Naomi out of the country of Moab. 7 She said, 'Please let me glean and gather after the reapers among the sheaves.' So she came, and has continued even from the morning until now, except that she rested a little in the house."*

From verse eleven, we learn that Boaz knows about Ruth but does not know who she is, now he puts a face to the name. It begs the question of why he has done so little for his relatively close relations when he has only heard good things about her? Bethlehem was not that big a place. The overseer,

---

43. Oswalt, Bārak in *TWOT*, 132.
44. Richardson, *Theological*, 33.
45. Block, *Ruth*, 51.

who is nameless, is described as a *naar*, the first of the young people in this chapter. The word covers a wide range of ages from an infant (Exod 2:6) to the mature Absalom (2 Sam 14:21). Rather than defining his age, we should see it as a contrast to old Boaz and therefore he is lacking the wisdom of age. In a book where names are at the very center, the overseer's lack of a name suggests to the readers, that this is going to be someone who does not embody covenant faithfulness. Running the harvest and maintaining discipline in the field would, I expect, (and the readers would expect,) to be the role of an older, responsible person. This is reinforced by Ziegler who suggests that after being given the title of an adult, the word *naar* is used disparagingly, with the storyteller wanting us to see him as someone who does not fulfil his covenant responsibilities.[46] To need to employ an overseer reflects Boaz's wealth.

At no point are we told Ruth is beautiful but there was something about Ruth that took the attention of Boaz, causing him to ask to whom she "belonged." She was conspicuous and rabbinic sources put this down to her modesty[47] but this need be no more than her Moabite attire. There is the expectation that a young woman would be attached to someone or even worse, that she was a slave. There is a hint that Boaz was asking if she was married[48] as a married woman should not have to glean like a pauper. Other cases where this expression occurs (Gen 32:17–20; 1 Sam 30:13–14) show it is a question that probes circumstances.[49] The question of Boaz regarding Ruth's "possession" and seeing her as less than a person in her own right, "fits his culture, but it does not fit this woman, who is in tension with that culture."[50] She can only be identified, not by a male lord but through her foreignness and through another woman.

Being a woman with no male protector, and a Moabitess on top, she was a social nobody and an easy target for sexual abuse while gleaning. Judge-like, Boaz will ensure Ruth is protected at least on his field. His question is the start of the process of taking Ruth from being unrecognized and unaccepted to integration into the Bethlehem community. When they arrived back from Moab, the residents asked, "*Hazot Naomi*" and showed no interest in Ruth. The question by Boaz also involves *hazot* and can be seen

---

46. Ziegler, *Ruth*, 214–15.
47. Ruth Rabbah: 4:6.
48. Evans, *Ruth*, 251.
49. Campbell, *Ruth*, 94.
50. Trible, *Rhetoric of Sexuality*, 176.

as the storyteller correcting the disregard of the others.[51] The townsfolk will take up this word again in their blessing in 4:12. As in chapter 1, Ruth's coming to Bethlehem is referred to as "returning" and is said to be the appropriate term for the "archetypical proselyte."[52]

Verse seven proves very difficult to translate. Campbell starts, "She asks, "May I glean" and then gives up and takes up the story at verse eight.[53] Block translates further into the verse but then only picks out individual words with enough missing to lose the full sense of the verse.[54] There is little agreement about the final translation of the Hebrew and Block believes that this is intentional on behalf of the storyteller. He believes it is an aid in characterizing the supervisor when he says, "Not only has the young man painted Ruth with negative brush strokes, but his stammering style at this point also conveys his own insecurity and nervousness before his boss."[55] He suggests the same stammering style in 3:2 to express Boaz's frustration that there is a closer kinsman than him.

From this lack of clarity with verse seven we see translators taking two different paths. The RSV sees her as being a diligent worker with the foreman saying, "So she came, and she has continued from early morning until now, without resting even for a moment." However, there is no indication that she has entered the field and the word *ta'amod* means "she has stood," not "she has worked"[56] which leads to an alternate understanding of events. The overseer knew Ruth was a Moabitess and should have been aware that the Law had clearly stated her right to glean and, conversely, Boaz's responsibility to provide for her needs this way. The Law went further, it was more than something he had to do, it should have been done unbegrudgingly. Leviticus 19:33–34 says, "When a stranger resides with you in your land, you shall not do him wrong. 34The stranger who resides with you shall be to you as the native among you, and you shall love him as yourself, for you were strangers in the land of Egypt; I am the Lord your God" (NASB). Did she find this love and acceptance? Not if she was made to stand and watch, somewhat if she was able to work from the time she arrived. Which was it?

---

51. Ziegler, *Ruth*, 200–201.
52. Eskenazi and Frymer-Kensky, *Ruth*, 32.
53. Campbell, *Ruth*, 85.
54. Block, *Ruth*, 25.
55. Block, *Ruth*, 128.
56. Allen, 'āmad in *TWOT*, 673–74.

The overseer has a lot to say to Boaz and, as mentioned previously, it is all critical. In telling Boaz that Ruth is a Moabitess, mentioning her ethnicity twice, he is hinting, if not outright declaring, that she does not really belong there. The overseer does not even acknowledge the bond that exists between her and Naomi. He just associates her with Naomi, against whom there may have been resentment for being in the fields of Moab, with their crops, when Bethlehem had famine.[57] The town was abuzz about Naomi returning with her daughter-in-law and in a small community there would have to have been some awareness of the family connection which is not mentioned.

The religious obligation of the landowner was not to harvest the corners of a field but, inside the field, the rights of a gleaner were limited to those stalks that were missed by the sickle blade or dropped from the palm of the hand when being gathered into sheaves.[58] The need to leave the corners unharvested shows what meagre pickings there were in the field itself when harvested by skilled workers. Only after the harvesters left the field did they have access to what was left standing or had fallen and any forgotten sheaves. The overseer adds one word to Ruth's request to Naomi in verse two. Instead of just asking permission to glean, she is now reported as also asking for permission to *'asap*, "gather" from among from the sheaves. Block describes it this way, "she intended to skim off ears of grain from the shocks the harvesters had created, a brazen act for this foreigner."[59] This makes her sound greedy and presumptuous, without directly saying so.[60] She sought permission from Naomi to glean behind the owner who was gracious to her, but the overseer has her asking to work among the harvesters.

Then the overseer said that Ruth has been standing since the morning. Gleaners do not stand, they move. They follow the harvesters, they sit and they glean. Why then does the overseer say that Ruth has been standing all day? Perhaps he is hinting that he ordered her to stand and wait until the master arrives and decides whether to give her permission to glean or not. In three brief sentences, the overseer has put Ruth down, and has shown off his own ability to keep unworthy strangers out—without quite saying a single explicitly negative word about her. Ziegler paints a picture of the

---

57. Ziegler, *Ruth*, 214.

58. Refer to Babylonian Talmud: Pe'ah, chapters 4 and 5 for the regulations regarding gleaning.

59. Block, *Ruth*, 127.

60. Ziegler, *Ruth*, 215.

overseer as a bigot who dislikes strangers.[61] To which I would add, it is a very big deal not to let her drink from the water jars and that, above everything, shows what was going on here.

A positive spin can be given to the foreman's word by interpreting *'amad* as "to remain" or "stay" in that she has not gone to another farmer's field, but this would be unusual. It also requires that the overseer, despite the poor picture he painted, has given Ruth privileges beyond what the Law required without first getting permission from Boaz. This all seems very unlikely.

> **8** *Then Boaz said to Ruth, "Listen, my daughter. Don't go to glean in another field, and don't go from here, but stay here close to my maidens.* **9** *Let your eyes be on the field that they reap, and go after them. Haven't I commanded the young men not to touch you? When you are thirsty, go to the vessels, and drink from that which the young men have drawn."*

Ruth had respectfully asked for permission to glean but she didn't find grace and favor with the overseer, and she must have been disappointed and wondering if she had made a good choice going to that field. But Boaz saw right through his overseer, ignoring all that he said and went to Ruth and was gracious to her, addressing her in the most tender way, "My daughter." This opening formula was used already by Naomi in 1:13 again in 2:2 also by her in 3:1. His following words are made up of two negative rhetorical questions. This is said to reflect their old fashioned, fussy way of speaking which places them in the same age group.[62] As their social and age distance required, Boaz started the conversation and used relatively long sentences while the replies of Ruth are short.[63] Despite the huge ethnic and social divide, "Boaz spoke with the grace and generosity that Ruth has hoped for . . . , in him biblical *hesed* became flesh and dwelt among humankind."[64] Three times in chapter 1 Naomi resolutely used *lekh* "go" to urge Ruth to return to Moab, (1:8, 11, 12). Ruth then used the word also when asking permission to go gleaning and Naomi, again using *lekh*, (far from enthusiastically,) gave permission so its use by Boaz in verse eight could not be more different. Starting with the same word used negatively,

---

61. Ziegler, *Ruth*, 213–18.
62. Eskenazi and Frymer-Kensky, *Ruth*, 34.
63. Block, *Ruth*, 129.
64. Block, *Ruth*, 129.

Boaz urges Ruth to remain, so with the one word "Naomi repels, whereas Boaz welcomes; Naomi pushes Ruth out, while Boaz gently tugs inward."[65]

Was this more than just a courteous greeting? Moore sees in these words a family patriarch assuming his responsibility to restore, "two displaced widows whose connection to kinship structure has been severed."[66] Without knowing Ruth personally, his subsequent actions on the field are father-like, going beyond what would be expected. Ruth, at this stage, is not aware of the family connection and she can see only that her hope for finding favor had been answered beyond any reasonable expectation.

The wealthy landowner spoke to "Ruth," without the addition of "Moabitess." He was not speaking to an unnamed young woman or a foreigner or an appendage of Naomi, but simply to Ruth. Her gratitude to Boaz in verse ten stems first from simply being recognized. This favor was more than could ever be hoped for. Not only was Boaz gracious to Ruth, ensuring her safety at work, he will go further. In verse twelve, he will bless this foreigner who, until a few days beforehand, had followed idols. There is no thought from Boaz that she was unclean as this would have made the drinking implements unclean. Rather, she was not just someone the Lord could bless, but in his opinion was someone the Lord should bless because of her faithfulness to Naomi. This is along the same lines as when Naomi asks the Lord to use the *hesed* of her daughters-in-law to model his kindness to them (1:8–9). But Boaz's starting point is different. The Lord is the one who blesses but for Naomi he is the one who afflicts. Ruth started the day hoping for human favor (*hen*) but will end it, not just with a hope of divine blessing but the actual experience of *hesed*. An indication that there was something different about this workplace is that the water has been drawn by the young men and not the young women. This was traditionally the work of women, (e.g., Gen 24:10–20), not the more able men.

After the arduous trek from Moab, the great uncertainty Ruth is facing about her future and lack of kindness, the storyteller hints at her future stability. Boaz told Ruth not to leave the field, which is literally "you shall not wander" (*'abar*). In 1:14, Ruth cleaved to Naomi who tried hard to push her away, now the same verb is used of how Boaz draws her in by wanting her to stay very close to the young women in the field. The storyteller intentionally picks up on this uncommon word and interweaves it into the narrative which, "implicitly applauds . . . [suggesting] Ruth receives a commensurate

---

65. Ziegler, *Ruth*, 219.
66. Moore, *Ruth*, 332.

return for her behavior."⁶⁷ In reality, by giving Ruth kindness, sound advice, safety in the fields, permission to glean every day and daily food and water, Boaz is really asking Ruth to cleave to him, a complete stranger.

By telling Ruth to glean with his own young girls, Boaz is sending the message that he views her in the more elevated position of a *naarah*, a young (servant) girl.⁶⁸ This is a position above a normal gleaner and almost as an employee, as he extends to her the same privileges he gave to his employees. The young men, *naarim*, a parallel to the new *naarah*, are instructed not to touch Ruth. While *naga'* can mean no more that simple touching, here it refers to sexual contact.⁶⁹ Sakenfeld sees the old man's comments as a concern for Ruth's safety and was advising her how to act in a Jewish field when she translates "watch the field" as meaning "keep your eyes down" when near where the men are working.⁷⁰ This is a further example of the ambiguities of the book. There may even be the implication through Boaz's triple request that Ruth not leave his field that something had already happened.⁷¹ If she is correct, (and it would have been sound advice in such a dangerous setting), it will be followed up with further counsel on appropriate behavior. Later that day she took her meal sitting beside the reapers who would not have been all female. His advice about only associating with the women had not been fully grasped! Finally, she is guided by Naomi to stay only with the young women (See my comments on 2:22). This makes the events of chapter 3 even more shocking. Her new status would help avoid unwanted advances or worse. Ruth's response is to fall down before her new male protector. In Judges 19, where there are striking similarities and contrasts to this chapter, the concubine "fell down" *napal* (same word) as a result of, "forced submission to a violent male."⁷² Here it is through respect and gratitude.

Boaz treated his employees fairly but was he typical? He recognized that it is not safe in other fields and even in his own fields he has to warn his workers not to molest Ruth. More than that, he had already told them not to molest her before he even knew that she was a relative. Perhaps he could tell she was a foreigner from her attire, or he just knew she was new. Either way, by instructing the workers to act with proprietary before he knew who

---

67. Ziegler, *Ruth*, 470.
68. Moore, *Ruth*, 332.
69. Coppes, Nāga' in *TWOT*, 551–52.
70. Sakenfeld, *Ruth*, 43.
71. Evans, *Ruth*, 253.
72. Moore, *Ruth*, 333.

the gleaner was, speaks volumes about Boaz. Over recent years in Australia, we have become aware in our own businesses that a safe workplace is much more than just guarding our machines. With our own Lockyer Valley fields largely being harvested by foreign backpackers, we must also be diligent now that the correct wages are being paid by the contractors we engage. Stories that have come out of recent years of underpayment in a wide range of industries have been shameful. Perhaps more shameful has been the disclosure of sexual harassment in the workplace of backpackers all the way up to high profile actresses.

The Book of Ruth is seen by Warren Wiersbe as a love story, claiming "that when he [Boaz] saw her it was love at first sight . . . and therefore took the first steps to meet her needs."[73] This makes his actions self-serving and not the natural reactions arising from his compassionate nature. However, there is no clear indications of any romance or attraction between Boaz and Ruth in chapter 2. But there are hints of the marriage to come, though these are only evident once we know the outcome of the story. Reading the second time through it is possible to see alternate meanings of words. Possibly the clearest hint is when Boaz allows Ruth to drink from the "drawn" water. With the mention of "drawn" water, a well is implied and with that, a setting that would have been familiar to the readers, a "type-scene" which ends in betrothal for Isaac, Jacob and Moses.[74] It is described this way:

> The expected-betrothal-type-scene begins when a man journeys to a distant land and there encounters a young woman at a well. As it turns out, she is a member of his extended family. Water is drawn from the well, and the young woman rushes home to tell her family about the man's arrival. The man is invited for a meal and a betrothal is concluded between the man and the woman.[75]

Allowing for the role reversal, this fits very accurately with the Book of Ruth.

---

73. Wiersbe, *Be Committed*, 36.

74. The scene-type is present also with Saul and the young women in 1 Samuel 9 but there, dynasty is not the focus but kingship and will result in Saul's first meeting with Samuel.

75. Ziegler, *Ruth*, 272–73.

> **10** *Then she fell on her face and bowed herself to the ground, and said to him, "Why have I found favor in your sight, that you should take knowledge of me, since I am a foreigner?"*
> **11** *Boaz answered her, "I have been told all about what you have done for your mother-in-law since the death of your husband, and how you have left your father, your mother, and the land of your birth, and have come to a people that you didn't know before.*
> **12** *May Yahweh repay your work, and a full reward be given to you from Yahweh, the God of Israel, under whose wings you have come to take refuge."*

Boaz and Ruth both speak twice. Each time that Boaz speaks Ruth responds with gratitude and self-consciousness of her social status. The first time she expressed her amazement and gratitude that, as a foreigner, she has not only been recognized by, but also found in Boaz, the favor she sought. We need to remember that in all this, Boaz is not taking the initiative. He is reacting to a woman who actively sought favor.[76] (While probably we would have expected him to have taken the initiative as he knew of his relative's predicament, there is no hint of censure of his slowness to act.) A simple "Thank you" was enough but Ruth draws Boaz into a conversation that revealed his motives. The storyteller uses a skillful word play as "foreigner" and "notice" have the same consonantal root *nkr*. The same root will be taken up again by Naomi in verse nineteen when she asks for a blessing on the man who has taken notice of Ruth. Yet again the word will be used on the threshing floor (3:14) when Ruth leaves before she can be "recognized." Recognition is a major theme of the Book of Ruth. Ziegler, after describing the period of Judges as a time, "defined by dissatisfaction and mutual estrangement" describes this act of recognition as, "a seminal moment, not only restoring Ruth's personal dignity, but also in guiding the townspeople to move past the period in which people do not properly see one another."[77]

Ruth's response of falling on her face and then followed by the word *wattistahu* for "bowed down" invokes the language of "worship,"[78] especially after calling Boaz her "lord." In the context of an inferior to a superior, it could be seen as just "servile submission," but it would seem contradictory

---

76. Trible, *Rhetoric of Sexuality*, 178.
77. Ziegler, *Ruth*, 203.
78. Yamauchi, Šāāḥ â in *TWOT*, 914–15.

to view a woman of noble character as servile. Block sees in this setting that she "bowed before a man who would play an extremely important role in the divine plan for Israel, and indeed humankind."[79] If it wasn't a rhetorical question, what answer was Ruth expecting? Unfortunately, in our own society, news reports have said that continued favor from some employers to foreign backpackers has depended on providing sexual favors (see comment on verse nineteen). Boaz's answer speaks volumes about the man.

In this, her second reply, Ruth accepts the implication of cleaving to the servant girls and calls herself as such, and longs for the favor to continue. The bar is raised even further from servant girl status when she is redefined by Boaz as a woman who has sought refuge under Yahweh's wings (2:12). Boaz's reply to Ruth's question "Why" starts with two separate verbs, "he answered" and "he said," one of which would seem unnecessary. These are the same verbs used by the overseer in verse six, though not together. When these two verbs occur together, they can have the effect of an official pronouncement. Rather than his words being a private conversation between Ruth and Boaz,[80] they were for the benefit of everyone harvesting in his field that day.

In helping Ruth, Boaz was directly helping Naomi. He was high in the chain of those who could be considered responsible for caring for a bereaved relative, yet it is only after Ruth enters his field by chance that he takes action to help Naomi. He answered Ruth that he had been told how she had left her country and parents. This is not just idle gossip, but the double words *hugged huggad li* can be translated, "it has been explained and reexplained to me."[81] Boaz has done his homework on the foreigner. Yet, until now, despite good things being said, neither the relatives nor the townsfolk have been moved to assist Ruth. Her comfort to Naomi and her desire to provide an heir to continue her dead husband's name may have been a moral obligation, but she, "was free not to fulfil the responsibility while at the same time being uniquely in the position to do so."[82] Orpah's reaction was the natural course of events, not Ruth's.

Boaz could have replied that his actions are simply those that would have been expected of someone who is at his very core, good and God honoring, and this would have been correct. A person's attitude to the poor reflects his attitude to God. To have acted any differently would have seen him acting

---

79. Block, *Ruth*, 131.
80. Ziegler, *Ruth*, 221. Examples are Gen 24:50; 27:37; 31:43; 40:18; Exod 4:1.
81. Moore, *Ruth*, 334.
82. Sakenfeld, *Meaning*, 43.

at odds to the covenant keeping God whose blessings he would call down and equally be willing to receive from others. This is clearly stated by his descendant Solomon in Proverbs 14:31, "One who oppresses the poor taunts his Maker, but one who is gracious to the needy honors Him" (NASB).

Instead, Boaz reverses the criteria, looking instead at Ruth's goodness. The explanation he gave was his recognition of how she "left your father, your mother and the land of your birth, and have come to a people that you didn't know before." These words mirror the journey of Abraham from Ur of the Chaldees. Likewise, the "reward" (*sekharka*) that was promised Abraham (Gen 15:1) is also reflected in the "reward" (*maskurtekh*) Boaz calls down upon Ruth. The link to the Patriarchs is also strengthened when Jacob used the word three times about his dispute with Laban (Gen 29:15; 31:7, 41). We see in the cycles of the Book of Judges that God maintained order among his people through punishment for sin, but Boaz had not lost sight of the other side of the coin, that he repays people for good deeds. The debt was such that only Yahweh could repay it.[83]

As well as Abraham's journey to Canaan, there are also echoes of Genesis 31:13–18 with the migration of the Patriarch Jacob back from Paddan Aram in upper Mesopotamia, again with great wealth. Similarities exist also to marriage in Genesis 2:24 with the reference to leaving mother and father and "cleaving." But in contrast to both the patriarchal allusions, there is the implication of Ruth possessing an even greater faith for she has no consolation of wealth, only the prospect of abject poverty. There is no promise of the presence of God or his protection. Naomi had also told her to abandon hope of marriage.

Boaz's actions have been daringly represented in Judaism as a role model for God, "Boaz comforts! Will I not comfort?!"[84] At the very least, God expects people to do their part in repairing the world: "Boaz did his [part] and Ruth did hers and Naomi did hers; [then] the Holy One said: 'I too will do mine.'"[85] This is not too dissimilar to the thought expressed in the Lord's Prayer over forgiveness. William Barclay says of it, "Jesus wants your disposition to be a good example to God. We invite God to imitate us." He then quoted Gregory of Nyssa who said, "Do thou the same as I have done. Imitate thy servant O Lord though he be only a poor beggar and thou art the king of the universe. I have shown great mercy to my neighbor,

---

83. Hubbard, *Ruth*, 166.
84. Ziegler, *Ruth*, 233.
85. Eskenazi and Frymer-Kensky, *Ruth*, lii.

imitate thy servant's charity O Lord."[86] In the end Boaz does not wait for God to act but himself does what he calls on God to do. Boaz will be the wings of God when he seizes the opportunity to be the redeemer.[87]

Judaism can portray Ruth as the opposite of Orpah, presenting her as paradigm of kindness and modesty—modestly bending down in the field[88] and not flirting with the young men.[89] Her experience in Bethlehem so far has not been good. The women have ignored her, the overseer puts her down before Boaz, the young reapers may well have harassed her and in chapter 4, her closest redeemer will rebuff her.[90] This is what would have been expected. What is not expected is that, against social norms, Boaz functions as a role model leading the people of Bethlehem in recognizing her.

It is always a pointed question, "What are we to believe or do in a world where God's presence is not self-evident?" It is even more so when we view the Book of Ruth from the perspective of the violent times of the Judges—What are we to do in a world pervaded by chaos and violence? The answer given in the Book of Ruth is, "a theology of *hesed*—generosity that goes beyond the call of duty. Human *hesed*, when rightly cultivated "for the sake of heaven" . . . , serves as a real power."[91]

Boaz is presented to us as a paragon of this *hesed* yet, "At the same time, however, some midrashim[92] perceive a disparity between his speech and his actions and view Boaz's *hesed* as motivated at least partially by his own interests."[93] It must be acknowledged that while Boaz spoke generously to Ruth, he only treated her with moderate generosity.[94] Although other biblical books explicitly enjoin Israel to emulate God, (e.g., Lev 19:2), Ruth seems to say more, it is almost as if human actions and words bring God into the world. God-centered people prompt God to show up, as it were.[95]

---

86. Barclay, *Lord's Prayer*, 110.

87. Block, *Ruth*, 52.

88. Babylonian Talmud: Šabb.. 113b.

89. Ruth Rabbah: 4:9.

90. Ziegler, *Ruth*, 46.

91. Eskenazi and Frymer-Kensky, *Ruth*, liii.

92. Midrashim are homilies on a passage derived by traditional Jewish exegetical methods and usually involve embellishment of the scriptural narrative.

93. Angel, "*Midrashic*," para. 37.

94. Angel, "*Midrashic*," para. 35.

95. Eskenazi and Frymer-Kensky, *Ruth*, lii.

Ruth

For all of Boaz's kindness, he did not claim to initiate it, acknowledging that he was only imitating Ruth.

Shalom is a well-known word which is usually translated as "peace." Boaz uses the verbal form *yesalem* for "repay" which could indicate an obligation upon Yahweh to pay an outstanding debt (as with the LXX). With an implication of measure for measure this would have been the flip side of an eye for an eye. But the alternate meanings of, "completion and fulfillment—of entering into . . . a restored relationship"[96] would be more appropriate in our story of *hesed,* where service is voluntary and motivated by love. Any "repayment" would likewise be motivated by love and not a measured response. The word is used a second time but as an adjective in verse twelve to describe the full or complete reward for sheltering under the *kanaph* "wings" of Yahweh.[97]

Yahweh is not just a rewarding God, even the pagans believed that of their gods, but he was a God who provided refuge under his wings. Given the deep Yahwistic faith of Boaz it would be expected that he had visited the tabernacle where the wings of the cherubim extended over the mercy seat, though the Ark was hidden from his view. His mother, Rahab, would have seen the Ark from her brothel window as it was carried around Jericho and could testify to the refuge offered to those who sought refuge under the wings of Yahweh, foreigner and Israelite alike. The wings of Yahweh could also be a metaphor describing the loving care of the God of Israel, to that of a mother bird offering her wings as protection for her chicks. This illustration is only found elsewhere in the Old Testament in Psalm 91:4. Jesus used the same illustration to describe how he wanted to gather up the people of Jerusalem and protect them (Matt 23:37; Luke 13:34). The ambiguity of this book allows us to see either illustration, or both at the same time.

Unlike the Levite from Judges 19 who found it, "easier . . . to look down his nose at Jebusite foreigners than to protect his concubine from Israelite harm,"[98] Boaz has allowed himself to be transformed by his faith. By rewarding Ruth and sheltering her from attack, his actions are more than Judge like. They are God like, wrapped in the frailty and fallibility of human flesh. Not only has he been transformed, Boaz also allows that God

---

96. Carr, Šālēm in *TWOT*, 930.

97. Ziegler sees in this dual reference to *shalem* a possible hint at kingship. *Shelemat* is the time of completion, security, reward and peace (1 Kgs 5:4–5) that is brought in by Solomon (*Shelomo*) from Jerusalem. Ziegler, *Ruth*, 229.

98. Moore, *Ruth*, 334.

can transform others. He is father-like in the way he steers Ruth away from Moabite practices into the modest ways of Jewish women. This is explored in my comments on verses twenty and twenty-one.

> 13 Then she said, "Let me find favor in your sight, my LORD, because you have comforted me, and because you have spoken kindly to your servant, though I am not as one of your servants."

Chapter 1 ends with the picture of Naomi who was empty but as Ruth eats at the invitation of Boaz, the storyteller emphasizes Ruth's fullness. An old man, an attractive younger woman, and a workplace where the propriety of the younger men couldn't automatically be guaranteed is prime ground for some very unsavory thoughts, if not comments. Despite the storyteller not saying so in as many words I think we can say that Ruth was attractive. Boaz saw an expression of her noble character in that she did, "not run after the younger men, whether rich or poor" which, no doubt, is easier for a woman to do if she is attractive. What Boaz and Ruth saw in that field was totally different. Both are described as people of moral substance and character and like recognizing like. His actions not only met the immediate needs of Naomi and Ruth, but Boaz went beyond any responsibility he had to a gleaner. Charity is too often called "cold charity" for a reason but that day on the field his words were kind and comforting. The meaning of, "you have spoken to the heart" (*leb*) is, on the face of it, referring to his comforting words but in light of the outcome of the next two chapters, the hint of the double meaning of "to entice a woman" can't be ignored.[99]

Ruth addresses the old stranger as "lord" (*'adon*) and calls herself a servant girl (*shifha*). The storyteller builds tension by using a cognate of the word used of "subtribe" to describe her family relationship to Boaz in 2:1.[100] Later, she will call herself Boaz's *ama* (3:9) a "maid-servant" or "female slave" and the two words can be synonyms. An *ama* though could have marriage prospects so its use in the next chapter hints at what's to come. The word she chose to use still abased her when Boaz had already raised her status to that of a young woman and not a foreigner (2:5). This word choice may reflect a poor self-perception which kindness had not fully erased. Combine this with Ruth falling on her face before this man and the

---

99. Campbell, *Ruth*, 100–101.
100. Campbell, *Ruth*, 101.

recognized danger of sexual assault in her workplace. This does not paint a good picture of the position of women in Israelite society at the time.

While Ruth thinks that she does not belong even in the lowest servant class of her protector's household, the readers are aware of her close relationship to Boaz. The translation reads, "though I am not as one of your servants" but it is literally, "and I will not be as one of your maidservants." After hinting at the language of courtship, there is in the alternate meaning of the storyteller's words, a hint at her desired status. As Ashkenazi and Frymer-Kensky say, "she not only acknowledges Boaz's graciousness; but also—at another level—distances herself from permanent subservience: she is not an actual maid-servant and will not become one."[101] Such is the ambiguity of the Book of Ruth.

Proverbs 31 paints a picture of a woman who is far from servile and subservient. There, a husband's reputation is built upon, and recognized by all to be built upon, the diligence, integrity, and hard work of his virtuous wife. The Proverbs portrait of the ideal wife sees her doing the things attributed to Boaz, purchasing fields, farming and ensuring the safety and security of her young women. The fact that there were very few such women, as Proverbs states, does not make the status quo in Ruth correct. In the Tabernacle and the temple of Solomon there would be no court of the women. All could come equally before Yahweh.

> [14] *At meal time Boaz said to her, "Come here, and eat some bread, and dip your morsel in the vinegar." She sat beside the reapers, and they passed her parched grain. She ate, was satisfied, and left some of it.* [15] *When she had risen up to glean, Boaz commanded his young men, saying, "Let her glean even among the sheaves, and don't reproach her.* [16] *Also pull out some for her from the bundles, and leave it. Let her glean, and don't rebuke her."*

While Naomi will recognize the ephah[102] of grain gleaned that day as the result of *hesed*, what she did not see, which was Boaz's actions with Ruth over the meal, embodied *hesed*, though not called as such. Boaz extended to Ruth all the rights that his other young female workers enjoyed, shelter, food, water and very importantly, companionship. She sits, as it were, at the

---

101. Eskenazi and Frymer-Kensky, *Ruth*, 40.

102. See the comments on verse seventeen for what this old measure represents.

master's table.[103] Food, which did not have to be given at all, was provided beyond what she needed. This level of generosity is seldom seen in the Old Testament. It is uncertain what *homes,* often translated as "vinegar" actually is but it was forbidden to a Nazirite (Num 6:3) so it is likely to be alcohol related. The Babylonian Talmud describes this item as good for countering the heat.[104] Boaz did not let his guest eat dry bread while he sat and ate something tastier in front of her. Here, under the shelter, Ruth is being introduced to Bethlehem society in an environment controlled by an employer whose own behavior set the standard of their expected conduct. Whereas Ruth may have been tolerated, Boaz moves the situation to active acceptance.[105]

At the mealtime she is elevated to being an invited guest of the landowner. The text is not clear who gave Ruth the food, the reapers or Boaz, but most translations have this as Boaz, (e.g., NIV, KJV, RSV) and the story will demand it—see my further comments on verses twenty and twenty-one. By feeding Ruth personally she knows how much she can take of the prepared grain without appearing greedy. It is very possible that Ruth had not eaten properly for some days, yet she is considerate. This may be indicated by the three verbs used in rapid succession in verse fourteen, *vatokhal* "and she ate," *vatisba* "and she was satisfied," and *vatotat* "and she left over."[106] She ate no more than she needed and took her leftovers home to Naomi. By sitting with men, in a setting where gender separation was practiced, the storyteller may well have been depicting Ruth reverting to Moabite norms.[107] Naomi will gently guide her in correct social behavior when she returns with her day's gleanings and the message will be taken to heart.

After the meal, the instructions given by Boaz direct to his workers, out of earshot of Ruth, are intended to return dignity to Ruth and go far beyond the requirements of the Law. These instructions are, given in an ABA'B' format:

103. Eskenazi and Frymer-Kensky, *Ruth,* 41.
104. Babylonian Talmud: Šabb. 113b.
105. Moore, *Ruth,* 340.
106. Ziegler, *Ruth,* 241.
107. Ziegler, *Ruth,* 261–62.

Ruth

A Let her glean even among the sheaves,

   B and do not insult her

A' Also you are to purposely slip out for her *some grain* from the bundles and leave *it*

   B' so that she may glean, and do not rebuke her (NASB).

Boaz restated his earlier instructions and gave more generous privileges to Ruth giving her permission to glean among the sheaves. The overseer said that Ruth asked to glean among the sheaves (*ba-'omarim*) which it appears he considered impudent for a foreigner. She may have been asking for a better position among the gleaners. The overseer's earlier disparaging remarks were ignored further after lunch when Boaz gave even more privileges when he said, "Let her glean among the sheaves" (*gam bein ha-omarim telakket*). The word *gam* means "also" but with our limited knowledge of harvesting practice in the field it is no longer clear what this privilege is.[108] Even when, "she deviates from accepted norms of gleaning"[109] she is not to be embarrassed.

It must be embarrassing for someone to be so destitute that they must glean to survive but Ruth's dignity is also being restored by Boaz ensuring, artificially and without her knowledge, that she takes home a bountiful harvest, rather than a day or two's provision. In his instructions to the reapers to drop extra stalks, Boaz uses *vaazavtem*, "leave" or "let" the same word he previously used of her leaving her parents (*vataazvi*) in verse eleven and picks up the same word in Ruth's pleading (*le'ozvekh*) to Naomi that she should not leave her (1:16).[110] Boaz goes even further in protecting Ruth's dignity, especially as she would be seen as having very special privileges over other gleaners. He had already given instructions that Ruth was not to be touched sexually, but someone on the bottom rung of society is still an easy target for a caustic tongue. No doubt there would have been a price to pay for disobeying these commands. Was there a price to pay for Boaz? In any small-town gossip is always an issue with people always trying to read between the lines, let alone workers who needed to be instructed on sexual propriety. His strong social position made it easier to be bold with his response of being the human face of God to his relative.

---

108. Eskenazi and Frymer-Kensky, *Ruth*, 41.
109. Ziegler, *Ruth*, 246.
110. Ziegler, *Ruth*, 246.

> ¹⁷*So she gleaned in the field until evening; and she beat out that which she had gleaned, and it was about an ephah of barley.* ¹⁸*She took it up, and went into the city. Then her mother-in-law saw what she had gleaned; and she brought out and gave to her that which she had left after she had enough.* ¹⁹*Her mother-in-law said to her, "Where have you gleaned today? Where have you worked? Blessed be he who noticed you." She told her mother-in-law with whom she had worked, "The man's name with whom I worked today is Boaz."* ²⁰*Naomi said to her daughter-in-law, "May he be blessed by Yahweh, who has not abandoned his kindness to the living and to the dead." Naomi said to her, "The man is a close relative to us, one of our near kinsmen."*

After a slow start for the day, particularly after, it appears, the foreman made Ruth wait for permission from Boaz, she was able to beat out an ephah of barley. An *ephah* by volume was about twenty-three liters and by weight about 15.5 to 17.7 kg.[111] While this was good, very good, the time available to glean was very limited. Comparing Exodus 16:16 and 36 where an *omer* appears to be a day's ration and as there are ten *omers* to an *ephah* this would normally be five days provision for the two women. That is unlikely as it requires eating almost 2.3 liters of grain each per person per day. Coming from another direction, on a subsistence diet of 1200 calories each and with about 350 calories to 100 grams of barley, Ruth brought home about twenty to twenty-five days' provision for them both if eaten frugally. The bounty she had from gleaning probably shows the extent of the reversal of fortune of this rural community when Yahweh remembered his people.

Ruth immediately gave her mother-in-law the leftovers from lunch before saying anything to Naomi about the day. The storyteller's skill is seen by using the word *yasa* "brought forth" which has as one of its possible meanings "to give birth"[112] and so possibly hinting at the final resolution of the story where Ruth's baby is handed to Naomi.[113] This must have looked

---

111. The weight is very imprecise and could be 12–13 kg. (Evans, *Ruth*, 254) or even as much as 21 kg (Campbell, *Ruth*, 104).

112. Gilchrist, Yāṣā' in *TWOT*, 394.

113. Some, e.g., Rauber, see a further suggestion of future pregnancy at the end of chapter 3 when Ruth carries home the grain in an apron held in front of her and the word of Boaz not to go empty. Rauber, *Literary Values*, 27–37. However, the allusion is not as

Ruth

like a distinct change in their fortunes and Naomi's question, "where" *eipho* rhymes with *ephah*. The result of her gleanings was obviously more than expected from a novice gleaner and Naomi calls, in words that echo Boaz's blessing on his workers, a blessing down upon this unknown benefactor. This is Naomi's first blessing in the Book of Ruth and is possibly the first dawning upon her that her God of *hesed* had been at work, even in her darkest hour.[114] The storyteller does not affirm whether God truly has been the instigator or whether it was after all, just chance.

Naomi's first question of where she gleaned is straightforward but the, "second question *ana asit* 'where did you do this' is decidedly vague, Where did Ruth do *what!!!*"[115] As Ziegler says, "it is difficult to imagine what act Ruth, a newcomer to town, could have done for a landowner in a field on her first day on the job."[116] The gleanings were large and beyond that, gleaners are not supplied with food. The possibility of an immoral act being rewarded with food may well have been on her mind. One Jewish source says it this way, "When her mother-in-law saw her, she became frightened and said, 'God forbid, she has clung to the licentious ones.'"[117]

Ruth's reply starts off equally vague. She does not concern herself with "where" and is repetitive until, and we can almost hear the drumroll, then she drops the name, Boaz. She answered, "Who." Just as in the introduction to chapter 2, the name Boaz is left hanging till the end of the sentence. Ruth didn't do anything for Boaz. Instead Boaz did something for her. Her bounty was from the favor she found with Boaz, a man above suspicion. She twice uses *asa . . . im*, "whom . . . with" in verse nineteen echoing Naomi's words, but this phrase can suggest sexual behavior, as with Amnon raping Tamar (2 Sam 13:16). Again, *asa* is used on the threshing floor incident suggesting, "an underlying sexual subtext."[118] Ruth returned to Naomi, "in her enormous and touching innocence" with little understanding of the significance of what had happened in the field. Naomi, for her part quickly grasped what had occurred and views Ruth in a new light. She no longer pushes Ruth away instead, for the first time, using the first-person plural, "our redeemer." Ruth has gone against culture

---

clear, as the item of clothing is uncertain and may have been carried on the back or head.

114. Moore, *Ruth*, 341.
115. Ziegler, *Ruth*, 250.
116. Ziegler, *Ruth*, 250.
117. Meir, *Ruth*, para. 21.
118. Ziegler, *Ruth*, 251.

in actively seeking favor and even being pushy on the barley field when looking for the best gleaning. Why did Naomi not seek out Boaz in the first place? Trible suggests that Naomi may be, "a woman of her culture who waits for a man to act first."[119]

The storyteller had left verse twenty deliberately ambiguous and in doing so, "intended to highlight the complex relationship between human and Divine action in Ruth."[120] We can't be sure if Naomi has seen the hand of God in her change of circumstances for the better, or is she blessing Boaz for his favorable treatment of Ruth and seeing in him a possible redeemer. A strong case can be made for both possibilities. While Ruth will ultimately be the bride, Naomi is already seeing in Boaz the potential redeemer for both of them. If this is human *hesed* that came from Boaz, it would be his response to Ruth showing *hesed* to her living and the dead. Kindness done to the dead can never be repaid making it the, "purest, most inspiring expression of kindness."[121]

The *hesed* that Ruth received in the barley field was based on a previous action and could be seen as deserving. Ruth has left her home to follow Naomi, going far beyond what was needed. The use of *hesed*, by Naomi is another case of ambiguity because it could either be the subject or object and the giver of *hesed* could either be Yahweh or Boaz. While the simplest interpretation is, "whose *hesed* has not forsaken the living and the dead"; where *hesed* is the subject, Sakenfeld argues for it being the object.[122] This would then read, "who has not abandoned his *hesed* with the living and the dead." The significance of this is that, if it is Yahweh doing the *hesed*, there is an implication of a relationship with the dead whose bodies are lying in foreign Moab. Generally, there is no relationship envisaged. The word for "living" is masculine and if only Naomi and Ruth were envisaged it should be feminine. Moore sees in Naomi's belief that God's *hesed* extends to the dead, a "statement . . . about as close to resurrection faith as one can find in Scripture"[123] or at least the Old Testament.

To avoid the implications of saying that this is the only case of divine *hesed* to the dead, Glueck says that this is human hesed with Boaz doing

---

119. Trible, *Rhetoric of Sexuality*, 179.

120. Angel, *"Midrashic"*, para. 39.

121. Ziegler, *Ruth*, 255.

122. Sakenfeld, *Meaning*, 105. This is based on uniform practice in translation to Greek and a similar structure in Gen 24:27.

123. Moore, *Ruth*, 342.

hesed for Ruth.[124] Against this, an argument from silence is not conclusive and the repetition of "the dead" from 1:8 is part of the use of key words and phrases which characterize Ruth. One argument against this being God's *hesed*, as Block maintains, is that Naomi's rapid change of disposition from all but cursing God to now blessing him is too sudden.[125] But, as was argued, there had to be a very significant degree of trust in the very fact of returning from Moab to abject poverty in Israel.

Ultimately, nothing definite can be said. The writer is ambiguous and perhaps intentionally so.[126] My preference would be to see this as Yahweh's *hesed*. To allow Ruth to glean, which was, after all, her right, and to give her some extra stalks of grain seems to fall short of fulfilling any responsibility Boaz may have towards his relatives, alive and dead. Boaz has only acted with the, "generalized responsibility for Ruth as a poor person."[127] He makes no mention of regarding her as a relative and indeed, his protection of her started before he knew she was a relative. Naomi could see this as Yahweh's *hesed* as he caused her to come upon Boaz's field by chance and there was a favorable response by him. Ruth could not have organized this by herself. The author, knowing the end of the story, is more likely to see this as Yahweh's *hesed*. If there is one overarching message about *hesed* from chapter 2 of the book and indeed a primary message of the Book of Ruth is that *hesed* is often not clear cut but ambiguous. It is tied into the extremely complex matter of human motivations. If human motivations are not complex enough, the boundary between an even more complex God and human action can be very blurred.

Naomi made Ruth aware of the family connection. Boaz is not just a relative, but close enough to be a potential "redeemer" (*goel*), the first mention of this word. The root *gaal* and the concept of a redeemer (as opposed to a Judge) does not appear in the Book of Judges at all but in the Book of Ruth it appears twenty-three times. It will appear seven times in chapter 3 and fifteen times in chapter 4 making it one of the overriding themes, along with *hesed* in the book.

There are two words for redeemer in Hebrew, the other *padah*, is used of redeeming the firstborn child (Exod 13:13–15) and livestock and property (Num 18:15–17; Lev 27). The *goel* is related to what we would call

---

124. Glueck, *Hesed*, 41.
125. Block, *Ruth*, 145.
126. Sakenfeld, *Meaning*, 106.
127. Sakenfeld, *Meaning*, 106.

"family law" and dealt with matters affecting the well-being of the clan. The Law laid out the responsibilities of the *goel* towards family members. It could be negative as in the "guiltless executioner"[128] of the murderer of a family member (Num 35:12–14) or positive in the redemption of land (Lev 25:25–28) or an Israelite slave (Lev 25:48–54). Of course, this only happened if he was, "a good and true man";[129] and Boaz had already demonstrated that he was such a man.

The use of *goel* here should probably be used in a general rather than a legal sense. In the next two chapters we see an expectation that the kinsman redeemer will marry the widow whose husband has died without an heir. It is estimated that 90 percent of the population of Israel at the time of the Judges was agrarian and accordingly the Law had extensive laws to protect the social, economic and spiritual life of such a society.[130] However, in all these laws there is nothing that required marriage of Boaz to Ruth and Naomi's plan in chapter 3 assumes that he will go beyond its minimum requirements. Conversely, the situation of these widows was a situation beyond anything anticipated in the Law and Naomi matched the need to the nature and resolve of Boaz. The Law had provided, "him with a covenantal worldview and an ethic that impelled him to seek the well-being of others."[131] That worldview started with a love of Yahweh (Deut 6:4–5), and caused Boaz to love those who he loved, the widow and the alien (Deut 10:17–19).

The word *goel* is used in the Psalms and prophets of the LORD who, "will stand up for his people and redeem them."[132] The Christian cannot help but see an image, veiled and imperfect as it is, of their own redeemer who would come through this good and true man.

It took courage to complete a day working hard in a situation in which in any other field she could have been molested. Her reward is to be embraced by Naomi as family, not the foreign daughter-in-law. The acceptance must have been healing for both of them.

---

128. Harris, Gāʾ al in *TWOT*, 144.

129. Harris, Gāʾ al in *TWOT*, 144.

130. Eskenazi and Frymer-Kensky, *Ruth*, xxvii.

131. Block, *Ruth*, 40.

132. Harris, *Goal*, 144.

> ²¹*Ruth the Moabitess said, "Yes, he said to me, 'You shall stay close to my young men until they have finished all my harvest.'"* ²²*Naomi said to Ruth her daughter-in-law, "It is good, my daughter, that you go out with his maidens, and that they not meet you in any other field."* ²³*So she stayed close to the maidens of Boaz, to glean to the end of barley harvest and of wheat harvest; and she lived with her mother-in-law.*

Boaz modelled appropriate conduct when he addressed Ruth as just "my daughter," without any reference to her Moabite origins, now finally Naomi does the same in verse twenty-two. Despite this acceptance, the storyteller still uses the Moabitess tag in chapter 4. On three occasions (1:22; 2:2, 22), it has been used in connection with Naomi and may be a reflection of how her daughter-in-law's Moabite birth influences Naomi's response to her.[133] Ruth, for her part, does not seem to have grasped the significance of what Naomi just said. As a Moabite she may not have known what a *goel* is or considered it unlikely that Boaz, "would flout public opinion and redeem her and Naomi."[134]

In verse twenty-one, she is again Ruth the Moabitess, and she misquotes Boaz's advice to cleave to his female workers for her safety, instead she has him saying to cleave to the young men! The third use of cleave is found in this verse. Ruth has been described as a woman of such striking beauty, "that whoever saw her would have an emission."[135] Despite allegedly having this effect on men, as has been mentioned, Judaism views Ruth as the model of Jewish virtue. This is pictured saying:

> As Ruth sat to glean with the reapers, she turned her face away, and not even a single one of her fingers could be seen, for when she saw a standing stalk, she would stand and take it, and when she saw a fallen stalk, she would sit and gather it.[136]

Ziegler argues that this extreme virtue may not initially have been the case. She was, instead, a Moabite convert familiar with Moabite norms but on the path to becoming someone with an understanding of

---

133. Eskenazi and Frymer-Kensky, *Ruth*, 45.
134. Ziegler, *Ruth*, 259.
135. Ruth Rabbah: 4:4.
136. Meir, *Ruth*, para. 17.

appropriate Jewish conduct.[137] This opinion is more grounded in reality than those of the legends.

Naomi now begins to understand that Yahweh's *hesed* had never departed, despite her calamity, and with this acknowledgment her whole thinking has changed. The words of encouragement and advice that should have started the day are now forthcoming. Both Boaz and Naomi will become united in their, "concern . . . for the safety of a young woman in an environment of young men."[138] Warnings about the dangers in the field and advice on appropriate behavior to minimize the risks would have been helpful before setting out in the morning.

We can understand from the words of Boaz and Naomi that the workforce was segregated or at least, largely segregated. In verse three, Ruth follows after the harvesters, not a case specific word, but would have included young men. This suggests she chose not to glean with the women workers and, of course, they may well have been antisocial as Boaz read the riot act to all his employees. Boaz advised her to follow the young women, in conjunction with informing her of the inappropriate behavior of the young men. In so doing it is possibly, "a conscious attempt to steer her away from her inclination to follow the male reapers."[139] At mealtime she sat with the reapers again and is called over to sit with Boaz. While the Book of Ruth must be interpreted in its culture, it must also be seen as, "a story that goes against culture as well as transforming it."[140] This is the same as the ministry of Jesus and should remain the constant ministry of the church.

This time Ruth did understand what Boaz and Naomi had said and she cleaved to the young women and in so doing desired modesty. This departure from the midrash's portrayal of Ruth's modest nature comes not only from an argument from the text but also a knowledge of real life. Ziegler is correct when she describes the process of conversion:

> The biblical text portrays Ruth as a typical convert, clumsily but determinedly navigating the complex pathways of Judaism . . . In this portrayal, both Boaz and Naomi guide Ruth's action, firmly but gently facilitating her entry into Bethlehem . . . The midrashim

---

137. Ziegler, *Ruth*, 261–63.
138. Trible, *Rhetoric of Sexuality*, 196.
139. Ziegler, *Ruth*, 261.
140. Trible, *Rhetoric of Sexuality*, 196.

disregard the process that a convert naturally undergoes in seeking to adapt to a new set of norms.[141]

If her conduct was not in keeping totally with Jewish social mores, we should not be surprised if Boaz looked past that and saw only that she had come to shelter under the wings of Yahweh. His mother, the prostitute Rahab, did the same so he, of all people, would know of the journey that the life of faith is for a convert. Because of his depth of character, Boaz would most likely also have understood that it was when working as a prostitute Rahab would become a hero of faith, not the sanctified wife of his father Salmon (Heb 11:31).

Naomi's later statement to Ruth that Boaz will not let the matter of redemption rest until the matter is resolved (3:15) indicates that she was aware of his character. So, her counsel to Ruth was to take Boaz's advice and, for her own safety both physical and sexual, only glean in the fields of Boaz. To have gone elsewhere after such kindness would have been ungrateful also. Naomi's advice is to avoid the whole group of young people but to stay only with the women, "going out" probably includes even going out from the city accompanied with them for safety. There is a change in Naomi's attitude to Ruth. Even in her correction she is "affectionate and maternal" even recalling Ruth's plea from 1:16, "do not harm me by making me leave you." In both cases the word *paga* for harm[142] is used. Like the use of "cleave" the word is used to show approval for Ruth's initial action and a just repayment through being able to glean in safety.

In verses eleven and twelve we learn that Boaz had been listening to what the people of Bethlehem had been saying about Ruth and it was all good. While Boaz may have been Judge like, Ruth had been like a Patriarch in the way she had left her parents and her land to shelter under the protection of Yahweh. In the next chapter he acknowledged that everyone knew Ruth to be a woman of valor, and with marital options (some not good) within that society (3:10–11). Yes, she was a Moabitess and that may have been a reason for Boaz initially being reluctant to fulfil his responsibility as a redeemer. But, "how do we justify his allowing her to beg in his field for so long? . . . It is impossible to understand adequately why Boaz did not see it fit to visit the widows and attend their needs."[143] Chapter 2 ends with Naomi and Ruth alone against the world, though not as perilously so

---

141. Ziegler, *Ruth*, 263.
142. Hamilton, Pāgaʽ in *TWOT*, 714–15.
143. Angel, "*Midrashic*," para. 31.

as at the end of chapter 1, as the imminent threat of starvation has passed. Chapter 3 likewise ends with the two women at home but with the hope of redemption. Ruth's faithfulness to Naomi has been proven.

If Ruth could return to the city each day with what she beat out on the first day, she may well have had sufficient food for a year for the two of them. With the barley harvest starting possibly late in March (early spring), and the wheat harvest finishing as late as mid-July,[144] there were many opportunities to glean. For Ruth to do this safely on Boaz's land all this time, he would need to have been a very large landholder indeed. This of course is the other meaning of him being a man of substance (2:1). At the end of the harvest, Ruth was no closer to the household of Boaz and he had made no ongoing provision for her. As Trible points out, the storyteller is in tension with the characters. At the end of chapter 1, Naomi's words speak of death but the storyteller hints at life, but here at, "the end of scene two Naomi affirms life but the narrator cautions death."[145] After interpreting the events on the barley field as Yahweh's *hesed* (most likely), she "begins to plan a face-saving way for Boaz to do what near-kinsmen are supposed to do."[146]

---

144. The Gezer Calendar said it was one month for the barley harvest and another month thereafter for a different crop thought to be wheat. Pritchard, *Ancient*, 209. In reality, the timing of the harvest was very variable as it was only planted after the early rains and ripening depended on the location. Masterman, *Barley*, 431.

145. Trible, *Rhetoric of Sexuality*, 181.

146. Moore, *Ruth*, 305.

Chapter Three

I HAVE TO ADMIT, as I write these words, even though I am now almost seventy years old, if I were to wake in the middle of the night and find a sweet smelling, attractive, much younger woman lying near or beside me, obviously not one of my employees and with at least the suggestion of availability, it would have my attention! It certainly had Boaz's attention too! In our permissive society there is little doubt which way this evening would usually end, and, in the immoral setting of the Book of Judges, there was little doubt also. Attention is one thing. What you do about it is an entirely different matter! In the continuing ambiguity of the Book of Ruth we are not told if our story is a continuation of the failure of Israel or its turning point towards the kingship of David and the line of the Messiah founded with two virtuous people. We are left to draw our own conclusion. I choose to believe that Boaz, who is virtuous in his dealings with his employees and Ruth when people were looking, shows the same virtue when he was alone.

Boaz chose to call a woman who visited him at night arguably dressed like a prostitute, "virtuous." What is the nature of her virtue? It was barely three months, if that, since Ruth forsook the gods of Moab and called the God of Naomi, the God of Israel, her God. This is far too short a time for a deep work of sanctification to have taken place. This virtue had to be a quality she possessed already in Moab and the source of her devotion to Naomi and Mahlon. Some time ago, I used to ship timber from Australia to Hungary and had opportunity to visit my client. I had seen images of her and knew already she was a strikingly beautiful woman. I was only in her presence for a few minutes when I became aware of a quality about her that I could only describe as "virtue." Was she a believer? I don't think so but, for all that, it was a delight to be in her presence because of what she was, not how she looked. I suspect that, with Ruth, we are looking at something very similar, something that is very tangible and set her apart from the other young women of the city. Even, dare I say, when dressed for seduction.

In chapter 1, with the two women alone on the road, there is the opportunity to choose what righteousness calls for and Ruth decided to abandon the idols of Moab and follow the living God of Israel. The events of chapter 2 were carried out in public and again there is the opportunity to do what righteousness calls for and Boaz ensured the safety and daily provision of his near relative's daughter-in-law. Now, in chapter 3, we are met with secrecy and privacy with just Naomi, Ruth, and Boaz. How we act at times when no one is looking (and we may hope that God himself is busy elsewhere or at least averts his eyes,) goes to the heart of who we are. But we will see that even in these most private of moments, in the shadows when no one recognizes the other, God is still in control through enabling Boaz and Ruth to choose to do what righteousness calls for, even in a highly sexualized context.

And the chapter is sexually charged and packed with double meanings, leaving the reader asking, "Did they, or didn't they?" I do not doubt for one minute that both parties wanted to be intimate, and the frequency of the double entendres is probably meant to reflect that, but their restraint shows that they were not animals driven by urges over which they had no control. It transpired that, despite what Naomi was planning, it would not become a romp on the threshing floor but a matter of whether things progressed according to the Law, Israelite customs and the requirements of lives governed by *hesed* living.

Much has been said in this commentary so far and more will be said about family and the continuation of the name, but Ruth's attachment to Naomi asks the question, "What is family about, is it just blood connections or is it about commitment?" We see in the Book of Ruth a singular reluctance of the nearest family members to commit to be what family members should be. Ruth had this commitment in spades. We might also ask, "Were there no eligible brides in Israel?" It would appear that there was not one with the commitment and virtue needed to start the task of national healing and lead it to the kingdom, one that would, in the wisdom of God, have no ending.

My own wife-to-be used to sit at my table in bible college and one day the Lord whispered into her heart that I would be her husband. I might add that she was none too pleased. The Good Lord got around to telling me by whispering into my heart something about the day's events that led to us keeping company. There is one thing that we cannot know about Boaz's highly unexpected response but is worth speculating upon. Boaz was a man who walked with God, so how much had God whispered to the heart of his friend about Ruth. This is alluded to in Targum[1] Ruth where it says, after Ruth enquires in the barley field why she has received such favor:

> Boaz replied and said to her, "It has surely been told to me concerning the word of the sages that, when the LORD decreed concerning them, he did not decree against any but the men. And it was told to me by prophecy that there will come forth from you kings and prophets."[2]

We sell our faith short when we don't acknowledge the possibility of there being more going on behind the scene than is spoken about.

> [1]*Naomi her mother-in-law said to her, "My daughter, shall I not seek rest for you, that it may be well with you?* [2a]*Now isn't Boaz our kinsman, with whose maidens you were?*

The structure of chapter 3 mimics that of chapter 2 which opened with a conversation at the two women's home, then followed by a longer agricultural scene where Boaz has a question about Ruth's identity and praises her *hesed*. Both chapters end with the two women back at their home talking about food provided by Boaz and the prospect of more to follow. Whereas the first encounter with Boaz was "accidental," the second will be carefully contrived and the women's roles as instigators reversed. Still, God does not allow himself to be seen and we are left with only the scheming of Naomi. But, without saying as much, we are left with only one conclusion, that Yahweh was the one who was primarily, "responsible for redeeming Ruth, Naomi, the family of Elimelech and the nation."[3] The agreement between Boaz's will and that of God illustrates the seamless agreement there is meant to be and can be, between man and God and sets a model for the future reign of human kings.[4]

1. A Targum is an ancient Aramaic paraphrase or interpretation of the Hebrew Bible from about the first century AD when Hebrew was ceasing to be a spoken language.
2. Targum Ruth: 2:11.
3. Ziegler, *Ruth*, 287.
4. Ziegler, *Ruth*, 287–88.

Up to the point that Naomi mentions Boaz's name, her words are similar to his to Ruth in 2:8 where he also calls her "my daughter" and likewise also uses two rhetorical questions. Boaz and Naomi have a distinctive way of speaking by saying something through asking questions. Campbell suggests that the age of Boaz is hinted at by both he and Naomi speaking in the same way, i.e., they are of the same generation.[5] Naomi's mind must have been in a far better place for her now to be taking parental responsibility for Ruth and calling her "my daughter." She was working towards a brighter future for her daughter-in-law, one that continues beyond her death. Any personal concerns Naomi had are unspoken, at least in our translations.[6] Forefront in what she says to Ruth is finding her a husband but it will, in the end, equally benefit her. Naomi does not mention Boaz's role as a *goel*, the "redeemer" of their land, but, as the story unfolds in chapter 4, he will be seen to have an entirely different agenda, at least publicly, providing an heir for Mahlon. Naomi never mentions the need to restore the male line and has seen this as an impossibility (1:11–12).

Naomi's prayer for both Ruth and Orpah in chapter 1 was that they would both find *menuah*, "rest" in the home of another husband. Orpah did just that but Ruth returned with her mother-in-law to Bethlehem to what could promise no more than a life of abject poverty. For Naomi, there can be no protection without a husband but, "the Book of Ruth gently, yet firmly, illustrated that Naomi's security depends first and foremost on another woman."[7] While their immediate circumstances have improved dramatically, there was no security going forward. The same word from 1:9 is found here also but with the emphasis of the rest that comes from security.[8] The speed with which this all happened must have surprised Naomi.

The second goal of her plan, *yatab-lak*, that it "may be well" with Ruth, would have been the hardest part. A rich husband would give financial

---

5. Campbell, *Ruth*, 118.

6. The Hebrew is not so clear. The MT has vowels that were added in the nineth to tenth century, the scrolls read in the synagogue only have very basic vowels. There can be a difference between the two and this is known as *keri*, what is read and *kethiv* what is written and in Naomi's speech there are a larger number than usual. What is read in her instructions are "you will go down" and "you will lie down" but what is written is "I will go down" and "I will lie down." Ziegler sees in this a possible intent by the Masorites to show us Naomi's motives. Ziegler, *Ruth*, 291–92. Campbell sees these as archaic second person endings. Campbell, *Ruth*, 120.

7. Eskenazi and Frymer-Kensky, *Ruth*, 49–50.

8. Coppes, Nûaḥ in *TWOT*, 562–63.

security, but without love and respect it would be a life of misery, not of wellness. The expression is used in Deuteronomy 4:40 where wellbeing is seen as the reward for covenant obedience. For Ruth, wellbeing would have involved a long life, a good marriage, prosperity and many children (Pss 127 and 128). On the journey back from Moab, Naomi wished that God would help her daughters-in-law find security, or a home with a new husband (1:9). Ultimately, security in that society, at least in old age, came not from the marriage but from progeny which resulted from it and Naomi's plans for Ruth, though not directly stated as such, are about children. Of course, should the night be successful, it was as much in Naomi's best interest too.

Naomi does not wish or pray and wait for God to intervene but instead she takes it upon herself to act to ensure such security by finding a home for Ruth. Has she usurped Yahweh's role in devising this morally questionable plan? Again, we are faced with the ambiguity, who is acting, God or is it the scheming of Naomi? We can see it as both at the same time but, even so, her plans, dubious as they are and without any mention of God, are grounded in having seen his hand at work in the kindness shown to Ruth by Boaz.

Ruth had found favor in the fields of Boaz but with him being an old man the situation could and most likely would, quickly change for the worse on his death. The book is written against the background of the Book of Judges where violence and injustice are pervasive. From the timeline of chapter 4, the natural death of Boaz could well have impacted them by the next harvest.[9] This is not just self-interest on Naomi's part as the relationship between the two women had changed. Ruth is no longer the "Moabitess" but a daughter, and Boaz is no longer a relative on her husband's side but a relative of both of them. Her ethnicity will not be mentioned again until the legal discussions of chapter 4. It has been suggested that, though not stated as such, the old woman is now acting in the role of a "wise woman," an honored biblical role.[10]

The hard realities of life in a society where much of life could be lived at barely above subsistence level meant that finding a permanent solution whereby Ruth could find "rest," meant finding a husband for her. Of course, this could equally be a two-way street with the husband needing the wife

---

9. The harvesting could have taken up to three months and, assuming Ruth married Boaz soon after the events of chapter 4 and conceived quickly would have taken the time up to the start of the next barley harvest. Boaz has exited the story by then and may well have died.

10. Moore, *Ruth*, 351–52. See the wise woman of Tekoa (2 Sam 14:4–11) and of Abel (2 Sam 20:18–19).

for exactly the same reason. I expect that there were other men who could have provided "security" but both women have more than just that in mind, although not mentioned at this stage. He must also be a close relative who could purchase their land and Boaz is the obvious choice. How much a levirate like marriage whereby the close relative could father a son for Mahlon was in mind is a moot point. It will not be mentioned in this chapter. In verse two Boaz is called a *moda'at*, "kinsman," as in 2:1 but thereafter he is called a *goel*, "redeemer." This first word is significant as it is based on *yada'* "to know" and Eskenazi and Frymer-Kensky believe that when Naomi chose to use an unusual form of the word that she had something other than redemption and levirate marriage in mind.[11] It is the first of what is called, "the much too frequent use made of the verb "to know" and its related nouns not to be noticed (also 3:3, 4, 10, 18)."[12] Of course, it is a word with many possible meanings but, with all the other innuendos such as "to lie" and "to go," the one that will come to mind to the listeners is to have sex.

In some respects, at this stage Naomi is acting more as the "guardian redeemer" than Boaz.[13] Naomi referred indirectly to Boaz's character as he was the master of the girls Ruth had been working with. She has had up to three months to assess how he treats his workers, particularly his most vulnerable. If there was a weakness in looking to Boaz as the answer to their problems, it was that he had allowed Ruth to glean for all this time.[14] He will need some serious prodding before he goes beyond his general duties to the poor and marginalized, let alone a close relative. He appears content to leave the providing up to God. There is no answer to the important question of why he didn't help earlier when he was aware of Ruth's outstanding character (2:11–12).

As for his future action, there is an answer. Ruth is not a book of, "good people doing good things, but rather an example of how ordinary people with mixed motives become extraordinary through the cultivation of *hesed*."[15] Naomi had not been enthusiastic towards Ruth, and Boaz only offered basic charity. It is only Ruth's acts of *hesed* that, "nurture their potential to go further."[16]

11. Eskenazi and Frymer-Kensky, *Ruth*, 50.
12. Campbell, *Ruth*, 131.
13. Evans, *Ruth*, 257.
14. Refer Ruth Rabbah: 5:11 for the three-month length of the harvest.
15. Eskenazi and Frymer-Kensky, *Ruth*, l.
16. Eskenazi and Frymer-Kensky, *Ruth*, l.

Ruth

It was Naomi's idea to match Boaz with Ruth, an older man and a relatively young woman, so what are we to make of that? Even Boaz is surprised by that possibility but in the end both he and Ruth are comfortable with it. It does beg the question that in selling one farm, on the death of Boaz does she gain two and possibly become the richest woman in Bethlehem? Most likely and Boaz was perfectly aware of the possibility and the public perception of "gold digging" yet still agrees. The description of the virtuous woman from Proverbs (31:10–31) is a life that is anything but restful, but it is secure. With Ruth matching this description[17] who better to entrust your life's work and future heir to? There is no indication of any children from a previous marriage of Boaz.

> *2b Behold, he will be winnowing barley tonight on the threshing floor.*
> *3 Therefore wash yourself, anoint yourself, get dressed, and go down to the threshing floor; but don't make yourself known to the man until he has finished eating and drinking. 4 It shall be, when he lies down, that you shall note the place where he is lying. Then you shall go in, uncover his feet, and lay down. Then he will tell you what to do."*

God's hand, seen first in the climate, then directing Ruth's "luck" when she chanced upon Boaz's field, is seen now in the dubious schemes of humans. The age difference between Ruth and Boaz and his relationship to the widows being somewhat distant may have caused the redeemer to think that help and redemption was the responsibility of a more suitable closer relative. Naomi's plan is fraught with potential problems, and while it would barely raise an eyebrow now, it would have been contrary to the prevailing custom and the accepted morality, even if it wasn't always followed. At the end of chapter 2, Naomi is seen as, "gently guiding Ruth to observe the modesty norms of Bethlehem society. And now she asks Ruth to flout those norms and act in an egregiously immodest manner."[18] She planned to make the widow as attractive as possible and so break down Boaz's resistance.[19] Naomi may also have had in mind that it was time for Ruth to end her period of mourning and get on with life[20] (see a similar

---

17. For a comparison between the two see Ziegler, *Ruth*, 322–23.
18. Ziegler, *Ruth*, 296.
19. Block, *Ruth*, 169.
20. Block, *Ruth*, 170.

situation with David in 2 Samuel 12:20) but this is unlikely. With so many suggestive words used it is difficult to see this as anything but festive, if not actually seductive. The word used for her clothing, *shimlah* is a very general term and can refer to a one-piece outer garment that virtually covered the entire body except the face and is used of male and female dress. Given the preparations and setting it demands that this was a special piece, not the clothes she gleaned in. Is it the dress of a prostitute? Only the timing and secrecy of what follows make it possible to see it as such.

Marital arrangements that are above board aren't negotiated on a threshing floor at midnight. Perhaps Naomi is thinking that a, "less formal and more personal arrangement"[21] which circumvents the rules of propriety is needed, as she thinks no one will be willing to marry a Moabitess. Why go to this trouble? Ultimately, we have little idea of what local customs and taboos were, so it is even suggested that, because this is all happening outdoors and presumably some distance from the workers, such actions may be more discreet and less risky than Ruth actually visiting the home of Boaz.[22] This may well be the case if it were Ruth meeting with Boaz but where would be the impropriety in two elderly relatives, Naomi and Boaz, talking together? I can only assume that the safe approach was considered likely to be rebuffed, perhaps because it was Naomi asking, as Boaz never makes direct mention of her. Was she considered as a traitor to her community?

While we must have questions about the wisdom and propriety of the plan, there are biblical examples of women who are, "depicted as deploying courage and creativity to ensure continuity."[23] Examples of courage are the midwives who defy Pharaoh and protect the Israelite children (Exod 1:15–21) and the three women who again defy Pharaoh to ensure Moses survives. As examples of creativity, a euphemism for "a moral minefield," are Lot's daughters having sex with their father and Tamar pretending to be a prostitute to have a child from Judah. Both these events lead to Ruth and Boaz and ultimately Jesus. None of these women surrendered to their fate and Judah would declare the righteousness of Tamar as greater than his (Gen 38:26). Perhaps Ziegler has a point when she says, "Naomi's bold plot, the peculiar mechanism that she employs to obtain continuity, is therefore an expected, and perhaps accepted, mode of action for a virtuous biblical woman."[24]

21. Eskenazi and Frymer-Kensky, *Ruth*, 49.
22. Eskenazi and Frymer-Kensky, *Ruth*, 51–52.
23. Ziegler, *Ruth*, 297.
24. Ziegler, *Ruth*, 301.

Ruth

In chapter 1, Ruth doesn't obey her mother-in-law and return to Moab, but an emphasis of chapter 3 is faithfulness to instructions. This faithfulness shown by Ruth to Naomi and then Boaz to Ruth includes actions that are morally questionable:

- v4. He will tell you what to do—Naomi to Ruth,
- v5. All that you say, I will do—Ruth to Naomi,
- v6. Did all that her mother-in-law told her—Narrator of Ruth,
- v11. I will do to you all that you say—Boaz to Ruth, and
- v16. All that the man had done for her—Ruth to Naomi.

Preparing the grain was a two-part process. The first stage was threshing which removed the grain from the stalk and was done soon after harvest. The second was to winnow which involved removing any remaining chaff and hopefully pests before the grain was stored. The chaff would be kept for animal feed. What is not clear is that the barley is winnowed up to three months after it was harvested. This delay could happen if the barley was harvested before it was fully ripe but Ruth was able to thresh hers on the day it was harvested. And why is Boaz only now winnowing the earlier crop, not the wheat? The MT reads, "he is winnowing the threshing floor of the barley" which suggests a winnowing floor for both wheat and barley which is unlikely.

Campbell makes a very reasonable suggestion of modifying the MT *se'arim* (barley) for the very similar *se'orim* (gate) making, "it the threshing floor by the gate." He describes the change this way, "just as barley has played its role up to the end of chapter 2, given the story tellers love for wordplay as well as giving hints of things to come, it is not surprising to have him introduce the gate in 3:2, close to his last use of barley in 2:23."[25] For another wordplay on gate and barley see 2 Kings 7, particularly verses one and sixteen to eighteen. In Hebrew manuscripts that only have consonants the word for barley, gate, and the suggested unusual unit of measure in 3:17 are exactly the same.[26]

---

25. Campbell, *Ruth*, 117–18. The threshing floor at Samaria was at the gate (1 Kgs 22:10) and the Jerusalem temple site was also a threshing floor. Jeremiah also associates the threshing floor with the city gates (Jer 15:7).

26. Campbell, *Ruth*, 13. Bush argues against this proposal in part suggesting that everyone knew where the threshing floor was, but I would expect that the farming community would need more than one threshing floor given that winnowing was such a slow and laborious process. This would make it logical to describe which field to go to.

How desperate was the financial plight of Naomi and Ruth at the end of the wheat harvest? With "Sunday best" clothes and perfume, I would suggest that the darkest days, when the shadow of starvation was cast over them had passed, especially if the LXX addition of, "and rub yourself with Myrrh"; is correct. The actions are now related to security, not survival. The work on the threshing floor of winnowing was hard and dusty so no one would expect that there would be a woman dressed for romance that night, and if not romance, at least what you would expect if you were presenting yourself as a potential bride.[27] With the harvest finalized for the year and all its backbreaking labor behind them, that night would have been a time of celebration and drinking for all involved. The mention of drinking combined with a Moabitess would have prompted the hearers to think of the story of Lot's daughters getting their father drunk and having sex with him and so starting her nation (Gen 19:30–38). Similarly, Tamar had feigned the role of a prostitute to seduce the Patriarch Judah to secure a child (Gen 38). Was this Moabitess behaving the same way as her nation's founding mothers? She was dressed for it. To the contrary, as the story unfolds, she will be portrayed as the antithesis of the national stereotype.

What exactly is Ruth not making any objection to? The whole proposal from Naomi is sexually charged. The suggestions can involve "tarting her up" and offering her to Boaz like a prostitute[28] or even encouraging the old man to sleep with Ruth, "believing that his integrity is such that he will then provide *a home* for her."[29] I deliberately used the expression, "tarting up" for its shock value because the expression used to describe Ruth in this chapter is "virtuous." Again, we will see that the story is ambiguous which forces us to choose. Was she "easy" or as Rabbi Chanin the son of Levi said: "She really was a Moabitess"[30] or the alternative that she was "virtuous," a worthy mother for the line of King David? Settle for the former and it also makes Naomi no better than she should be.

There is clear but very subtle reference to sex in verse three in Naomi's instruction, "Don't let him know (*yada'*) you are there." The word, "to know," used twice in short succession, as was mentioned earlier, is a euphemism for sex. The similarities between Judges chapter 19 and Ruth have already been

---

Campbell, *Ruth,* 149–50.

27. Evans, *Ruth,* 257.

28. Evans notes though does not accept the idea. Evans *Ruth,* 259.

29. Evans, *Ruth,* 259.

30. Ruth Rabbah: 5:11.

made (see Table One) but Moore sees a further connection. He sees the low point of this word's use in that chapter with its destruction and violence when the Gibeonites demand that the Levite be brought out that they might "know" him. Contrasting this, in his opinion, is the high point of its use where Ruth is patient and gentle by not making herself known too quickly to Boaz.[31]

The double entendres continue in verse four which contains four sexually charged words "to lie," "to go in," "to uncover" and "his feet." To "lie" is just like our own use of the word and, apart from the three occurrences in verse three, it is found a further five times in verses seven, (twice) eight, thirteen, and fourteen. The only other place where there is such a concentration of the use of this word is in the story of Lot's daughters having sex with him which results in the ancestor of the Moabite nation (Gen 19:30–38). It is possible that the storyteller intends the readers to link the two events.[32] Either way, this proposed action would have been considered scandalous.

The second of these four words found here and in verses seven and fourteen, *bo'*, "to go into," or "come" can also mean to have intercourse[33] and is used this way in 4:13 when the marriage to Ruth and Boaz is consummated. To uncover (*galah*) can refer to uncovering someone's nakedness and have illicit sex (Lev 18:6–19). All of these words can be completely innocent if it were not for the frequency of their use (refer Table Two) and the setting, but the reference to Boaz's feet is probably the most direct innuendo.

A large part of this negative picture of what Naomi was proposing is drawn from a reference to *regel* (feet) which can be used as a euphemism. In Judges 3:24 and 1 Samuel 24:3 it refers to going to the toilet and in Isaiah 7:20 of pubic hair.[34] A more direct example is found in II Samuel 11:8, where King David told Uriah to, "Go down to your house and wash your feet"; where the reference is clearly to have sex with Bathsheba. But the storyteller has her not just merely saying "feet" but using the more unusual *margelot*, "place of the feet," which is still a possible euphemism for his private parts. The form of the word does soften the innuendo to possibly be no more than the ground around his feet.[35] Table Two contains a list of those words which have sexual connotations.

---

31. Moore, *Ruth*, 348–49.
32. Eskenazi and Frymer-Kensky, *Ruth*, 53.
33. Martens, Bô' in *TWOT*, 93–95.
34. Coppes, Rāgal in *TWOT*, 831–32
35. Eskenazi and Frymer-Kensky, *Ruth*, 53.

Word	Verses	Times used
Know	2, 3, 4	3
Lie	4, 7, 8, 13, 14	8
Go in to	4, 7, 14	3
Expose	4, 7	2
Feet	4, 8	2
Heap	7	1
Spreading the robe	9	1
Go after	10	1
Poured out	15	1

Table 2. Use of double entendres in chapter 3

It is reasonable to say that the storyteller is playing with the expectation of his hearers, especially as in the ancient Near East immoral practices were common at harvest time as part of fertility rites of some religions.[36] The only word missing is "seed" which is a little surprising given the setting is all about seeds. As the story unfolds in the opposite direction, the storyteller would probably say, using our vernacular, that, "You shouldn't have such dirty minds." Block maintains that "although these look like the actions of a prostitute this overtly sexual interpretation seems to read more into the text than is intended."[37] Most likely what is intended is that Ruth simply was to uncover his lower legs, leaving his genitals covered and to lie down beside him and see what happens.[38] Either way, to uncover any part of a man's body at night was highly suggestive, as was lying beside someone as husband and wife. If the plan was to act like a prostitute, she is not likely, as the story unfolds, to have been called virtuous by Boaz. However, there is no escaping the conclusion that the plan was risky and morally

36. Morris, *Ruth*, 287.
37. Block, *Ruth*, 172.
38. Block, *Ruth*, 172.

and socially unwise, to say the least. Her encounter was one in which she could, "have returned home broken in body and bruised in spirit"[39] had Boaz interpreted her actions incorrectly. It was also one from which Naomi could extricate herself with a few comments about the morals of Moabites.

What Naomi proposed was a very private encounter, but it was going to happen in a very public place, albeit at night. Moore says of the threshing floor, "People stream through them constantly, buying and selling goods of all sorts, not just threshed grain . . . Festivals are celebrated there (Deut 16:13–17). Prostitutes also ply their trade there (Hos 9:1).[40] What Naomi expects from Boaz in such a compromising situation is not spelled out nor what Ruth is to say, it is more like, "Go with the flow." But what she does expect is for, "the man will take over; that is the least one expects."[41] How much passion there could be without waking the workers is another matter but the whole encounter was risky How much was sexual is not explicitly stated but it certainly was morally ambiguous.[42] Nevertheless, the two women were, "enacting time-honored roles, and they knew exactly what they were doing."[43]

> **5** *She said to her, "All that you say, I will do."*

Jewish Law based on the Talmud stated that converts were not to be reminded of their previous lifestyle so as not to offend and hurt them.[44] Though this was developed at a later stage, the obvious wisdom of this injunction is timeless. Naomi's plan would appear to be built upon her preconceived perception of Ruth as a Moabitess and requires, indeed even expects, her to return to the ways of her countrywomen.[45]

In chapter 3, here and in verse seventeen there are two cases of words spoken by Ruth, *elai,* "to me" that are not written in the MT but are read because they are implied. Here it is everything you say "to me" and in verse seventeen he gave these six measures of barley "to me." Ziegler sees this double occurrence of Ruth taking herself out of the sentence as significant.

---

39. Block, *Ruth*, 173.
40. Moore, *Ruth*, 348.
41. Trible, *Rhetoric of Sexuality*, 182.
42. Block, *Ruth*, 52.
43. Moore, *Ruth*, 352.
44. Mishneh Torah: *Laws of Repentance*, 7:8.
45. Ziegler, *Ruth*, 304.

By removing "to me" may indicate that Ruth is aware that what is proposed probably serves Naomi's interests more than her own[46] yet she still agrees to go ahead. She says of Ruth's decision that she, "is the ideal candidate to produce kingship because of her extreme selflessness; she disregards herself and her personal needs."[47]

> 6 *She went down to the threshing floor, and did everything that her mother-in-law told her.* 7 *When Boaz had eaten and drunk, and his heart was merry, he went to lie down at the end of the heap of grain. She came softly, uncovered his feet, and laid down.* 8 *At midnight, the man was startled and turned himself; and behold, a woman lay at his feet.* 9 *He said, "Who are you?" She answered, "I am Ruth your servant. Therefore spread the corner of your garment over your servant; for you are a near kinsman."*

The scene on the threshing floor is a far cry from the famine that starts the story. Boaz was in good spirits (*wayyitab libbo*—literally, "his heart became merry") when he lay down at the foot of the pile of grain. (The same expression is found in Judges 19:9 when the Levite's father-in-law tries to stop him from leaving.) As another "stroke of luck" he lay at the corner of the threshing floor, offering some privacy for what is to occur. Presumably, he had eaten well and quite possibly drunk heavily so it could almost be assured he would sleep deeply. This is not to say Boaz was drunk as the expression is used in a positive way to describe a "state of euphoria and well-being" (1 Kgs 8:66; Prov 15:15; Eccl 9:7) but also negatively to refer to a state where poor decisions can be made (1 Sam 25:36).[48] The storyteller is ambiguous as to his sobriety that night. His state suggests either another obstacle for Ruth to overcome or hints at Naomi's, "intention to take advantage of a mellower-than-usual condition."[49] As the sexual tension rises the storyteller introduces us to another likely innuendo *arema*, "a heap of grain," which is very close to *arom* which means "nakedness."[50] Ruth lay "at his feet", as already mentioned, it can be a, "euphemism for "beside him" or

46. Ziegler, *Ruth*, 305.
47. Ziegler, *Ruth*, 113.
48. Campbell, *Ruth*, 122.
49. Campbell, *Ruth*, 122.
50. Ziegler, *Ruth*, 295.

"very close to him"[51] so the sexual connotations cannot be avoided. Naomi's instructions of verse four are repeated precisely, showing that Ruth was following her mother-in-law's instructions faithfully. The authority that Naomi's words held with Ruth is revealed by her use of *tzivvattah*, the verb form of the word "commandment," as in the Ten.

The story hinges on verse eight where both of the players are stripped of their names and their identity. Boaz is simply a man and Ruth is just a woman. The words, "and behold a woman" appear exactly the same in Proverbs 7:8 where, "it introduces a woman who is a harlot and has come to seduce a man."[52] Are these two sexual beings, who find themselves in a highly charged situation going to act in the way the storyteller has prepared, that the old man will succumb like Judah and Lot. Alternatively, will they prove worthy of being the redeemers of Israel through David or whether, "deliverance for the Jews will arise from another place" (Est. 4:14). The story will move from a nameless man and woman back to one on the major themes of Ruth, identity, when Boaz asks, "Who are you?" and elevates Ruth from being just an object for sexual gratification. His first question of identity in chapter 2 was about who possessed her and now his question is about her personal identity.

When he shuddered, *hared*,[53] at "midnight," probably because of the cold, Boaz was aware that someone was present. The scene is dark with just enough light to see that there is a woman close by but not recognize who it was. How close was she? Very close indeed as Boaz did not sit up to see Ruth. The word used is *wayyilapet* (translated as "turned himself") from the root *lapath* which is seldom used but has a meaning of, "twist, turn or grasp with a twisting motion."[54] Campbell prefers "groping" in this case rather than the common translation of "trembled."[55] This would give a situation where Boaz would discover her as he, "groped about for his mantle, to cover himself from the cold."[56] Midnight is pictured as the time of mystery, peril and possibility, the same phrase, "in the middle of the night" is used

---

51. Evans, *Ruth*, 257.

52. Ziegler, *Ruth*, 295.

53. Usually associated with "emotional agitation before an unusual circumstance" both good and bad. Bowling, Ḥārad in *TWOT*, 321–22.

54. Kaiser, Lāpat in *TWOT*, 481.

55. Campbell, *Ruth*, 122.

56. Campbell, *Ruth*, 118.

of the tenth plague when the firstborn of Egypt died (Exod 12:29) and of David praising God (Pss 119:62).[57]

Robert Hubbard sees in this night scene that, like, "the human characters, God himself seems incognito, unrecognizable, throughout the scene. One even feels that God is looking the other way, thereby leaving the actors completely on their own."[58] Is he right? Yes, there is no theophany or an angel telling Boaz what to do, but they were anything but operating without guidance in a moral vacuum. No angels were necessary, as he knew exactly what to do. They, "lay that night in the crucible of temptation . . . [and] emerged the heat morally unscathed."[59] Before meeting Ruth on the barley field, he had heard time and time again how she left her country and family and did *hesed* to Naomi. Since that meeting, she must have been the topic of conversation on many occasions as he will say that everyone knows she is virtuous. Despite what she looked like he knew exactly what this woman at his "feet" was. And he knew exactly who he was. He was a man whose faith was rooted in a covenant-keeping God who showed *hesed* and expected no less of the nation he had called and no less of him. He had publicly recognized that Ruth had this very Jewish trait in abundance and had governed his actions towards her. There was the need for a *goel*, a means of relieving the distress of a widow which was every bit as real as leaving grain for gleaning. It was something equally within his power to grant. It wasn't a matter of committing Ruth's request to prayer or doing the sums as Joe Blow will do in chapter 4, but simply acting on a life that had been guided by the Law but led by the Spirit.

On waking, Boaz asked who she was, the same question that will be put to her by Naomi in 3:16, but Ruth's reply turns the question around. She told him that who he is was more important.[60] In the previous chapter, when he asked the same question, she is called a Moabitess by the overseer, stressing her foreign birth but Boaz countered that. At that time, he gave, "her a name and an identity beyond her Moabite, alien status"[61] while at the same time protecting her from being an object of pleasure for the men of Bethlehem, at least in his fields. This acknowledgement of Ruth, not as an object, but as someone with an identity, sharply contrasts the sexual degeneration seen with the nameless concubine from Gibeah (see Table One).

57. Ruth Rabbah: 6:1.
58. Hubbard, *Ruth*, 195.
59. Hubbard, *Ruth*, 74.
60. Evans, *Ruth*, 260.
61. Ziegler, *Ruth*, 310.

As mentioned, Naomi's plan to wait till Boaz had drunk suggests the actions of Lot's daughters who got their father drunk. Dressing in a manner of a prostitute brings images of Tamar. Both Lot and Judah did not know that they had been seduced (Gen 19:33, 35, 38). They were deceived because they did not ask who was beside them but Boaz refuses to be deceived. Ziegler points out how Lot's apathy and refusal to act to secure his future forced his daughters to act. Likewise, Judah was willing to give up his identifying symbols, his seal and staff to a prostitute he would probably never see again. She describes this attitude behind both saying, "they did not enquire, presumably because, having abandoned Abraham's path and rejected their destiny, neither wished to know."[62] In this vein Boaz is seen as someone who does not want to be deceived, he wants to know.

Judaism draws a valid comparison between the moral weakness of Samson and the strength of Boaz. Samson was born after an angelic visit and is set aside as both a Nazirite and military savior of Israel (Judg 13:3–7). When needed to do mighty feats, the Spirit fell on him and gave him supernatural strength. His role as a Nazirite should have made him a religious leader and this, combined with his strength, should have seen him be not just a military deliverer. Israel needed a social and religious deliverer as well. But Samson's passions ultimately overpower him and, in turn, lead to his captivity and failure. He is saved from capture after a visit to a prostitute in Gaza in the middle of the night (*bahatzi halayla*). This term is rare and evokes the final plague in Egypt that led to Israel's national deliverance but for Samson it is deliverance from the consequence of his own lusts.

At the same time setting, at the "midpoint of the night," *Boaz* exhibits enormous restraint and, as a consequence he, "succeeds in reversing several societal defects that characterize this period, including the rampant sexual decadence."[63] A further connection to the Samson story and Boaz is the previously mentioned word *wayyilapet*, "groped" which caused him to find Ruth beside him. This word is only found here and when Samson groped (Judg 16:29) for the pillars of the temple of Dagon. His death between the twin pillars "spells the end of leadership in the Book of Judges and the termination of any hope of a leader who can reverse the downward spiral of the book."[64] Samson's last act is to destroy a "house," while in the next chapter Boaz will be seen as a "house" builder with five references to

62. Ziegler, *Ruth*, 313.
63. Ziegler, *Ruth*, 321.
64. Ziegler, *Ruth*, 320.

the word (4:11–12). The only other building which is mentioned as having twin pillars is the Temple of Solomon and one of these is called Boaz.

Ruth's approach is a subtle combination of deference and confidence. She had called herself Boaz's *shipkhah* "servant girl" in 2:13 but now, when answering this question, Ruth did not reply using that word or that she was an "unworthy foreigner" (2:10) but that she was his *ama*. This is a very positive change in her perception of herself, but still deferential. As was mentioned, the words can be used interchangeably but an *ama* could have marriage (or concubinage) prospects. Her mother-in-law's instructions, which she promised to obey, appear to have been to seduce Boaz. But she moves away from Naomi's instructions which required her to be passive and silent and, instead of doing what Boaz told her, Ruth takes the initiative and told Boaz what needs to be done by asking for no more than she rightfully deserves.[65] Ruth upended Naomi's plan for seduction by appealing to Boaz's role as a *goel*, something not mentioned by Naomi and turns it into secret legal business.

But unlike the meeting in the barley field, where she was nameless to the overseer and unknown to Boaz, here on the threshing floor she regains her name and the process of regaining Mahlon's name through a levirate like marriage has started. The first part of Ruth's request is open to different understandings, and it could mean as little as cover me from the cold night air,[66] but from the context it is a none too subtle suggestion that Ruth is asking Boaz to marry her. This is the way he understood it. At no point here or in chapter 4 is the terminology of levirate marriage mentioned. If it really was a levirate marriage which was hers by right, she should not have needed to revert to a midnight meeting. She will not deceive the old man but rather asks him to make good on his blessing of 2:12 where she is commended for taking shelter under the "wings" *kenapayw* of Yahweh. She now takes control and asks Boaz to shelter her under the corners (or wings) of his garments *kenapeka*. A similar passage in Ezekiel 16:8 where betrothal is clearly intended says:

> Then I passed by you and saw you, and behold, you were at the time for love; so I spread My garment over you and covered your nakedness. I also swore an oath to you and entered into a covenant with you so that you became Mine," declares the Lord God (NASB).

---

65. Ziegler, *Ruth*, 326.
66. Block, *Ruth*, 180.

Ruth

While there are a few cases where *kanaf* refers to sexual relations (Deut 22:30, 27:20), Boaz did not take Ruth's presence as a request for sex but as an, "invit[ation] . . . to become God's agent."[67] With this understanding, the setting is turned from the highly charged sexual setting to a legal one.[68] Defying custom, an Israelite man is being called to account by a Moabitess, and she is asking for no more than he is capable of providing.[69] Again Boaz will be reacting to female initiative. The word *goel* will be used six times in rapid succession.

This multiple use of *goel* causes Ziegler to see redemption through Boaz as coming on three levels. First there is the immediacy of what is happening on the threshing floor, the "redemption of the house of Elimelech."[70] But the introduction of the genealogy through to King David at the end of chapter 4 allows us to agree that this was the start of national redemption from the time of the Judges. Equally important, it set into motion the process leading to the appearance of the ideal king who will grow from the stump of Jesse, David's father. We know this king as Jesus. Redemption is present for Ruth, future for the nation and long-term future which I would call "eternal" for the redeemed.[71] Failure to see these three levels of redemption, would be to fail to see a significant part of the story and miss its theological aim.[72] I have to agree.

Just as Naomi wished and prayed for Ruth's security in chapter 1 and then moved to take an active role in fulfilling her hopes, so it is now time for Boaz to take an active role in fulfilling his wishes and prayers for her. This request of Ruth shifts the responsibility for her care and security from God to Boaz, who is asked to take personal control for the situation.[73] When Boaz is first introduced (2:1) he is a relative of Naomi's husband, in 3:2 he is "a relative of ours," now Ruth identifies him as a *goel*. While Ruth asks for redemption, which strictly relates to the family land, Boaz will go further in chapter 4 and offer marriage where real security lies. What is surprising here is the combination of a levirate like marriage in chapter 4 and the duties of the *goel* "redeemer," as they are two separate things in the

---

67. Eskenazi and Frymer-Kensky, *Ruth*, 59.
68. Trible, *Rhetoric of Sexuality*, 184.
69. Trible, *Rhetoric of Sexuality*, 184.
70. Ziegler, *Ruth*, 342.
71. Ziegler, *Ruth*, 344.
72. Ziegler, *Ruth*, 342.
73. Ziegler, *Ruth*, 327.

Law. Only in Ruth are they combined, and not just that, everyone takes it for granted that they are combined (4:5). Even Joe Blow will not complain about the linking of the two.

All parties were moving in an area outside of the case law delivered by Moses which forced Naomi and Ruth to interpret the Law to their unique situation. Ruth is asking for redemption and Boaz is determined to redeem her, but redemption was about land and slavery (Lev 25:25–28, 47–50) and Ruth did not own the land nor was she his relative nor was she an Israelite slave. When at the city gate with the elders and Joe Blow, he does not mention his role as *goel* but changes the verb to *qanah* "to claim" (4:5). Naomi raises the possibility or, more correctly, the impossibility of levirate marriage in chapter 1, but at no point is levirate marriage with the preservation of Mahlon's name mentioned in this scheme. The success of the plan could only be guaranteed if all parties understood the spirit undergirding the Law and, while guided by its letter, were all driven by its spirit and by the Spirit.[74] Block describes what is happening as a bending of the rules of redemption but observed that, "genuinely godly people do not need laws to do the right thing."[75]

The role of the redeemer is meant to be driven by, "caring responsibility for those who may not have justice done for them by the unscrupulous, or even by a person who lives by the letter of the law."[76] This responsibility extends not just to the unfortunate family member but also to their property and is exercised within the family circle. Levirate marriage operates on the same principals as redemption, but while the provision of an heir and the retention of the property in the family is important, so the care of the widow is just as important. In the Book of Ruth, it is the main driver. James would later define the care of the widow as one of the key ways to identify true religion—always was, always will be.

Naomi linked Boaz to their own future by using the personal pronoun "our" redeemer, but Ruth does not say that he is "my" redeemer. Perhaps an impersonal appeal to his responsibility may have been better received. By being called "a" redeemer *goel*, not "the" redeemer, it leaves open a possibility that there was no guarantee that the social security system operating in Israel was actually going to lead to the outcome of Ruth marrying Boaz. This would give a situation where that night on the threshing floor

---

74. Block, *Ruth*, 55, 46.
75. Block, *Ruth*, 194–95.
76. Campbell, *Ruth*, 136.

was intended to get things started among the circle of redeemers.[77] Boaz makes no attempt to usurp, "another man's right to act responsibly."[78] While a little ahead of ourselves, verse twelve is difficult to translate because of its vocabulary and syntax with the second *ki im*, "that I am" found in "it is certainly true that I am a kinsman redeemer." Rather than see this as a clumsy shorthand for the preceding *ki 'amenam* (now it is true). Block suggests that it represents stuttering (similar to the overseer in 2:7). If so it, "reflects Boaz's own frustration because there was a kinsman redeemer who was a closer relative than he."[79] This would, if correct, be the closest we see to romance between the two. Love (*ahav*) between the two is not mentioned in the book but what we see is respect, admiration and gratitude.[80]

> **10**He said, "You are blessed by Yahweh, my daughter. You have shown more kindness in the latter end than at the beginning, because you didn't follow young men, whether poor or rich.

The response of Boaz to such an unexpected and culturally objectional approach has been described this way:

> In a moment the process of understanding is completed. Everything culminates and merges in this image of ingathering: the wings of the LORD sweeping into himself the people, the arms of Boaz gathering into himself the maiden Ruth, the arms of the young men drawing into the barns the grain. It is a moment of imaginative splendor and depth.[81]

Naomi had pictured a life of unmarried widowhood as all that Ruth could have expected should she return with her to Bethlehem (1:11–13) but Boaz saw her as a woman with very good prospects. By commending her for not "going after," *habbahurim*, from the word "to choose" indicating virile young men,[82] rich or poor suggests that in his opinion she could take her pick of husband or at least a male provider. Ruth had rejected marriage for love (poor) or money (rich) choosing instead to sacrificially follow

---

77. Campbell, *Ruth*, 123.
78. Campbell, *Ruth*, 137.
79. Block, *Ruth*, 184.
80. Ziegler, *Ruth*, 335.
81. Rauber. *Literary*, 33.
82. Oswalt, Bāḥar in *TWOT*, 100–101.

family loyalty.[83] Boaz acknowledged that there was more involved in the night's encounter than "gold digging" as there were only a limited number of men who could be a *goel*. The term, *leket 'ahare* "go after" is often used of worshiping other gods or, "to establish illicit sexual activities."[84] Moore describes the wonder of what is going on that night, saying, "Evidently somewhere between the crass manipulation and spiritual regeneration, kindness for Boaz is something that enables him to experience the joy-filled wonder of discovering, on a public threshing floor of all places, that Yahweh intends to place a beautiful woman in his life." The only appropriate response is that he be a man who can "live up to the privileges of his responsibilities."[85] How old was Boaz? Block suggests that he wasn't an old and withered man because he could work a full day with his workers winnowing and then sleep in the open.[86] But attending the winnowing as the landowner is a far cry from actually doing the work. Given that he seems to be quickly off the scene he could well have been very old. Ruth Rabbah says he was eighty![87]

From Boaz's standpoint, Ruth's previous *hesed*, would refer to 2:11 where he told her that he had been informed of her comfort to Naomi and now includes her desire to provide an heir to continue her dead husband's name. At that time, she obligated herself with an oath, just as Boaz does for her. These were acts combining responsibility and freedom and were far beyond what could be expected from a foreign wife. By faithfully obeying Naomi in this seriously compromising situation, ahead of her own interests, she was again going far beyond her legal obligation. The latest act of *hesed* is directed towards Boaz but from which Naomi will also benefit. The events will prove to be levirate like, which was the responsibility of the male, but by taking it on herself to initiate it she was, in effect, acting like a kinsman redeemer. Orpah's return to her own people was what would be expected so the personal relationship between Ruth and Mahlon must have been powerful.

What is remarkable is that Boaz is able to see in the actions of a woman dressed and for all intents and purposes, acting in a way similar to that of a prostitute, an act of extraordinary *hesed*. He is able to see the act of self-sacrifice behind Ruth's actions and he thinks more of her rather than

---

83. Hubbard, *Ruth*, 214–15.
84. Block, *Ruth*, 182.
85. Moore, Ruth, 305.
86. Block, *Ruth*, 182.
87. Ruth Rabbah: 6:2.

less.[88] Perhaps also he sees Naomi's handiwork in all this. An ordinary man could be more expected to curse instead of blessing her for violating his personal integrity.[89] With a mother as a one-time prostitute, he should have been aware of the desperate economic pressures that can lead a woman to sell her body to survive and how people can change. If her initial acts of *hesed* warranted full payment of her wages to use the metaphor of 2:12, how much greater a reward should she now receive.

> [11]*Now, my daughter, don't be afraid. I will do to you all that you say; for all the city of my people knows that you are a worthy woman.*

It would have taken great courage to leave Moab and its god/s for Israel and now, with this plan of Naomi's, even greater courage was needed. It could all have gone disastrously wrong as:

> Boaz could have treated her as Moabite trash, scavenging in Israel's garbage bins, and then corrupting the people with her whorish behavior. But with corresponding *hesed*, he sees her as a woman equal in character and equivalent in status.[90]

Fortunately, Boaz reassures Ruth with the traditional words, "Do not be afraid." Ruth said to Naomi in verse five, "All that you say, I will do" and now Boaz repeats the same words only adding "for you." By doing this he upends the social order by saying he would act as Ruth's servant, not her master. Naomi does not even rate a mention in all this.

Boaz diffuses this private sexually charged scene where they were accountable to each other's opinion, by broadening the scene to the opinion of those in the gate, and this public view of Ruth is important to Boaz.[91] The setting is prepared for chapter 4 when Boaz refers to "all the city" which is literally "the gate of the city" Among the "legally responsible body of the town"[92] that sat at the gate entrance, where legal transactions are made, the opinion there was that Ruth was a "virtuous woman," *'eset hayl*. She had certainly been noticed and her character was outweighing any racial prejudice that would have existed and unfavorably influenced the legal

---

88. Ziegler, *Ruth*, 315.
89. Ruth Rabbah: 6:1.
90. Block, *Ruth*, 184.
91. Ziegler, *Ruth*, 330–31.
92. Campbell, *Ruth*, 124.

proceedings. This favorable opinion did not translate into positive help though but would have made the legal proceedings in chapter 4 much easier. This exact word is only found elsewhere in Proverbs 31:10 with the description of the virtuous woman. It is not likely that Boaz would have retained his high opinion of her if he considered she was out for, "a one-night stand."[93]

This reference to Ruth being virtuous connects Ruth and Boaz but it is not the only one. There is a definite linking of the two and is outlined in this table:

Word	Ruth	**Boaz**
Natan (Give)	Used once of giving food to needy Naomi (2:18)	Used once of giving food to Ruth for needy Naomi (3:17)
Hesed	*Hesed* done to the deceased (1:8)	*Hesed* done to the deceased (2:20)
	Sacrificed dignity to help another through gleaning (2:1)	Sacrificed dignity to help another through serving Ruth food on the field (2:14)
	Hard working as she gleaned from morning to evening (2:7, 17)	Hardworking as he visits his fields and threshing floor (2:4; 3:2)
Anokhi (I am)	Used three times to describe herself (2:10, 13; 3:9) with movement from anonymity to identity	Used three times and always in relationship to his role as a redeemer (3:12, 13; 4:4)
Hayil (Virtuous)	Ruth is Virtuous	Boaz is Virtuous
	Blessed in the name of God (3:10)	Blessed in the name of God (2:20)

Table 3 Mirroring of Ruth and Boaz[94]

Boaz was introduced as a man of standing but quickly we came to see that the alternate meaning of a man of noble character better described him. Now we see that Boaz described Ruth with the same word. Economically,

---

93. Evans suggest that the events on the threshing floor may refer to some local custom. Evans, *Ruth*, 261.

94. Ziegler, *Ruth*, 466–69.

they are worlds apart, but Evans describes them as being of the same social class.[95] I don't think that is the right word, rather they share the same spirit making them perfectly matched, as it will give them courage to break the social strictures that bound this close-knit community. Ruth is the embodiment of the perfect helper of Genesis 2:18. Despite their age difference this shared quality is what, "makes sense of his view that she was doing him a favor by agreeing to marry him, and her view that he was doing her a favor."[96] Immediately after the storyteller shows them to be ideally matched, he throws in the complication of a closer relative.

> *12Now it is true that I am a near kinsman. However, there is a kinsman nearer than I. 13Stay this night, and in the morning, if he will perform for you the part of a kinsman, good. Let him do the kinsman's duty. But if he will not do the duty of a kinsman for you, then I will do the duty of a kinsman for you, as Yahweh lives. Lie down until the morning.*

Boaz was willing to act despite the obstacles in the way and the biggest was a closer relative. The fact that he was prepared, "to let Israel's social security system run its course" and not usurp the role of the closer relative shows that this was not a case of being swept away by a pretty face.[97] In fact we are not told that Ruth is attractive, unlike other matriarchs. There has been adequate time since they arrived home for Naomi to determine which of her relatives were alive or dead. While Ruth knows nothing about Joe Blow, Naomi surely must have. Had he been on the scene, and he should have been with at least some charity, cold or otherwise, Ruth would have been aware of his existence. If he couldn't do a small thing in the capacity of being Naomi and Ruth's closest relative, there is little chance he will take on the role of a *goel* which would involve real cost.

While this is in the realm of thinking aloud, if the field was productive enough for two men to line up to purchase it, there was no way that it would have been left fallow once the rains returned. With the rightful owner not on the scene and for all they knew very likely dead, who would its use have fallen to? I would expect it to be the closest relative. A less than generous attitude towards Naomi would have prompted her to bypass

---

95. Evans, *Ruth*, 261.
96. Evans, *Ruth*, 261.
97. Moore, *Ruth*, 357.

him all together. But of course, this is conjecture, but not unreasonable all the same. It would also explain the need for the very public nature of the transfer of ownership later at the gate.

Whether my conjecture is correct or not, the reason for approaching Boaz first is that Naomi knew that going up the avenue of the closest relative would be a waste of time, especially after Boaz's initial reaction to Ruth and their meals for the coming year being secured through him. It could well be that, "Ruth regards Boaz as her only hope, the only man in Bethlehem confident enough, pious enough and strong enough to withstand the social inclination to ostracize the Moabite woman."[98] Though he was not the closest relative he committed to resolve the matter, with or without him being the *goel*. Very likely he knew Joe Blow's nature even better than Naomi and the offer of Ruth with the land may only have been a formality. The Law certainly foresaw that the *goel* would not do his duty (Deut 25:7).

But a closer relative was not the only hurdle. The age gap was another and has already been discussed but what of her being a Moabitess? When commenting on the marriage of Mahlon and Chilion to Ruth and Orpah, I mentioned that some rabbis made a valid distinction between a Moabitess and a Moabite. Only the Moabite was excluded. Be that as it may, human nature so often exhibits racism and will always have an excuse. I have attempted to show the overseer as racist and no argument, no matter how reasonable, will get past bigotry. It would not matter that Ruth had converted, had shown righteousness and could be viewed as an Israelite at heart. Boaz must have had a different outlook towards foreigners given that his mother was Rahab, a Canaanite prostitute (Matt 1:5). Boaz may have, and certainly should have, had a much earlier understanding of what Paul acknowledged in Romans chapter 2 when he said:

> 28*A person is not a Jew who is one only outwardly, nor is circumcision merely outward and physical.* 29*No, a person is a Jew who is one inwardly; and circumcision is circumcision of the heart, by the Spirit, not by the written code. Such a person's praise is not from other people, but from God.*

Boaz may have been color-blind to her race when he looked at Ruth's faith. Her race is not even mentioned. Here in the privacy of the threshing floor he is going to perform the role of the *goel* for Ruth's sake but in public he will use the cover of restoring the family line.

---

98. Ziegler, *Ruth*, 328.

To return home in the dark could have been dangerous so Boaz, accepting the role of the potential husband to be, is now careful about her physical safety. Ruth is invited to sleep at his feet, the same word that is used in verses four and seven and, "it is inescapable that this position is next to Boaz"[99] so enhancing the sexual tension in the story. The remainder of the night is told in a chiasm:

A Remain this night, and when morning comes
  B if he will redeem you, good; let him redeem you.
  B' But if he does not wish to redeem you, then I will redeem you, as the LORD lives.
A' Lie down until morning (NASB).

We are not told that Boaz did actually spread the corner of his garment over her in the sense of committing to be the *goel*. His commitment to Ruth at this stage is not to marry her but to do the work of a kinsman redeemer if the nearest relative will not do his part. In Boaz's mind, this went beyond simply marrying Ruth but redeeming the whole family situation which included security for both widows, retention of the land in the family and restoring the names of the dead. He did so with an oath, "as surely as Yahweh lives" which is a common oath formula in Judges, Samuel, and Kings. There are only six other women in the Old Testament who are blessed individually, Rebecca (Gen 24:60), Leah and Rachel (Gen 31:55), Jael (Judg 5:24), Hannah (1 Sam 1:17) and Abigail (1 Sam 25:32–33) but only Ruth is blessed using Yahweh's name.

What would Ruth have thought that night? She was happy to marry Boaz who she knew was a virtuous man, even if there was a big age difference. He could be relied upon to treat her well and give her security, but what of this new person of which she knew nothing? She was facing the possibility of being the virtual property of a man who had not shown basic humanity. In the morning, she could have found herself trading a life of abject poverty for one of abject misery.

A hint of the outcome of the event is found in Boaz's instruction to Ruth to stay with him during the night. It was not the usual word to lie with its sexual overtones, but from the root *luwn*, to "lodge." This was the same word used by Ruth in 1:16 when she promised to live where Naomi lived.

---

99. Campbell, *Ruth*, 126.

This word is free of innuendos.[100] Ruth's pledge to lie where Naomi lies is also alluded to. Campbell sees the question of whether they had sex on the threshing floor as irrelevant.[101] Should they have had sex that night would the outcome have been any different? Certainly, if there is any truth in the story that Boaz died on his wedding night presumably doing, or as a result of doing the deed.[102] By focusing on the likelihood or otherwise of a sexual encounter we can miss the big picture which is that Boaz has taken on his responsibility to care for the two widows.

> **14** *She lay at his feet until the morning, then she rose up before one could discern another. For he said, "Let it not be known that the woman came to the threshing floor."* **15** *He said, "Bring the mantle that is on you, and hold it." She held it; and he measured six measures of barley, and laid it on her; then he went into the city.*

The sexual imagery associated with feet is strong (see earlier comments) and obviously, to lie with someone also has a clear sexual image. The Jewish sages have made a comparison between Potiphar's wife (Gen 39:7) and Ruth. The Egyptian acts like a bitch on heat[103] demanding that Joseph have sex with her, but Ruth said nothing explicit to Boaz, but only modestly hints. Rising just before daybreak we see the same modesty in Boaz who shows concern for Ruth's reputation. How different this is from Judges 19 where the mob, "bellows loudly and publicly"[104] to rape, first the Levite, then settle for his concubine. Not all were like the Gibeonites and appropriate behavior was known and understood, if not followed.

By proposing in a very public place, Ruth has taken a very public risk which could easily be misconstrued.[105] The comment about not letting it be known, a parody of Naomi's instructions, that a woman came to the threshing floor could be directed to Ruth; but could also be a command to any of his employees who rose early. But the use of the masculine verb

---

100. Campbell, *Ruth*, 138.
101. Campbell, *Ruth*, 138.
102. Ginzburg, "Boaz," 278.
103. See Genesis Rabbah: 87:7 where the reference is to acting like a beast.
104. Moore, *Ruth*, 355.
105. Moore, *Ruth*, 348.

in, "let it be known" suggests that he could have been talking to himself.[106] When saying, "give me the wrap" it is read in the feminine but it is written in the masculine. Should anyone be awake, there was less reason to think, in the semi darkness, that a woman came to the threshing floor, as he was speaking as if Ruth was a man.

Boaz poured out six "barleys" (*seorim*) for Naomi. In "poured out" again we have possibly another word suggestive of sexual relations.[107] What these units are is very uncertain. It should be evident when a commodity is mentioned, here seemingly barley and a number, what the unit is and the one mentioned already, is *ephah* in chapter 2. With an *ephah*, measuring 23 liters approximately, that is approximately, 140 liters of barley which would weigh about 90 kg.[108] She would have to have been "built like an ox" to carry that. The shawl, if that is what it is, also would have been more of a blanket, not something that is in keeping with her finest clothes. An *'omer* or a tenth of an *ephah* would have been too small, making this a little over half of what she gleaned in a day which would be far from generous. A *seah* which is roughly a third of an *ephah* is still very heavy.[109] Campbell suggests that we should see this as a lost unit of measure possibly referred to in Genesis 26:12 (100 *searim* translated 100 fold).[110] Whatever the measure, it was so heavy Boaz had to lift it onto her and proved a tangible sign that he had received Naomi's message.[111] A woman carrying a quantity of grain early in the morning might be viewed as being about her proper business.[112]

Some Hebrew manuscripts say that "she" went to the city and others say "he" and either could be right. While the preceding two verses set the scene for Ruth leaving for the city with her grain, having Boaz leaving for the town sets the scene for chapter 4. It would show how keen Boaz was to settle the matter. It would not do to miss Joe Blow if he left the city for his field very early.

---

106. Block, *Ruth*, 186.

107. Eskenazi and Frymer-Kensky, *Ruth*, 66, (refer footnote 154).

108. The measures are very imprecise, and Campbell gives a possible weight ranging from 174 lb (79 kg) to 285 lb (129 kg). Campbell, *Ruth*, 127.

109. About 27 to 45 kg, and still probably too much for a cape. Block, *Ruth*, 187.

110. Campbell, *Ruth*, 127–28.

111. Evans, *Ruth*, 262.

112. Eskenazi and Frymer-Kensky, *Ruth*, 66.

> **16** When she came to her mother-in-law, she
> said, "How did it go, my daughter?"
> She told her all that the man had done for her. **17** She
> said, "He gave me these six measures of barley; for he
> said, 'Don't go empty to your mother-in-law.'"
> **18** Then she said, "Wait, my daughter, until you know what will
> happen; for the man will not rest until he has settled this today."

While some translations, (e.g., NIV, RSV, MEV) have Naomi's greeting to Ruth as, "how did it go?" or similar, this is really an interpretation of her greeting which was, "who are you?" (KJV). She may have been surprised that Ruth came home in the semi darkness. The preceding verses were about leaving before being able to be recognized and the reference to "my daughter" may just mean that she recognized a female figure. More likely it is a question about whether Ruth had sex with Boaz or whether there had been a change to her marital state. Something obviously happened as she was out all night. This would mean she was asking, "Are you Mrs. Boaz?" a woman with a new identity.[113] In a sense she did have a new identity as, "by now we have learned she was recognized by the townspeople as a noble woman."[114]

The three questions asked about Ruth's identity show her progress in Bethlehem's society. When Boaz asks, "Who is she?" (2:5–6) she is simply a Moabitess. On the threshing floor she is Ruth the relative who needs a *goel*, and now she is going to be the bride of an Israelite by the time the day is out.[115] There is possibly a connection with the question, "Who are you my daughter?" to the same question asked by Isaac when Jacob impersonated his brother Esau, "Who are you my son? (Gen 27:18)." There an older mother plotted to deceive an old man in a setting with limited visibility, with a plan that was very dangerous. Both stories also include an unrecognized person bringing food to the family head.[116]

Naomi called herself *Mara* or "Bitter" complaining that Yahweh had returned her to Bethlehem "empty" (1:21). The storyteller returned to this word with Ruth saying that Boaz had said that she is not to return to her mother-in-law empty. While there is no mention of Naomi on the

---

113. Ruth Rabbah: 7:4.
114. Block, *Ruth*, 190.
115. Hubbard, *Ruth*, 224.
116. Block, *Ruth*, 190–91.

threshing floor the storyteller avoids repetition and maintains the pace by telling us part of the conversation not recorded in the previous scene. This is a characteristic of the storyteller (see also 2:7 and 2:12). There is no need to see this as a fabrication to make Naomi feel better.[117] If it were so, it would make the journey from emptiness to fullness somewhat hollow. Importantly, Boaz is not called the *goel*, but "the man," probably referring to the potential problem of the nearer relative. Boaz's relationship with Ruth is only indirect. His legal responsibility is primarily to Naomi, so it is fitting that the gift is for her. Ruth only tells what Boaz did for her and says nothing about what she asked of him. Giving all the credit to another is likely another example of a life governed by *hesed*.[118]

Chapter 2 concludes with a pause in the story with a form of the word *yashab* "to sit or remain" and likewise another delay is introduced here with another form of the word used for "wait" or "sit still." The scene closes with Naomi showing she has a clearer understanding than Ruth of the events unfolding. Ruth can now wait because Boaz will not. In the first two verses of the next chapter, the storyteller will take this theme and first have Boaz sit, then Joe Blow and then the ten elders as they sort out her future. She knows the nature of Boaz and his commitment to keeping the covenant requirements. By the end of the day, she will be married, one way or the other but economics, not children have been the thrust of this last conversation. When there is a child in chapter 4 it will be for Naomi's security.

There are now two men on the scene, one desirable and the other not and again, despite the good will of a virtuous man, we are introduced to the element of luck with the expression, "how the matter falls" as with a die.[119] But will it be luck? Campbell points us in the right direction when he says, "Are we not to see the same hidden hand behind 'how the matter will fall out' as controlled the "luck" in 2:37."[120] That very expression *eikh yipol davar* "how the matter or word will fall" recalls God whose *davar* (word) does not fall (Josh 21:45; 23:14; 1 Kgs 8:56; 2 Kgs 10:10). In the background of the negations between the two potential *goels* is the true *goel* of Israel, Yahweh. God will be the source of Boaz's power to redeem and will ensure that Ruth's future is not subject to luck.[121]

---

117. As suggested by Ziegler, *Ruth*, 355–56.
118. Eskenazi and Frymer-Kensky, *Ruth*, 67.
119. Hubbard, *Ruth*, 227.
120. Campbell, *Ruth*, 129.
121. Ziegler, *Ruth*, 358–59.

The chapter ends as it starts with the two women alone in their house talking about their security and Naomi believing that any lasting safety can only come through a man. Chapter 4 will challenge that.

Chapter Four

SOME YEARS AGO, I was visiting a close friend, an assistant professor at Addis Ababa University, when we went for lunch with his Head of Department. After lunch, my friend's boss said, "Did you notice that I left a large tip?" I had not, but he proceeded to tell me a moving story. When he was a young boy, he secretly helped two of his uncles who needed money. His father eventually heard about it and called his son to him. Rather than reprimand his son, he told the boy to kneel before him, placed his hand on his head and asked their heavenly father to bless him. He added the prayer that his son would always have money to give away. From that point onwards money has always come to him from unexpected sources, and he always gives it away in line with his father's blessing.

What is the power in a blessing? Perhaps we have little idea because we may have done it so infrequently. But this is something that some, at least, in Bethlehem were not guilty of nor do they seem unaware of its power. Ancient Israel had its High Priest and the Levitical priests who were required to bless the descendants of Jacob but in Ruth, blessings flow freely from the lips of all. But not quite all—they did not flow from the two nameless characters, the overseer who was racist and Joe Blow whose actions were driven by commerce and expediency and neither did they receive a blessing. In this chapter the fruit of the blessings are fulfilled:

- In return for the *hesed* shown to her, Naomi asks Yahweh that her daughters-in-law would also receive his *hesed* and find rest in the home of another husband (1:8–9),

- Ruth is fully rewarded for seeking refuge under the wings of Yahweh (2:2),
- The generosity of Boaz in acts of *hesed* towards the dead and their widows is rewarded by adding Elimelech's property to his own, gaining Ruth as his wife and having a son (2:19–20),
- Ruth's acts of *hesed* are rewarded by having the legal processes proceed in such a way that her veiled request that Boaz marry her is fulfilled (3:9–10), and
- Naomi's concern that Ruth finds security was rewarded by a grandson, Obed who would provide her with security (1:9, 3:1).[1]

The final chapter of Ruth leaves us with a picture of perfect justice with no unresolved questions. Every good act was fully rewarded, especially the unwavering compassion of Ruth which resulted in her marriage to a wealthy man of equally noble character. Through all of this Boaz a man who, like Enoch, walked lockstep with God, recognizes his will and acts as a conduit for Yahweh's blessing. His response to Ruth on the barley field had initially been of giving her favor but here and continuing through chapter 4 will be way beyond what could be hoped for or expected.

If everyone in this world responded as Boaz did it would be a far better place but, after all, he was responding to family, by birth or marriage, and was motivated by the acts of compassion shown by Ruth. Jesus commanded his followers to go beyond their families and their friends and even bless their enemies who curse and abuse them (Luke 6:27–28). All Christians, not just the professional ordained clergy are commanded to bless (Rom 12:14) but the Apostle Peter goes even further, declaring this act of blessing is to be the Christian vocation (1 Pet 3:9).[2] This is how we can fulfill our calling to be salt and light in our community.

There is a similarity between the little town of Bethlehem with its Moabite widow and my farming valley, in that it is having its British and Germanic roots changed by an influx of "foreigners." Likewise, we have to consider what constitutes citizenship. Our government has decreed it is an act of parliament and a piece of paper granted after mastering the language and living in Australia for at least four years. Such people have all the rights of citizens. As I write in the start of the corona pandemic the nation has been appalled at reports of new "citizens" purchasing desperately

1. Block, *Ruth*, 244–45.
2. Block, *Ruth*, 244.

needed personal equipment and shipping back to their countries of birth. How this contrasts with Ruth's pledge, "Your people will be my people." In a community where you have to live for twenty years, after moving from another part of Australia, to be considered a local (or so the saying goes), formal citizenship has not always been the same thing as community acceptance. But Ruth received her citizenship in as little as three months in a society that was probably more parochial. For Ruth's part she took on the responsibility of citizenship and submitted her rights to the needs of others who were just as needy as she was. We see in chapter 4 that true citizenship, where acceptance as fully one of "us," is grounded not in a declaration by a person or a government but is also affirmed through the approval of the population as a whole. A wise person, as Ruth was, also finds it in the acceptance of the Living God.

Boaz had no idea that he was doing something that would lead to the redemption of Israel through its greatest king, David, let alone the savior of all the earth, Jesus. He did not live to see any of this, and he may not have lived to have even seen the birth of his son Obed. He just lived his life guided by the Law but led by the Spirit. He did what he understood to be the right thing. But more than that, he did not give up easily when problems stood in the way and would do it to his own detriment. May we all be blessed to live such a life.

> [1] *Now Boaz went up to the gate and sat down there. Behold, the near kinsman of whom Boaz spoke came by. Boaz said to him, "Come over here, friend, and sit down!" He came over, and sat down.*

In chapter 2, I included a table that showed the similarities and differences between the raped concubine of Judges 19 and Ruth chapters 1 to 3. The similarities to that especially dark period of the Book of Judges did not end there but continued through chapters 20 and 21. In the same vein, Table Four shows the similarities of the civil war of chapter 20, that almost saw the destruction of Benjamin, to the four chapters of Ruth. The similarities are strongest with this chapter.

Judges 20	Ruth 1—4
Wants to resolve the wrong done to him v5	Boaz is not concerned about damaging his inheritance
Children of Israel arise (*alu*) v3	Boaz goes up (*ala*) to the gate 4:1
Takes ten men v10	Takes ten men 4:2
Body is distributed to every field and inheritance v6	Resolves the inheritance and the fields
Wage war against their brothers v13	Their brother 4:3
Nage'ah (to touch) (NIV come) has led to evil (*haraah*) v41	Boaz commanded youth not to touch Ruth (*Nogekh*) is good for her 2:9
To cleave (*davak*) signifies the hot pursuit of the enemy v42, 45	Ruth is encouraged to stay safe by staying near the female workers 2:8, 21, 23.
Mashhit refers to annihilation of the population v42	The close relative is concerned he will destroy (*ashhit*) his inheritance 4:6
Menuha is either a town name or place Benjamites rested v43	Naomi wants her daughters-in-law to find rest (*menuha*) with a husband 1:9. Also with Boaz (*Manoah*) 3:1
Benjamite men of valor (*anshei hayil*) defend tribesmen from their own dreadful actions 44, 46	Boaz a man of valor (*ish hayil*) has a noble spirit 2:1 Ruth is a woman of valor (*eshet hayil*) 3:11.

Table 4. Similarities and differences between Judges 20 and Ruth 2—4.[3]

Chapter 4 starts with a man of Judah who is said to "go up," *ala* which hints at the twice asked question of Yahweh in Judges, "Who will go up (*yaaleh*) first for us" with the answer, "Judah shall go up (*yaaleh*) first" (Judg 1:1–2; 20:18). Ziegler sees in this, "tantalizing hints that Boaz is the leader twice alluded to by God at the beginning and end of the Book of Judges."[4] Perhaps that is a stretch too far but certainly it will be through Boaz that the

3. Ziegler, *Ruth*, 53–56.
4. Ziegler, *Ruth*, 46.

leadership vacuum, solved by kingship, does come from the outworking of his going up to the city gate that morning. It was of more consequence compared with anything that had preceded under the Judges.

The focus has shifted from Naomi and Ruth to Boaz and his character is more fully fleshed out and his virtuous nature is even more clearly seen. Boaz had made an oath in chapter 3 using Yahweh's name that the matter of Ruth's redemption would be resolved that day. Acting immediately upon his promise he went up to the gate to wait for the closer relative. What is unusual is that a man who greets his workers in Yahweh's name and freely blesses Ruth with it also, does not use his name at all in this chapter. Does the storyteller do this to reflect on the opportunity lost to the *goel*? He will turn down the greatest blessing Yahweh could offer anyone in Israel at that time, to be the great-grandfather of David and ultimately the Messiah.

The city gate was likely the only area of any size inside the city walls where people could socialize and conduct legal business. And, in this space, decisions were made that secured the fate of Naomi's land and of the two widows. Just as Ruth happened to chance upon her husband-to-be while out gleaning (2:3), Boaz just happened to sit down in the gate as the nearest kinsman passed by. Again, the ambiguous theme of chance is brought to play but this is where chance ends in the fate of Ruth. It is now up to the players to make decisions. While it is true that if Boaz went to the gate early enough, he would had to have met Joe Blow. Anyone going to work in the fields had to go through the gate, but as Campbell says, it "miss[es] the impact of the Hebrew construction, which . . . conveys a hint of God's working behind the scene."[5] Judaism sees the direct hand of God and it is said, "Boaz made his thing and Ruth did her thing and Naomi did her thing and the Holy One, blessed be, He said: "So I will do my thing."[6]

After the morally dubious and secret meeting on the threshing floor, the scene has moved to the most public venue available. Everything is now open and above board. Boaz firmly took control of the "chance" meeting with his relative, saying "come over," "sit down" and Joe Blow obeys as the elders also will. Our translation and others, e.g., RSV call this close relative "friend" but this misses the point. Given the importance of names and identities in the Book of Ruth it is very significant that he is not given a name. The meaning of the words used, *peloni almoni,* is uncertain so translators

---

5. Campbell, *Ruth*, 141.
6. Ruth Rabbah: 7:7.

look to the context and to the way the versions treat it.[7] The LXX translates with a word meaning "secret" or "hidden" as the only other places it is used refers to locations that are military secrets (1 Sam 21:3; 2 Kgs 6:8). It has been suggested that what we have is an onomatopoeic wordplay like helter-skelter.[8] Block suggests, given the context, that there is probably a wordplay between *almoni* and *almanah*, the word for "widow"[9] which, surprisingly, does not occur in the book.

I have referred to the closest relative as Joe Blow, others use different terms, e.g., "so and so"[10] but, either way, his name is deliberately omitted. In a book concerned with identity he proved not to be worthy of one and, like the nameless characters of Judges, is "relegated to the obscurity of history, uncelebrated and unidentified."[11] This is along the same vein as the brother who refuses to undertake levirate marriage to continue the name of his deceased brother and who in turn is given a new shameful name, "The House of the One Who Removed His Shoe" (Deut 25:10). The delinquent brother is in effect committing a form of fratricide because, not only is he refusing to allow his brother's name to live on, his actions ensure he inherits his brother's land.[12] For this, and causing the widow to live in appalling conditions, he is called to account. It is the very opposite of *hesed*. While Joe Blow won't be pilloried like this, he certainly won't be honored either.

While Boaz refers to Elimelech as a "brother" to both he and Joe Blow, it need not be the case. As the closer relative and as a justification for levirate marriage the unnamed man is said to be a brother of Elimelech and Salmon the father of Boaz[13] (see genealogy in Table Six) so making Boaz a cousin of Elimelech. Perhaps. The word is used by people in a wide range of relationships, generally in a covenant relationship. An example is when David refers to Jonathan as his brother (2 Sam 1:26). It can also be as loose as referring to another Israelite.

---

7. Campbell, *Ruth*, 141.
8. Moore, *Ruth*, 361.
9. Block, *Ruth*, 206.
10. Evans, *Ruth*, 265.
11. Ziegler, *Ruth*, 374.
12. Ziegler, *Ruth*, 402.
13. Babylonian Talmud, B. Bat. 91a

Ruth

> **2***Boaz took ten men of the elders of the city, and said, "Sit down here," and they sat down.* **3***He said to the near kinsman, "Naomi, who has come back out of the country of Moab, is selling the parcel of land, which was our brother Elimelech's.* **4***I thought I should tell you, saying, 'Buy it before those who sit here, and before the elders of my people.' If you will redeem it, redeem it; but if you will not redeem it, then tell me, that I may know. For there is no one to redeem it besides you; and I am after you."*
> *He said, "I will redeem it."*

The similarities of the Book of Judges to Ruth continues as it moves into chapter 21 when the Israelites realize that they have done a dreadful thing in the way they punished Benjamin. They then try and ensure the tribe's continuation by providing wives in an even worse way. The bloodshed and kidnapping of brides of chapter 21 contrasts to the peaceful resolution of all matters at the gate of the city of Bethlehem.

Judges 21	Ruth 1–4
Sit in mourning till evening, v2	Ruth works to obtain food till evening 2:17
Lift up voice and cry, v2	Ruth and Orpah raise their voices and cry 1:9,14
Make an oath not to give their daughters, v1	Ruth makes the only oath 1:17
Genuine regret *(niham)* for the remnant *(notarim)*	Refers to Ruth having sufficient food and giving remnant *(notar)* to Naomi 2:18
Lack prospects of marriage, v7, 16	Lacks prospects of marriage 1:11–13
Elders propose plan, v16	Boaz's plan is assisted by the elders 4:2
Not be erased from Israel, v17	Boaz acts so Mahlon's name is not cut off from his brothers 4:10
First solution was violent—to kill the inhabitants of Jabesh Gilead and spare the virgins, v8–12	Solution is peaceful

Judges 21	Ruth 1–4
Second solution was to kidnap innocent young women, v20–22	Solution is peaceful
Survivors return to their inheritance (*nahala*), v24	The inheritance is resolved (*nahalatow*) 4:10

Table 5. Similarities and contrasts of Judges 21 to Ruth.[14]

To go up to the gate[15] was an idiom for "to go to court" and, with the twelve men sitting, it would have been clear to anyone passing that Boaz had come to transact legal proceedings. The fact that there were ten elders has been taken up in later Judaism as the quorum for reciting the marriage benediction[16] and the minimum number for a community.[17] Criminal matters were the subject for judges who are different from the elders of the gate referred to in Deuteronomy 22:15. The elders appear to be given five areas of responsibility, all related to family law. These are:

- Blood redemption (Deut 19:12),
- Expiation for unsolved murder (Deut 21:1–9),
- Rebellious sons (Deut 21:18–21),
- Defamation of virgins (Deut 22:13–21), and
- Levirate marriage (Deut 25:5–10).[18]

The root *g-ʿ-l*, from which *goel* is derived is used in Ruth at a much higher rate than any other book in the Bible.[19] While its twenty-one uses relate to human redeemers, no Jew would fail to bring to mind the familiar *goel Yisraʾel*, the "redeemer of Israel." He was the one who redeemed Israel from slavery in Egypt with an outstretched hand (Exod 6:6). In a similar

14. Ziegler, *Ruth*, 55–57.

15. Excavated gates at Gezer and Dan comprised a large open space, like a plaza, with stone benches along the wall.

16. Ruth Rabbah: 7:8.

17. Eskenazi and Frymer-Kensky, *Ruth*, 73.

18. Moore, *Ruth*, 361.

19. Eskenazi and Frymer-Kensky gives this comparison, twenty-one times in the twenty-seven chapters of Leviticus and twenty-five times in the sixty-six chapters of Isaiah. Eskenazi and Frymer-Kensky, *Ruth*, lv.

way to delivering the nation, Yahweh delivered the worthy from distress (Pss 72:13–14). If the God of Israel was a redeeming God then the act of redeeming the poor from distress was more than an act of charity, it was at its core intended to be a spiritual act,[20] not merely the commercial transaction that will govern the closest redeemer's action in this story.

This business at the gate (1–12) is all done by males and reflects a male point of view in a male dominated culture. For all that, the work has been done by women behind the scene. (Was it ever otherwise?) A very different approach is given in verses thirteen to seventeen when the women have the final say (and dare I say, was it ever otherwise) and view the events that occurred at the gate from a female perspective, and the whole is harmonized. While we have in verses three to eight an ancient equivalent of a court transcript, our understanding of what transpired is limited as we have an incomplete knowledge of Israelite customs relating to widows, inheritance and redemption.[21]

While Ruth is sitting at home, Boaz, Joe Blow and the elders sit down in the gate to transact a legal matter to secure her security or her fate, depending on which close relative redeemed her. God's hand is seen in legal matters. Despite the uncertainty of their outcome from a human perspective, "in the mind of the narrator God has determined the result from the beginning."[22] The story does not allow for a discussion between Naomi and Boaz to determine what she intends. Campbell suggests that he may have made it up as part of his plan to marry Ruth.[23] But equally, Ruth could have mentioned it on the threshing floor or, from her invitation to marry her. It was just how things were done once Ruth mentioned the need for a redeemer. But as Boaz addressed the *goel* and the elders, the question of who or what is to be redeemed is not initially clear. On the threshing floor Ruth only spoke of redeeming herself.

Boaz stamped his authority on the proceedings, "he commands, and others obey without question."[24] He immediately focused on the problem of the land though it is common to reverse the order of the sentence, as our translation does, to appear that he was more interested in Naomi and

---

20. Eskenazi and Frymer-Kensky, *Ruth, liii*.
21. Block, *Ruth*, 207.
22. Block, *Ruth*, 49.
23. Campbell, *Ruth*, 144.
24. Ziegler, *Ruth*, 380.

therefore her welfare.²⁵ Naomi's indiscretion in abandoning the town during famine is minimized but not overlooked and his primary concern, Ruth, is hidden. Boaz's commitment to redeem Ruth was made clear on the threshing floor and then by his totally focused actions but, quite possibly, he knew his relative well enough to appeal to his own financial gain and not to his good nature on the basis of charity. At that point Boaz was conducting business, not welfare.

Up to verse three we are given the opinion that Naomi is completely destitute, and Ruth needs personal redemption from the abject poverty that drove her to glean daily however there is a field. It is not just any field that Naomi is selling. It is described as *helqat*, a "portion" a word commonly used to describe, "the share or division of land made to the various tribes of Israel after the conquest."²⁶ This portion of land has come to the family of Elimelech by lot as a gift from Yahweh but neither he nor later Naomi was the owner as the land was Yahweh's. Israelites were to consider themselves foreigners and strangers in what they would otherwise consider their own land. Their relationship to the land that they were to adopt was as tenants not owners. Land could not be sold in perpetuity and, in the event of hardship, close relatives were expected, through the process of redemption, to step in and ensure the family's connection to the land was not lost. In the very worst of situations, land that was sold reverted to the family in the Year of Jubilee (the year following seven cycles of seven years) (Lev 25:23–28).

Further on, in verse five, the land is referred to by the term *nahalah* frequently translated as "inheritance" and then it is used again in verse six and ten. The root can be used to speak of Israel as Yahweh's "inheritance" (Deut 4:20; 9:26, 29) which put them in a very special relationship with him. Furthermore, it also means that their relationship with each other should also be different. For this reason, they should not possess one another (Lev 25:47) and by implication, the widow was Yahweh's widow and needed protection. As well, the land of Canaan is spoken of as Israel's "inheritance." Further the word can be used of the land allocated to the tribes, (Num 36:9; Josh 14:3) and even down to the allocation to individuals (Num 27:7; Josh 17:4; Judg 2:9). Our understanding of inheritance is something that comes to us after the owner's death but Yahweh, the owner, is eternal. As the rights to the land could be passed down through the generations it was only inheritance-like so it could be spoken of this way. The view

---

25. The actual order is reflected in the NEB.
26. Wiseman, Ḥelqâ in *TWOT*, 2902–3.

of Boaz was that Yahweh retained ownership of the whole land of Israel and the individual portions were, "divine grants to be administered on his behalf [and] since the land had been granted to the clans in perpetuity, . . . it had to be redeemed and restored to the clan."[27] In this vein, Block prefers the cumbersome, "divine grant of land" to inheritance to understand the nuance of the word.[28]

The storyteller introduces yet another wordplay in verse four when he asks the *goel* to *galah* ("redeemer" to "uncover") when he says, literally "uncover your ears," i.e., inform you. It also hints back at the seductive use of this word on the threshing floor. Forms of *goel* will then be used five times as the verse continues and a further three times in verse six. His ears must have tickled with the prospect of purchasing land when he was the only person with the right to make an offer. With the transaction occurring in public, it has minimized the chance of Naomi being forced to accept a bad offer. With an urgent seller and a keen backup redeemer already in place should he decline, a quick decision was needed, and he decided the offer was too good to resist. At no point is the price mentioned meaning that the human drama is what is important here, not the land.

The women have no active role in the proceedings so exposing a society that is paternalistic but not completely so. The land is not being forcefully taken from Naomi. More to the point, it is hard to imagine viable land remaining fallow and, if so, the farmer who was using the land, as I fully expect, does not have a right to its continued use and so overriding ownership by a destitute widow. She owns and is selling the land, but Ruth appears to be described as "property" in the transaction. The words, *qanah* "buy" and *makar* "sell" are commercial terms and are almost always used in purchasing land or slaves.[29] So this has a serious implication for the "acquisition" of Ruth, is Boaz purchasing a wife and so she will become no better than a slave? Campbell argues that this is not "strictly "purchase" or "gain by purchase." Rather it can be paraphrased, "marry as part of a legally valid commercial transaction."[30]

Chapter 3 was all about marriage and the first mention of Naomi's land does not occur till verse three and when Boaz manipulated the situation to

---

27. Block, *Ruth*, 207.
28. Block, *Ruth*, 216.
29. Campbell, *Ruth*, 145.
30. Campbell, *Ruth*, 147.

his own and Ruth's ends.[31] There is mixed opinion as to whether Naomi was simply selling the land that she owned or whether she is redeeming the land that she had to sell when she went to Moab. Land stayed within the family and any sale outside it would be similar to what we know as leasehold.[32] This situation would have Boaz negotiating the sale, or rather redemption of land that had been sold by Naomi. The tense of *makhera*, "sold," usually means an action that has already occurred[33] but a slight vowel change can make the word "is selling" and makes the best sense here.[34] Redemption could only take place if the land was actually sold and given the desolation during the famine there may not have been anyone with the finances to do this. If this were the case, it would have been Elimelech who sold it before leaving for Moab, i.e., not Naomi. If she had sold it on her return, they should not have been destitute. "Redemption" in this case may be being used loosely, as it was on the threshing floor. But, as Joe Blow has to purchase the land from Naomi, not a leaseholder, it is best to consider that she retained full ownership.

Scavenging for a living in a stranger's field at risk of sexual attack while at the same time owning land is unexpected. Our knowledge of the customs and laws relating to widows is fragmentary, which causes some to say that Naomi could not own the land she wants to sell. Certainly, the Law said nothing definite about women owning land and, in that void, no doubt they were often taken advantage of when they became widows. For anyone, "who had an agenda of grace"[35] the sentiment, if not the proverb itself would have been known, "The LORD will tear down the house of the proud, but he will set the boundary of the widow" (Prov 15:25 [NASB]). Block is very likely correct in saying that whoever was farming the land had harvested it (assuming custom dictated that whoever worked the land had the rights to the harvest). That would mean that only now was she able to sell the land, her only practical option, as managing the land would have been impossible for two otherwise destitute widows.

The storyteller's use of *sadeh*, "field" is very deliberate. It is used sixteen times in the book, of these, seven are used of the fields of Moab, and

---

31. Evans, *Ruth*, 265.
32. Evans, *Ruth*, 265.
33. Ziegler prefers to read this as a legal declaration in essence saying, "Naomi is hereby selling." Ziegler, *Ruth*, 374.
34. Eskenazi and Frymer-Kensky, *Ruth*, 73.
35. Block, *Ruth*, 221.

seven times of the search by Ruth for a field in Bethlehem in which to glean. The other two times are here in verses three and five with the sale of the land. Ziegler sees this seven-fold use of the fields of Bethlehem with the fields of Moab as emphasizing Boaz's generosity to Ruth by overlooking Naomi's actions in abandoning the fields of Bethlehem.[36] Boaz uses the root *sdh* twice in verse four, first to refer to Naomi who has returned from the fields of Moab. The fields of Moab have been mentioned a number of times already (1:1, 2, 6 twice; 2:2,) and this may be a subtle rebuke. But equally, the second use is a reminder to the town where, whatever they thought of their departure, they had to uphold the Law.[37] The story of the Shunammite woman in 2 Kings 8:1–6 shows a woman could own land and reclaim it after a seven-year absence.

> 5 Then Boaz said, "On the day you buy the field from Naomi, you must also marry Ruth the Moabite, the widow of the dead, in order to preserve the name of the dead in connection with his inheritance."
> 6 "I cannot buy it for myself without spoiling my own inheritance," the near relative said. "You take my right of buying it as a relative, because I cannot do so."

The deliberations between Boaz and the nameless relative who should be stepping up to take on the role of redeemer unfolds in two stages. The first is when it is presented as just a matter of purchasing land. Standing in front of the elders he did not have the opportunity to go away and think about it, but he may not have needed to. Joe Blow was aware of his rights as the closest relative so may well have considered purchasing Naomi's land. He jumped at it without hesitation, expanding his farm must have been seen an excellent business opportunity. It also gave him the opportunity to increase his standing in the community. Without any children on the scene there was no chance of the land reverting to its original owner in the Jubilee year. The social welfare issue of caring for the widows does not receive a mention in the original proposal put to him by Boaz. Profit not charity has driven the man who at no time receives a blessing. Why should he consider marriage to Ruth as a necessary part of the deal if he, like Boaz, considered she was free to marry whomever she wished? His response,

---

36. Ziegler, *Ruth*, 385.
37. Ziegler, *Ruth*, 385.

while calculating, was honorable. If there was an inkling that he had to marry someone, surely it was Naomi, the owner of the land, and she was past bearing children. As for Ruth, after all, despite her verbal commitment to Israel she was still considered a Moabitess.

Was Ruth, a Moabitess, a co-owner of the land with Naomi? Her role in the purchase is distinguished from that of Naomi. The land is purchased, "from the hand of Naomi" and what is expected is and, "from the hand of Ruth" but Boaz says literally, "from with Ruth." While Naomi had the primary rights, Ruth does have secondary legal interest in the land.[38] Despite that, she has only expressed an interest in redemption through marriage.

Boaz then delivers the fine print; when purchasing the land, it comes with responsibilities as he also, in effect, "purchases" Ruth the Moabitess which will be a levirate, or more likely, levirate-like marriage.[39] However, the Deuteronomic law stipulated that this was the responsibility of a brother of the deceased, not close relatives and he obviously did not see this coming. The first-born son will be counted as Mahlon's and the purchased land revert to him sooner than the Year of Jubilee. The syntax of verse five is awkward and convoluted. It could be that Ruth is being purchased or the field and it could also be that Ruth, a Moabitess, is a legal joint owner, further complicating matters. Legally, Boaz did not have a leg to stand on when he said that Joe Blow must marry Ruth. While Boaz had committed himself to a moral obligation to marry Ruth, he could not force this same obligation upon his relative.[40]

Ziegler suggests that the "clumsy syntax reflects the flimsy basis for interweaving these separate matters."[41] No one objects because it simply made sense, as this way Elimelech's land can be maintained as a separate entity and Mahlon's name be continued over the families allotted field (4:10), for both were considered sacrosanct. Boaz uses almost identical language to the provisions of the levir in Deuteronomy 15:5–6 which are intended to being both land and name together and fulfil a moral and family responsibility, if not a legal obligation to act. The suggestion by Rashi is

---

38. Block, *Ruth*, 213.

39. The linguistic similarities between Deuteronomy 25:5–10 are too numerous (Ziegler lists 8) to not see a close association to the practice but there are also significant differences (Ziegler lists 5). In the end, for all the allusions it may ultimately be best to see this as a widower marrying a widow. Ziegler, *Ruth*, 395–98. The key word for a levirate marriage *yibbum* is missing and in 1:8–13 Naomi indicated that there was no eligible levir.

40. Block, *Ruth*, 214.

41. Ziegler, *Ruth*, 388–89.

simply that, "Ruth will not relinquish the field unless the redeemer marries her"[42] and this is probably what was happening.

The sacred nature of the land allocated by lot has already been discussed as for the sacred nature of a person's "name" it was more than just a tag by which someone could be identified, and their achievements remembered and honored. The later Jewish and then Christian, understanding of an afterlife has "scant attention"[43] in the Old Testament (Josh 7:9; 1 Sam 24:21; 2 Sam 14:7; Isa 14:22). What is clearer is a belief that a person lives on in their children so, to establish Mahlon's name, is to give him a posthumous existence. Hence the shame attached to the brother who would not perform the role of the *goel* as he was denying the closest to him an afterlife while, at the same time taking his possessions.

Joe considers the process will *shakhat*, literally "destroy"[44] his own inheritance but we are not told how; it seems melodramatic to use such a strong word as it is the language of warfare (2 Chr 35:21). His excessively strong language exposes his motives as being purely for personal gain and not family restoration. The Law does not outline when the profit earned from the land would have reverted to Mahlon's heir instead of staying within Joe Blow's family group. There were no banks where a "college fund" could be started on the birth of a child and likewise no double entry bookkeeping systems to track profit and loss. I would expect that with reasonable harvests, the cost involved could reasonably be recouped by the time the child was old enough to farm it himself, but obviously not an ongoing commercial profit. It would be a very poor field that could not feed two mouths and provide a little extra. Keeping peace with a probable first wife[45] or concern for the racial purity[46] of his line may have been the real reason. A further consideration would be that any offspring would dilute the inheritance to existing sons.

Twice Boaz mentioned that Ruth is a Moabitess, indicating it could be a problem in wider community and quite possibly for Joe Blow, though not for him. Some inhabitants could take a strict understanding of Deuteronomy 23:3–5 where Moabites were not accepted into Israel. But for all that, Joe Blow's decision is shown to be purely commercial. The purchase

---

42. Quoted in Eskenazi and Frymer-Kensky, *Ruth*, xxxviii.
43. Block, *Ruth*, 215.
44. Hamilton, Šāḥat in *TWOT*, 917.
45. Block, *Ruth*, 218.
46. Ruth Rabbah: 7:10.

of the land only, would have been equally attractive to Boaz also but he has the added incentive of Ruth, a woman who was his equal. Is it love? Attraction can occur quickly but I expect it more likely to be the potential, welcomed by both parties, for love to grow. At this stage he is not driven by the sentimentality of pity or by economics but by moral conviction of the responsibilities of a close relative to the dead,[47] i.e., *hesed*. Behind the commerce and the affairs of the heart, Moore ultimately sees his faith saying:

> "Boaz's proposal is a bold attempt to apply the tenets of Hebraic Yahwism to the needs of the desperately vulnerable family. Boaz believes that his God, Yahweh, is a God of justice (see 1:1), a God determined to save the landless as well as the landed, foreigners as well as Israelites, women as well as men."[48]

Whatever the opinions of Joe Blow and the worthy citizens of Bethlehem were about a mixed blood marriage, from Boaz's perspective, "Ruth the Moabitess, the wife of the dead" was doubly unfortunate.[49] This marriage will be the due recompense for her *hesed* for which he prayed in 2:12. If race was an issue, Boaz was prepared to pay a much steeper price than money for the land. He was prepared to sacrifice his reputation to marry his mirror image. Ziegler puts it thus:

> "Boaz's selflessness mirrors Ruth's selflessness. The union of two uncommonly altruistic and generous individuals is designed to produce a dynasty of kings devoted to their constituents, without regard for their personal need."[50]

The matter of the need for a *goel* has now been raised in public and also a marriage with a clear allusion to the levirate provisions of Deuteronomy 25:7 so there was no getting away from it now. It may well be that the financial implications were what caused the closest relative to be absent during the three months or so of the barley and wheat harvest. He quickly passes what could well have become a "hot potato" to the next in line. Just as Naomi knew Boaz's nature, he in turn would have known the nature of his close relative and skillfully moves him to a situation where he would refuse the offer.

Joe Blow's second speech in 4:6 has a well-crafted chiastic structure:

---

47. Block, *Ruth*, 214.
48. Moore, *Ruth*, 363.
49. Campbell, *Ruth*, 160.
50. Ziegler, *Ruth*, 407.

A I cannot redeem it for myself,

   B otherwise I would jeopardize my own inheritance

   B' Redeem *it* for yourself; you *may have* my right of redemption

A' since I cannot redeem it (NASB).

The use of "for myself" and the multiple use of "I" in his refusal contrasts the difference between the closest relative and Boaz who always acts in other people's interest. Boaz may himself have committed a Freudian slip. Our translation follows the *kerey* (what is read), "you acquire" but what is written (*kanita*) is, "I acquire" and usually what is read is correct but probably not in this case. His intentions may have been revealed to all present, something for which Joe Blow would have been grateful as it would have given him an honorable excuse. But it may not have been a slip but intentional. If "I acquire" is correct, the end result is the same in dissuading Joe Blow. It would have meant that the sale of the land and the marriage of Ruth are two separate items that had to be resolved that morning. Joe Blow can purchase the land if he wishes but, come what may, Boaz is going to marry Ruth. If Ruth then has a child by Boaz and it is claimed as Mahlon's, the field still reverts to the child on the Year of Jubilee.[51]

Either way, the right of redemption is passed on to Boaz. The man who refused the role of redeemer is shown as, "an ordinary, decent person, not a villain"[52] and like Orpah tries to do the right thing but eventually gives up. Still, while he may not be a villain, his actions were not what the readers, let alone his society or his God, expects. As Trible says, the "redeemer dies to the story in order to live to his own inheritance, and the judgement upon him is adverse. After all, she is not a foreign woman but the nearest of kin. Thus, he passes away with the infamy of anonymity."[53] His actions serve only to show the big heart of Boaz.

---

51. Eskenazi and Frymer-Kensky, *Ruth*, 76–77.
52. Eskenazi and Frymer-Kensky, *Ruth*, 78.
53. Trible, *Rhetoric of Sexuality*, 191.

> **7** *Now this used to be the custom in Israel: to make valid anything relating to a matter of redemption or exchange, a man drew off his sandal and gave it to the other man; and this was the way contracts were attested in Israel.* **8** *So when the near relative said to Boaz, "Buy it for yourself," Boaz drew off the man's sandal.*

The practice of taking off the sandal as a visible sign of a completed deal had obviously passed into history by the time the book was written. The editorial note here, just as in 1:1 setting the story in the time of the Judges, means that the final version of the story that we read dates at the very least to well into the reign of King David, a span of at least 100 years. This may also suggest that the core of the story is much older. These comments add further information rather than forming a necessary part of the story. The passage is deeply ambiguous which intentionally allows for multiple meanings, each of which contribute to our understanding of the story.[54] The practice of removing a shoe to seal a deal was obviously used in a wider range of transactions than just redemption.

In Deuteronomy 25:9 there is a similar practice which was meant to expose contemptable behavior, but this was done by the widow who also had to spit in a recalcitrant *goel's* face. Here it is no more than a way of acknowledging, "a consensual gentleman's agreement."[55] It seems best to consider the two practices similar but not the same. It is not clear who removed his sandal, Campbell thinks more likely Boaz as a pledge of payment[56] while Block is adamant it is the other way around following Deuteronomy 25:9.[57] Still it could well have even been reciprocal, like each stepping into each other's shoes.[58]

In the Deuteronomy 25 case and here, the removal of the shoe could point to something that is legal but an, "acknowledgement of the less-than-honorable decision of the redeemer."[59] It would be reasonable to assume that Joe Blow's concerns about the inheritance relates to his being married and already having children. Boaz appears to be childless (1 Chr 2:10) and,

---

54. Ziegler, *Ruth*, 417.
55. Eskenazi and Frymer-Kensky, *Ruth*, 79.
56. Campbell, *Ruth*, 150.
57. Block, *Ruth*, 219.
58. Campbell, *Ruth*, 148.
59. Ziegler, *Ruth*, 415.

with him ready to step in immediately and take up the role of the *goel*, there is not likely to be the level of reproach we see in Deuteronomy 25:

> ⁵When brothers live together, and one of them dies and has no son, the wife of the deceased shall not be *married* outside *the family* to a strange man. Her husband's brother shall have relations with her and take her to himself as *his* wife, and perform the duty of a husband's brother to her. ⁶It shall then be that the firstborn to whom she gives birth shall assume the name of his *father's* deceased brother, so that his name will not be wiped out from Israel. ⁷But if the man does not desire to take his brother's widow, then his brother's widow shall go up to the gate to the elders, and say, 'My husband's brother refuses to establish a name for his brother in Israel; he is not willing to perform the duty of a husband's brother to me.' ⁸Then the elders of his city shall summon him and speak to him. And *if* he persists and says, 'I do not desire to take her,' ⁹then his brother's widow shall come up to him in the sight of the elders, and pull his sandal off his foot and spit in his face; and she shall declare, 'This is what is done to the man who does not build up his brother's house!' ¹⁰And in Israel his family shall be called by the name, 'The house of him whose sandal was removed'(NASB).

From this point onwards, Joe Blow is not spoken to or spoken of again; he is dismissed nameless, just like the overseer in chapter 2. Boaz spoke only to the elders and the people. Joe had the opportunity to show *hesed* to Ruth but in the end only proves to be a foil to contrast how remarkable Boaz was. He at least would not fail in upholding the Law and his covenant responsibilities. The closest relative disappears, just like Orpah before him as he was just too ordinary to be the husband of Ruth.

The storyteller's use of the root *gal* is as deliberate as his use of the word *sadeh* (field). In chapter 4 it is used fifteen times, fourteen of these, in two lots of seven are in reference to Joe Blow. The first seven uses relate to him initially jumping at the opportunity to purchase the land, where Boaz uses *gaal* five times in quick succession (4:4). The second set of seven relate to his refusal to marry Ruth, again quickly using the word five times (4:6). The fifteenth reference, somewhat unexpected, is spoken in the blessing of the women and is referred to in my discussion of verse fourteen.[60]

---

60. Ziegler, *Ruth*, 419.

> ⁹Then Boaz said to the elders and to all the people, "You are witnesses at this time that I have bought all that was Elimelech's and all that was Chilion's and Mahlon's from Naomi. ¹⁰Moreover I have secured Ruth the Moabite, the wife of Mahlon, to be my wife, in order to perpetuate the name of the dead in connection with his inheritance, so that his name will not disappear from among his relatives and from the household where he lived. You are witnesses this day."

A crowd must have gathered around as Boaz no longer addressed the elders and his relative but "all the people." His speech has changed from the conversation between relatives to using legal language to make public his commitment to purchase the land and Ruth. In a largely oral society, the role of witnesses and actions like the sandal were critical. Boaz's declaration, "You are my witnesses" begins and ends his declaration (see Joshua. 24:22 for a similar use of "witness"). Despite the legal formulation, the gathered witnesses were left in no doubt that Boaz was not driven by the commercial considerations of Joe Blow but, at least publicly, for the continuation of Mahlon's line. The welfare of the two widows came as a consequence of, not its primary intent. Trible, a feminist scholar, hones in acutely at the injustice here. She compares the situation at the gate to the later words of the women of Bethlehem and says, "the men shifted emphasis from justice for living females with justice for dead males." The emphatic and irreversible nature of this transaction is underlined by Boaz saying that these things will happen "today." The double reference to "today" reminds us of the promise to Ruth (3:13), and the assurance of Naomi (3:18) that her future would be resolved that day.

After mentioning the purchase of the land and not just the land but the totality of everything the family owned, Boaz then raises before the assembled witnesses the more important part of his actions that morning,[61] he is, "buying" Ruth the Moabitess. The name of the deceased could not be established on the land without Ruth bearing a son. Ruth's purchase is mentioned in a separate verse to the purchase of the land and is introduced by *vegam*, "and also" which suggests the two were separated in the mind of Boaz.[62] Campbell sees this term as emphasizing this part of the transac-

---

61. Campbell, *Ruth*, 151.
62. Ziegler, *Ruth*, 423.

tion and translates it as "more importantly."⁶³ The land is purchased out of obligation; but Ruth is married out of *hesed*.

This is not the language of purchasing a slave but is used of acquiring wisdom, which no amount of money can secure (Prov 4:7; 15:32; 16:16) and also may well be associated with redemption. In the song of Moses and Miriam in Exodus 15 we read:

> ¹³ In Your faithfulness You have led the people whom You have redeemed;(*gaal*).
>
> ¹⁶By the greatness of Your arm they are motionless as stone,
> Until Your people pass over, LORD,
> Until the people pass over whom You have purchased (*kana*) (NASB).

In this hymn of redemption *gaal*, the work that Joe Blow refused to do and *kana* "to purchase" are linked to describe the act of redemption of Israel by Yahweh himself. Rather than recoil at the "purchase" of Ruth, in the overall context of the divine national redemption that flows from the union of Boaz and Ruth, Campbell's words regarding this "purchase" are apt:

> If God is confessed as both redeemer and the one who does whatever *qnh* means in the "declarative praise" section of this ancient triumph song, a human being who does these actions in Ruth 4:1–10 is therefore praiseworthy as well.⁶⁴

With Joe Blow, the land came with strings attached. He was to be forced to marry Ruth but for Boaz, the fine print of marrying Ruth was that he had to purchase the land. Boaz is specific about his relationship to Ruth, she will be an *ishah*, "wife." He had other lesser relationships available, but she is not considered a concubine, young girl, slave girl, or foreign woman.⁶⁵ Boaz did not call her "my wife" but "a wife" which leaves open the greater role she was to fulfil, continuing Mahlon's line and securing his name on the field.⁶⁶ By mentioning the noble aim of ensuring Mahlon's name continues he may well be countering any criticism relating to marrying a Moabitess. Whatever was involved with "acquiring" or "buying" Ruth, Evans points out "that the relational tone of the rest of the narrative is the

---

63. Campbell, *Ruth*, 151.
64. Campbell, *Ruth*, 160.
65. Moore, *Ruth*, 367.
66. Block, *Ruth*, 224.

writer's way of indicating that, although this was the view of society, it was not how they or Boaz, or by implication Yahweh, really saw it."[67]

Throughout Old Testament history, marriages have been private family affairs, but it is possible that we have in verses nine to thirteen, the only example where the community is involved. These verses contain all the elements of a legal Rabbinic marriage (apart from a written contract) which are:

- The intent of the groom in front of witnesses (4:9–10),
- the transfer of possessions with affirmation of witnesses (4:11), and
- consummation in the home of the groom (4:13).[68]

Moore points out that the drought wrought its effects on many more than just Elimelech's household, but that Bethlehem was a community of survivors in a brutal world. They must have been inspired to witness at least one family overcome the ravages of famine, death and childlessness.[69] However, the point of the marriage given by Boaz was to maintain the name of the dead husband, but this seems to be little more than a negotiating ploy. In the genealogies in 1 Chronicles 2, and the Gospels, their son, Obed, will be counted as Boaz's son.

> 11 *Then all the people who were at the gate and the elders said, "We are witnesses. May the* LORD *make the woman who is coming into your house like Rachel and Leah, who together built the house of Israel. May you do well in Ephrata, and become famous in Bethlehem.* 12*From the children whom the* LORD *will give you by this young woman may your household become like the household of Perez, whom Tamar bore to Judah."*

The storyteller reverses the order from verse nine where it is the elders first and then the people, so forming a chiasm. They reply with a single word, "witnesses" because biblical Hebrew had no word for "yes." The wholesome praise of those in the gate could contain an element of kowtowing to a man of status and authority in their small community but more likely could be genuine acknowledgement of his praiseworthy action He

---

67. Evans, *Ruth*, 268.
68. Eskenazi and Frymer-Kensky, *Ruth*, xxxi.
69. Moore, *Ruth*, 367.

had "followed through on legal responsibilities others had avoided."[70] The hope for many children like that of Rachel and Leah who, with their slaves, bore the twelve children that would become the tribes of Israel, would include the hope for children that Boaz could call his own. This suggests that he did not have living children of his own.

The names of Naomi's sons in 1:2 are Mahlon and Chilion and the order in which the wives are mentioned is Orpah and Ruth suggesting Ruth was married to Chilion. In 4:9 the order is reversed, and we find that Ruth is married to Mahlon. In this legal transaction it would be reasonable to assume that Mahlon was the younger son, in the least favored position. This would put Ruth as, "the least in rank of the story's characters, [yet] who is now to receive the reward of her faithfulness."[71] Leah was the first sister that Jacob married but is mentioned after Rachel. This could be an allusion to her extended period of childlessness and/or that her grave was said to be in Bethlehem. Leah's inheritance through Judah was in Bethlehem.

Their prayer for blessing by the people at the gate in Yahweh's name is in the form of a chiasm:

A May the LORD make (*yiten*) the woman who has come into your house
  B Like Rachel and Leah, both of whom built the house of Israel;
    C And may you achieve wealth in Ephrathah,
    C' And be famous (call a name) in Bethlehem.
  B' Moreover, may your house be like the house of Perez whom Tamar bore to Judah,
A' through the descendants whom the LORD will give you (yiten) by this young woman" (NASB).

This chiasm voiced an expectation that Yahweh, the unseen and virtually un-acknowledged one, would be active in their marriage because this is what a God, who kept *hesed* with his children did. Because these few lines are very important in understanding the union between Boaz and Ruth, I will deal with them in more detail. The townspeople's prayer for Boaz in 4:11, *yitin yhwh* "may the LORD provide" for childless Ruth who is entering her husband's home comes as an answer to a similar prayer of Naomi in 1:9. There she says, *yiten yhwh*, "may the LORD provide" rest, in the home of a

---

70. Evans, *Ruth*, 268.
71. Campbell, *Ruth*, 152.

husband. Despite these words being a blessing, it is crafted to acknowledge the unorthodox nature of the marriage.

In A, the opening words, God's favor is directed towards Ruth and in A' it is towards Boaz. Surprisingly, the "seed" *hazzera* often translated as "offspring," comes as a gift from Yahweh through Ruth, not Boaz. The almost universal use of this word attributes this word to men, and the womb was regarded as a bed in which the male seed germinated and grew.[72] As a woman who provides the "seed" she is placed alongside Eve in Genesis 3:15 whose "seed" will crush Satan's head and Rebecca who married Isaac (Gen 24:60). The unexpected praise by indirectly associating the Moabitess Ruth with the matriarchs is expanded in B and B' of this chiasm.

Naomi had given up any hope of ever establishing a house for her daughters-in-law and urged them to go back to their mother's house. On their arrival in Bethlehem, the storyteller has been careful not to mention any house that the two women lived in, perhaps emphasizing their lack of stability.[73] The house is finally mentioned in the next section B and B' and the blessing hopes for similar fruitfulness as their ancestors who built a house, i.e., they have a family. First are the wives of the Patriarchs who built the nation and then in B' the tribal house of Judah, again keeping the female participation first. That the people at the gate would ask Yahweh to give a Moabitess a place alongside the matriarchs of Israel is astounding and shows her complete acceptance by the community.[74]

Their hope in B is that the couple will be as fruitful as Rachel and Leah and in B' that their union will be fruitful like that of Tamar and Judah. The child of Tamar, Perez will prove to be the line of kingship (Gen 49:8). This acknowledges children as a gift from God, not just the effort of humans. The women they mentioned reminded Boaz of the unconventional marriages in his family's past. (Laban passed off Leah as her sister Rachel at her marriage to Jacob before he eventually married his true love.) Marriage to sisters was forbidden in the Law (Lev 18:18) so strictly, the whole nation was built on an illicit marriage, not just, potentially, David's line. Tamar was the Canaanite woman who bore a child to Judah because he would not do his duty through his sons under the levirate custom. This reference to the ancestors suggests that the stories were well known, and that levirate

---

72. Block, *Ruth*, 227.

73. Ziegler, *Ruth*, 431.

74. Hubbard lists eleven similarities between Ruth and the Patriarchs/Matriarchs and Judah in particular. Hubbard, *Ruth*, 40.

practice was well established before Moses. But why, when dealing with virtuous people, refer to the skeletons in the family closet? Bright answers, arguing from the lesser to the greater, "if YHWH had blessed immoral Judah doubly through the birth of twins and if he had flourished through Perez, how much brighter might the prospects be for Boaz and Ruth."[75]

The central part C, C' is where the blessing is focused and it uses two words that are used a number of times in this story and form the very essence of what the book is about, *asa*, do, in C and *kara* "call" in C'. Prior to 4:11, *asa* is used twelve times, ten of them in relation to Ruth (mostly in reference to her kindness to Naomi, e.g., 2:11) and the other two times it refers to Boaz's kindness to her. The suggestion is that the kindness and generosity that they both exhibit will also flow through to their offspring. The first line of this couplet also expresses the hope for the couple's "prosperity" *(hayil)* which in Deuteronomy 8:17–18 means to acquire wealth. As it is the same word used to describe Boaz as a man of substance and virtue (2:1) and Rachel as a virtuous woman (3:11), its meaning goes far beyond simply acquiring wealth. Their hope is grounded on the reasonable expectation that their upright character should be rewarded in this life. This was, after all, part of the promise by Yahweh for covenant faithfulness. While Ephrathah is simply the old name for Bethlehem, the word's association with the tomb of Rachel and Ephrat being the wife of Caleb, the ancestor of Boaz, an intentional female link may also be intended.[76]

The second line, C' builds on the first and explains what the previous line means by, "acting nobly in Ephrathah."[77] The line uses *kara*, "call," and the symmetry in which it is used is again striking. "Call" is used seven times in total and six of these refer to Naomi. Three of these are in her own bitter accusation against God to the women of Bethlehem (1:19–21). The fourth time is here in the blessing and the remaining three are spoken by the women of Bethlehem where they declare how completely Naomi's fortunes had changed.[78] A similar arrangement occurs with the word *shem* or name. It occurs three times in chapter 4 before the blessing (five, ten twice) and three times afterwards (fourteen, seventeen twice). The one who is to be worthy in Ephrathah and have his name called in Bethlehem could

---

75. Block, *Ruth*, 227.
76. Eskenazi and Frymer-Kensky, *Ruth*, 84.
77. Block, *Ruth*, 226.
78. Ziegler, *Ruth*, 427–28.

be Boaz, or the union of both the houses of Boaz and Ruth.[79] It may also be a reference to the names that were lost being called again in Bethlehem, which would be a noble act. This is part of the ambiguity of Ruth.

As Ruth draws to a close with the emphasis on building a house and as a consequence the rebuilding of the nation and the establishment of the monarchy, the contrast to the end of the Book of Judges could not be starker. There, the emphasis is on the destruction of a house (Samson and the temple of Dagon) the collapse of specific families and the social and spiritual collapse of the house of Israel.[80]

Just as Boaz's statement opened and closed with the same words, their response has an opening and closing phrase, "May the LORD give." No one is being critical of the age gap though we are reminded of it when Ruth is called a *naarah*, like the young girls who worked in his fields. Her very youth is what can give the opportunity for the blessing to come to pass, and for Boaz, perhaps in recognition of his age, for fertility.

The mention of the ancestor Perez, whose name means "breach" or "break" points to the unorthodox arrangement of this marriage and how it "breaches the wall that excludes Moabites."[81] All of Judah came from an illicit union and a failed levirate marriage yet it was blessed with twins (Gen 38). (Ruth's line also is portrayed as the result of incest.) For all the mention of continuing Mahlon's line, the people will speak of the child as if it is from Boaz. Also, the genealogy that concludes the book and 1 Chronicles 2:12 lists Obed as the son of Boaz, not Mahlon. The example of the levirate arrangement between Judah and Tamar should have seen their twins, Perez and Zerah, counted as descendants of Er, Judah's son but Genesis 46:12 and Matthew 1:3 shows Judah as father. Either the person who finalized this book had no idea about what went beforehand, or simply that the offspring of Levirate marriage were seen as having dual paternity.[82]

The council in Mizpah in Judges 20 (see Table 3) badly mishandled the situation of the rape and murder of the concubine from Bethlehem as it resulted in war and death, while the "solution" here leads to restoration and healing. The elders who sat to transact legal business and those townspeople who were witnesses at the gate became prophets. But the house would not

---

79. Ziegler, *Ruth*, 426–27.
80. Ziegler, *Ruth*, 432.
81. Eskenazi and Frymer-Kensky, *Ruth*, 85.
82. Campbell, *Ruth*, 161.

be "like" that of Perez. It would be far greater, as King David and his eternal throne through the Messiah would come from them.

> ¹³So Boaz married Ruth, and she became his wife; and the LORD gave to her a son.

The pace of the story quickens and in one verse we have the marriage, consummation, conception and birth of the heir. Very quickly, the life that Naomi viewed as cursed was turned to blessing and her emptiness to fullness. God, who Naomi had seen as the agent of death now becomes the agent of life. At no point up to this, "has the divine world intruded upon the narrative by speech or by miracles. Clearly, the human struggle itself is divine activity, redeeming curse through blessing."[83] Key words from this verse, *vitikah*, "took" and *vatehi*, "became" will be used again in verse sixteen and applied to Naomi. Verses thirteen to seventeen recount the consequences of the legal proceedings at the gate but there is no hint of what prompted the hearing and their blessing. This was the redemption of the land, preserving the name of the deceased and the status of Ruth as a national matriarch.[84]

Ruth has come the whole circle in what she calls herself. She is no longer a foreigner (2:1), maidservant (2:13), servant girl (3:9) but now a legal wife, no longer of a dead man but of one of the wealthiest landholders in Bethlehem. Likewise, her conversion is now complete, having first had the approval of Boaz, then the townsfolk and now finally of Yahweh himself. She is no longer Ruth the Moabitess but simply Ruth. The extraordinary power of love in the form of *hesed* and the audacious acts of kindness it motivates have created a community into which someone would want to bring a child.[85] The biblical word for marriage is "took," *lakah*, but by "taking" Ruth, it does not mean that she was, "a passive object to be taken or given at will"[86] but simply reflects that the woman moved to her husband's home. When Naomi's sons married Ruth and Orpah, the word used in 1:4 is *nas'a* which is different from here, that word is only used in the Bible for mixed marriages (Ezra 9:2, 12; 10:44). The change of word represents

---

83. Trible, *Rhetoric of Sexuality*, 195.
84. Block, *Ruth*, 197.
85. Eskenazi and Frymer-Kensky, *Ruth*, xv.
86. Eskenazi and Frymer-Kensky, *Ruth*, 87.

the community's acceptance of Ruth. This was not simply a matter of Boaz taking Ruth as his wife. It was a two-way street, with Ruth actively involved and so becoming his *isha*.

Both parties exhibited true covenant righteousness, and a fruitful womb was promised as a consequence (Deut 7:13; 28:4, 11). The story of Hannah, the mother of Samuel (1 Sam 1) and the mother of Samson (Judg 13) prevent us from seeing Ruth's conception as an automatic result of their goodness. Verse thirteen is only the second time in the four chapters that God's action is acknowledged—both times with the word *natan*, "gave." The first was in 1:6 when Naomi heard that Yahweh visited his people with bread and now with the birth of Ruth's son Obed. God's hand that was rumored to be present in the favorable climate is now acknowledged in reproduction. There had previously been barrenness (though she is never called barren) or Mahlon's infertility. Although God plays a role in several important birth narratives elsewhere in the Bible the words here *vayiten la herayon*, literally, God "gave her pregnancy," are unique.

God's role in pregnancy is never depicted quite this directly and this may be a, "modest reference to a miracle."[87] Throughout this story, Boaz has been reacting to the initiative of women and even in this matter, "the power of the story is not transferred to him."[88] Yahweh may have been the God of Israel but his care for his people did not stop at the border. He who gave conception to Ruth in Bethlehem is the same who had withheld it from her in Moab. The destiny of the redeemer of Israel in the form of King David and then the world through David's greatest son was controlled by what happened in the bed of Mahlon and Ruth which, like the land he left, was unfruitful. It is all presented as a gift in which Boaz is only, "a conduit, distributing the food and seed . . . that God provides."[89] In this way Boaz acts as a model for the future kingship. Yet again, another prayer for blessing has not gone unanswered.

> 14 Then the women said to Naomi, "Blessed be the LORD who has not left you at this time without a near relative, and may his name be famous in Israel. 15 This child will restore your vigor and nourish you in your old age; for your daughter-in-law who loves you, who

---

87. Block, *Ruth*, 234.
88. Trible, *Rhetoric of Sexuality*, 196.
89. Ziegler, *Ruth*, 432.

> *is worth more to you than seven sons, has borne a son to Boaz!"* ¹⁶*So Naomi took the child in her arms and cared for him as if he was her own.* ¹⁷*The women of the neighborhood gave him a name, saying, "A son is born to Naomi!" They named him Obed. He became the father of Jesse, who was the father of David.*

We meet the townswomen again in verse fourteen and again they only address Naomi. We are given a male view of the situation in verses one to twelve in verses fourteen to sixteen the entirely different female perspective is given using words that echo that of the witnesses at the gate. Naomi's plans were to secure Ruth's future (3:1) and Boaz's promise was to be Ruth's redeemer (3:11) but the men of the town saw this only as securing the deceased male line. The women return the focus and true motivation of the events as benefiting the living. In chapter 1, they were initially surprised at the return of Naomi and all they could say is, "Can this be Naomi?" They offered no assistance and ignored Ruth but now she is married to a prominent man of the town and had his child, their tune changes and they are accepting of Naomi again. For all their mention of Yahweh in their blessing, how much of this acceptance is driven not by a Yahwistic faith but through the rise of their social standing?[90] There is no mention of Ruth's Moabite roots and this is the first time she is actually called Naomi's daughter-in-law by any of the participants.[91] Their inconsistent attitude to the widows is very different from that of Boaz.

In chapter 1, the word *shuv*, "to return" or "restore" is found twelve times and is used only once in the causative tense, when childless and a widow, Naomi complains to the women of Bethlehem that Yahweh has caused her to return empty. The word virtually disappears (it is only used again in 2:6, and 4:3) until the women use it, again in the causative, to declare that her *goel* will be a returner or restorer of life.[92] As mentioned, the men had seen this child merely as a restorer of a name![93] The woman in giving the blessing in a negative sense, "he has not left you without a redeemer" mirrors Naomi's accusations against God on her return to

---

90. Evans, *Ruth*, 270.
91. The seventh in total, all otherwise used by the storyteller.
92. Ziegler, *Ruth*, 448.
93. Trible, *Rhetoric of Sexuality*, 194.

Bethlehem (1:21).[94] What was empty is now full but it is the women of Bethlehem who vindicate God, not Naomi. The emptiness was caused by God, just as her fullness is. Although the baby does nothing but lie in Naomi's arms, he is somebody as he is the key to the domestic unit.[95]

Boaz has a reputation in the small locality of Bethlehem, but the townspeople ask Yahweh that his son will become famous in Israel. In so doing he will eclipse his father but also show that this story has a national rather than local or tribal interest. Considering the hopeless situation Naomi was in, one that only Yahweh could remedy and did remedy, it is not surprising that the child would be seen as having a special destiny, which is fulfilled in the genealogy that follows.[96] Eventually, both Boaz and Obed will become famous in Israel and though Boaz is the near kinsman who redeemed Naomi and Ruth at the gate, the *goel* "redeemer" that will secure Naomi's future into old age is Obed. The word is not used in its true technical sense. It is quite possible that Boaz, already advanced in years, was now dead. Despite the critical role of these two, the true source of the renewed life and her sustenance is Yahweh whom they bless. In effect it is a synonym for praise for his *hesed* towards the two widows. The *goel's* role of "restoring life" *meshiv nefesh* is exclusively the role of Yahweh in Psalm 23 where David calls the shepherd Yahweh, the one who refreshes his soul.

In the final verse of the book (excluding the genealogy), the key word "name" is used to introduce Obed, the son of destiny, a man with a name and a shared destiny with those on the list that follows. The first two words used by the women of Bethlehem in the expression, *veyikarei shemo beYisrael*, "his name shall be called in Israel" would normally require the addition of an object which would be the name of the child. This very expression is often used in synagogues when naming a child. The name of the brother who refuses to do the duty of marriage to his deceased brother's widow shall be called in Israel, "The House of the One Who Removed His Shoe." What will Ruth's son be called by these women? We are not told at this point. Boaz had used a different word for "called" in verses five and ten when referring to perpetuating Mahlon's name. He points to this child not being regarded as, "an heir to the deceased men of the house of Elimelech."[97]

---

94. Block, *Ruth*, 234.
95. Block, *Ruth*, 249.
96. Hubbard, *Ruth*, 20.
97. Eskenazi and Frymer-Kensky, *Ruth*, 89.

Ruth

Ziegler sees in the blessing of the women, not a declaration of what his name is, but rather something which is not as important as the fact that the child *has* a name in Israel. The Book of Ruth has been reversing the namelessness of the last chapters of Judges. She points to Exodus where there is an absence of personal names until Israel discovers God's name (Exod 3:13–15; 6:2–3). Then, "its members can themselves reacquire their own names, lost in the turmoil and mire of slavery and alienation from God."[98] The greeting of Boaz to his workers in Yahweh's name and enquiring of their welfare, used in Judaism as the basis of the practice, is evidence, "of the importance of recognizing each other and regarding one's fellow by name."[99]

What is surprising is that the storyteller has the neighbors giving the name Obed, not the parents or Naomi. In a sense the child did not belong to Boaz and Ruth. Boaz was raising a son for Mahlon and Ruth bore a son for Naomi. Names, in the Old Testament particularly, are significant and can refer to their very essence and destiny. Normally an explanation of significance of the name would be given but none is here. By the community naming the son they took on the responsibility of ensuring that he fulfilled that destiny. It really does take a village to raise a child. Ziegler sees in this a statement, "that the king does not belong to his family, his tribe, or even his parents. His name, essence, and purpose are the property of the nation he serves."[100] Alternatively, others view the double naming of Ruth's child as simply a corrupted text.[101]

Ruth is finally acknowledged for whom she is. She was, "more than a fertile womb [as her] life challenges the corrupt values of a sick culture."[102] This destitute foreign widow is now considered of more value than seven of Israel's finest sons[103] which was considered the ideal family (1 Sam 2:5; Job 1:2; 42:13). David also was a seventh son (1 Chr 2:14). Her devotion to Naomi is described as "love," a covenant commitment that actively seeks the well-being of the next person[104] and should govern all family relationships. This affection comes on top of her earlier praise by her husband-to-be on the threshing floor for her *hesed* (3:10) and for being a virtuous woman

---

98. Ziegler, *Ruth*, 446.
99. Ziegler, *Ruth*, 446.
100. Ziegler, *Ruth*, 453.
101. Hubbard, *Ruth*, 15–16.
102. Moore, *Ruth*, 370.
103. Moore, *Ruth*, 370.
104. Block, *Ruth*, 52 and 108.

(3:11). Here, 'love,' *aheb* is not an emotional feeling but actions, "expressed in covenant commitment demonstrated in action in the interests of the other person."[105] In a book dealing with marriage, it is surprising that this is the first time that this word appears and it refers to Ruth's action towards Naomi, not Boaz, and it has been the anchor of the story all along.[106] The women of Bethlehem were saying that the bond through *hesed* that Ruth had with Naomi was better than relationships with men. David spoke the same way of Jonathan's love for him (2 Sam 1:26).

This kind of love was meant to be at the core of the Israelite being. They were to love Yahweh with all their heart (Deut 6:5) and their neighbor as themselves (Lev 19:18). Difficult as that can be at times, they were also commanded to love the stranger as themselves also, (Lev 19:18). Yet Ruth, the foreigner was the one who showed Israel what that meant. This is at the core of the teaching of Jesus when asked what the greatest commandment is, he answered with these two verses (Matt 22:36–40). Again, with the example of the Good Samaritan, a despised foreigner showed what it was like to love the foreigner in their midst (Luke 10:25–29).

The storyteller uses the same verbs to describe Boaz taking Ruth as his wife *vitikah*, "took" and *vatehi*, "became" to describe Naomi's actions towards the child. Ruth's final act is, totally in keeping with her complete self-sacrifice throughout this book, to "gracefully exit the story, allowing Naomi to adopt the child as her own. Naomi places Ruth's baby in her bosom and becomes his foster mother causing the women to proclaim the final spoken words, "a child has been born to Naomi."[107] The baby is called a "child," *yeled*, (not *ben*, "boy") to reflect the word *yalad* to "give birth" in verse thirteen and later in verse seventeen and "fathered" in the following genealogy. This remarkable change of affairs has come despite her lament in chapter 1 that she is too old to have a child. The women who heard her lament and renunciation of her name declare the restoration of her name and family. The story that started in despair ends in hope.

18 *This is the genealogy of Perez:*
Perez was the father of Hezron,
19 *Hezron of Ram,*

---

105. Block, *Ruth*, 237.
106. Ziegler, *Ruth*, 449.
107. Ziegler, *Ruth*, 18.

Ruth

> *Ram of Amminadab,*
> [20]*Amminidab of Nashon,*
> *Nashon of Salmon,*
> [21]*Salmon of Boaz,*
> *Boaz of Obed,*
> [22]*Obed of Jesse,*
> *Jesse of David.*

It is easy to see this list of the all-male ancestors as something just tacked on the end and destroying the female-centric story that preceded it, but it is written as a continuation of what went before. The female members of the line were not totally ignored as the townspeople gave an abbreviated female ancestry. This little book has given an insight into the background work of woman behind the simple line, "Boaz begot Obed."[108] The line continues down to the birth of David, the last word of the book, this it can be argued is the very reason for the book's existence. He is, apart from Moses, the most significant character in the Old Testament as its messianic hope is all through him (2 Sam 7). His history takes up 41 percent of Samuel and Kings while only covering 9 percent of its time.[109]

The ten names are all but unknown with at most only a few of them having a mention in the Old Testament record. Their lives could be viewed as insignificant as would be that of Boaz had we not had this book. Through generations of drought, prosperity, slavery, warfare and moral decline, Yahweh had kept safe the line of King David and through him the Messiah. Into this mix was introduced another even more insignificant person, the foreign widow Ruth. Despite her unimportance, "This foreigner, guided by compassion and unparalleled devotion, will navigate the nation's path to a functional society and launch the monarchy, an institution designed to establish social unity and fidelity as well as faithful social interactions."[110]

The use of the *tholodoth*, "these are the generations" formula suggests a continuation of the Genesis narratives where the word occurs eleven times.[111] Ziegler sees its use in Genesis as referring to periods of filtering where the, "chosen nation is culled from the nations of the world, not to

---

108. Eskenazi and Frymer-Kensky, *Ruth*, 89.
109. Block, *Ruth*, 254.
110. Ziegler, *Ruth*, 33.
111. Block, *Ruth*, 45.

offer them special privileges but rather to recruit them into service of God, to be the nation that calls on the name of God and promulgates His name in the world."[112] This expression then only occurs twice outside of Genesis where two families were selected for service. Here in Ruth the genealogy of kingship is introduced and in Numbers 3:1 where we are presented with the priestly line.

We are introduced to the third phase of biblical history with a list of births which would be more expected at the beginning of the story, which instead was dominated by deaths. The first phase was Adam to Noah, recorded in Genesis 5, followed by Shem to Abraham in Genesis 11:10–26. In this third epoch, Boaz slots in at the seventh position which corresponds to Enoch and Peleg in the Genesis lists. By giving them the seventh position, a place of special honor, it places them at, "a watershed of human history."[113] Like Enoch, Boaz showed what it was like to walk with God. David is in the tenth place, the place of completion. What is not explained is why the genealogy, which follows that of 1 Chronicles 2, starts with Perez and not Isaac, or Jacob, or especially Judah who are left out entirely. In Eskenazi and Frymer-Kensky's opinion starting the list with a name meaning "breach," "signals a subversive dimension to the book, undermining a flat reading of the text."[114] The exclusivism of Ezra 9–10 and Nehemiah 13 that rejected marriage to foreign women has been rejected in favor of the inclusion of Isaiah 56:6–7.

> 6"Also the foreigners who join themselves to the LORD,
> To attend to His service and to love the name of the LORD,
> To be His servants, everyone who keeps the Sabbath so as not to profane it,
> And holds firmly to My covenant.
> 7Even those I will bring to My holy mountain.
> And make them joyful in My house of prayer.
> Their burnt offerings and their sacrifices will be acceptable on My altar;
> For My house will be called a house of prayer for all the peoples" (NASB).

---

112. Ziegler, *Ruth*, 457. R.K. Harrison makes an excellent case for this word being used in Genesis as a colophon, used at the end of ancient tablets which he believes are the source of the book, both views can hold true. Harrison *Introduction*, 543–48.

113. Block, *Ruth*, 45.

114. Eskenazi and Frymer-Kensky, *Ruth*, 93.

Ruth

Again, that the line of King David did not stretch to Judah is surprising, as the line of kingship was to come from him (Gen 49:8–10). It suggests that the focus was on David and the storyteller counted backwards from him which gave Boaz the significant seventh position. If David's position, or his Dynasty, was not secure you would expect the list to start at Judah. It also stresses the levirate start to this branch of the family. The list follows the true blood lines and gives symmetry by dividing it neatly into five generations prior to Moses (Perez to Nahshon)[115] and five after (Salmon to David). Had the marriage of Ruth to Boaz been a true levirate marriage, Obed's father should have been listed as Mahlon which would then have added Elimelech to the list also. Joe Blow's opportunity has been lost also.

Place	Phase 1	Phase 2	Phase 3
	Gen 5	Gen 11:10–26	Ruth 4:18–22
1	Adam	Shem	Perez
2	Seth	Arphaxad	Hezron
3	Enosh	Shelah	Ram
4	Kenan	Eber	Amminadab
5	Mahalalel	Peleg	Nahshon
6	Jared	Reu	Salmon
7	Enoch	Serug	Boaz
8	Methuselah	Nahor	Obed
9	Lamech	Terah	Jesse
10	Noah	Abraham	David

Table 6. Three genealogical lists

---

115. Nahshon was the tribal leader of Judah during the exodus (Num 1:7).

The stage is set for 1 Samuel with the coming kingdom of David. Saul's kingship would intervene, but he did not build a continuing dynasty because of character flaws, something David also had in full measure. Ultimately, Saul was not from the tribe of Judah of whom Jacob would prophesy that the scepter would arise, (Gen 49:10). In David, the prophecy of the men at the gate in this book that his name would be famous in Bethlehem (4:11) and the blessing of the women, that he would be called famous in Israel (4:14) would be first fulfilled.

Application

WHAT LESSONS CAN BE drawn for the twenty-first century from the Book of Ruth that draws on events and values from over 3000 years ago? Importantly, we do the Book of Ruth a grave disservice when we treat it as a work with the same unquestioned authority as when a prophet says, "Thus says the LORD," or with the authority associated with the words of Jesus. Instead, it tells us the story of how two women were saved from abject poverty through marriage to an influential rich man. There is no outside narrator saying that such and such an action occurred because either God was pleased or displeased. While the story is free of the violence of Judges, the community is far from idyllic and presenting a perfect role model. It just tells the story of imperfect people in an imperfect society trying to deal with difficult issues where there was no clear legal precedent. We are asked to draw our own conclusions from the events and words that at times are very ambiguous, and apparently intentionally so. We are forced to make judgement about what is good but needs reinterpreting in our own society but also what is not good and should be condemned and resisted. Boaz did this and was a social disrupter in his own society.

I recall reading in 1970 the words of President Nyerere of Tanzania who said how his country was, "condemned by history to the management of abject poverty." The society in which Naomi, Ruth and Boaz lived was not all that different in that it too lived on a knife edge. Similarly, it was dominated by men and security for women came through a male protector. There are many societies where this is still the case. One theology that cannot be taken from the Book of Ruth is that this is the heavenly ordained natural order that is to be maintained with the full authority of God's word.

Wishful thinking does not change the reality that, for countless women, their lives are blighted and their opportunities to rebel against these patriarchal societies are limited. In impoverished agricultural areas with no social safety net, the amount of physical hard labor needed to eke out a subsistence living demands the partnership of a man and a woman. But even so, in the Book of Ruth there is an upending of the status quo. The same amount of work still has to be done but, as the model of the virtuous woman in Proverbs 31 shows, it is the husband that needs such a wife and Boaz willingly becomes Ruth's servant and not her master. The tabernacle that they both may well have visited had no court of the women. Both men and women alike could come and worship in equality before God. This is clearly spelled out in the New Testament where we are told that God does not regard gender or race (Gal 3:8). Perhaps in its zeal to correct grievous wrongs in society we have erred too far in promoting the total self-reliance of the individual without the need of a partner. In my opinion, the union of a virtuous man and virtuous woman, linked and yet each with their own individually earned identity and respect, remains the best model for the relationship between a man and the woman.

Later, Jesus said that we will always have the poor with us, but its inevitability is very different from the indifference we have observed. In the eyes of the Bethlehem community Naomi may have made bad choices in leaving Bethlehem in the famine, now she was too old to marry and produce children and appears not able to glean. Not only could she contribute little to society, she also did not keep the best of company. Of what value is such a person who now only consumes without providing? To Joe Blow, it was an economic waste to feed such a person. The Book of Ruth has, front and center, the responsibility of the community to feed the poor, whoever they are and to ensure they have safety and are treated with respect. But more than that, because they are vulnerable, they are to be protected and the protector has the responsibility to be worthy and not violate that trust, as could easily have happened on the threshing floor. At the other end of the scale, children who are equally vulnerable, are to be treated in the same way and not as a drain on limited resources.

Australia has been running a policy of multiculturalism which assumes that vastly different cultures can coexist peacefully in the one society. With the concentration of different ethnic groups in specific locations it is almost as if one group is all but irrelevant to the other. Ruth also speaks to us about a different path, the inclusion of those living on the margins, but presents this as a two-way street. Ruth has been, "'pushy' towards being included."[1] She won't go back to Moab. She won't accept the poorest gleanings. She is forthright in seeking marriage. While she pushes for acceptance, Boaz freely breaks social boundaries that may have been in place and draws her in and eases her entry and acceptance into her new country. Inclusion in Ruth was on the basis of race but each society must face its own interpretation of this. My own valley is dependent on foreign backpackers for the harvest but when the crop is picked, they all return to the town in the minivans and the valley returns to its largely homogenous roots. My own church, situated in a potato field has, in its membership, a number of successful farmers and has been called, "the church with the expensive cars." A study about fifteen years ago which compared National Church Life Survey data with the national census, showed that there was another group in our valley. No doubt they are as "white" and Australian as our church but of lower socio-economic status living in the surrounding hills. Our church from the flats was having little impact on them. It is as if both groups are irrelevant to each other and no one was "pushy" to link the two. Our church is not unique in not being able to bridge the gaps in society but bridged it must be.

We see in the Book of Ruth, someone who fed the hungry, comforted the grieving, and entered into unlikely relationships drawing in those on the outer. We see this in its fullness in the life of Jesus. Both lives, "invite us to love loyal kindness and to follow the God in whom dividing walls of hostility are still being broken down."[2]

---

1. Sakenfeld, *Ruth*, 87.
2. Sakenfeld, *Ruth*, 88.

Technical Matters

Date, Authorship, and Purpose

THERE IS NO HINT in the book as to whom the author may have been. The Talmud ascribes Samuel as the author[1] but, as he was dead before David became king, that can safely be ruled out. There is no reason why the author could not have been a woman as the insights into a woman's world are keen and would have required an especially sensitive man to know them. A date somewhere between 1400 and 1100 BC has been suggested for the setting of the events in the Book of Ruth.[2] The conflict between the Old and New Testament timelines make it extremely difficult and probably impossible to reasonably pinpoint this book in time without considering who wrote it. (See below for a discussion of this conflict.) The genealogy of the book has only two generations from Obed to David who is thought to have lived C. 1050 to 950.[3]

As for when the book was written in its present format, it had to be completed well after the setting as it starts referring to a time when the Judges led and explains the old custom of removing a shoe (4:7). The genealogy places the final form of Ruth at least well into the time of David. When we review the structure of Ruth, we will see that this section is almost an appendage to the definite structure that Ruth has. Indeed, some would see it as a later appendage, as with the comment about the shoe. This leaves us free to say that the core of the book could be almost contemporaneous

---

1. Babylonian Talmud, B. Bat. 14b.
2. Evans, *Ruth*, 219.
3. Evans, *Ruth*, 220.

Ruth

with events, but was it? The reality is that scholars find this book very difficult to date.

Should you hold to the documentary theory for the compilation of Genesis and Deuteronomy, and as the author of Ruth has an awareness of these documents, then Ruth must be fairly late. This places the authorship of Ruth after the exile in the fifth century BC. On the other hand Hubbard sees authorship as being compatible with the period of Solomon and allows for it to be drawn up from palace records.[4] Campbell places it during the time of the kings somewhere between 950–700 BC.[5] They look to archaic word forms as a basis for their opinion but others can look at these same word forms and say it was a late work written to appear old.[6] Ultimately, any attempt to date the book is going to be a fruitless exercise. Eskenazi and Frymer-Kensky suggest a fifth century BC date but acknowledge the strong arguments from all sides and say, "an earlier or later date cannot be ruled out entirely."[7] What is said to govern the postexilic date is the apparent presence of a number of Aramaic words, but many of these are largely now discounted as being loan words.[8] If a late date is chosen for actually writing the story, that does not mean that it was not transmitted orally for centuries.[9]

A curious grammatical feature which is found seven times (1:8, 9, 11, 13, 19b; 4:11) in Ruth may point to the age of the text. This is a masculine plural with a feminine antecedent. As this occurs when there are two women, it points to an early feminine dual suffix—*m*. This is cited as evidence of, "archaic composition or at least of composition in a dialect retaining an otherwise lost grammatical feature".[10] It would be a dry gully to try to base an interpretation of these four chapters on a proposed later date, other than to simply accept it for what it purports to be.

If the book is seen as putting a brake on the actions of Ezra and Nehemiah who excluded foreigners, the book must then be dated as postexilic. That seems unlikely as the canon would have been compiled by their supporters and it is hard to imagine that they would have included a book

---

4. Hubbard, *Ruth*, 23.
5. Campbell, *Ruth*, 24.
6. Eskenazi and Frymer-Kensky, *Ruth*, xvii.
7. Eskenazi and Frymer-Kensky, *Ruth*, xvii.
8. Hubbard, *Ruth*, 27. He cites one study reducing this to two at most. Morris cites opinions that these are instead Canaanite words. *Ruth*, 237.
9. Morris, *Ruth*, 237.
10. Campbell, *Ruth*, 65.

attacking their position. If, on the other hand, it is seen as buttressing David's dynasty's claim to the throne then it has to be very close to the events. Then, who is going to be swayed by the personal character of his great grandparents.[11] If the purpose is just to write down a homily that shows us how to live and how to treat foreigners, without initially having any major political thrust, it could be very early indeed in its original form. In this way it could be considered as an Old Testament version of the parable of the Good Samaritan.

But why do we look for a purpose and not see it first and foremost as a ripping yarn of a poor foreign girl who made good. I attempt to demonstrate in the section below on Structure how the story is very skillfully and artistically put together. By looking first for a purpose such as edification, or to support the inclusion of foreigners, we fail to see, "the author of Ruth as an artist in full command of a complex and subtle art, which art is exhibited in almost every word of the story."[12] That is not to say that the storyteller had no purpose but to see the book as an extremely skilled creation allows for a number of minor and major themes to coexist at the same time. As for what scholars see these themes to be, largely, I expect, either governed by their perception of the dating or in an equally circular argument, perceptions of purpose governing dating. Rather than find a single time and therefore reason for writing, Sackenfield suggests that in the way that it addresses exclusivism, we should remind ourselves, "that the story of Ruth addresses a perennial issue in the human community."[13] Even, it might be said of my own church community in rural Queensland who, with their German heritage, all had past relatives who knew what it was to be strangers in a foreign land and to be treated with suspicion.

Theological Message of Ruth

Boaz linked two topics that are entirely separate matters in the Law, inheritance of land and the remarriage of a childless widow. If this book is only or even primarily about land and levirate marriage it is no more than an historical curiosity and serves no purpose for today. While the land tenure system we see in Israel during the Judges has long gone, many Europeans living in Australia still feel a very close association with family-owned land.

11. Sakenfeld, *Ruth*, 3.
12. Rauber, *Literary*, 37.
13. Sakenfeld, *Ruth*, 5.

Ruth

For our Australian Aborigines, the connection is said to be closer and even spiritual but for both, modern legal practice now controls ownership after death. Our pensions and charity systems ensure, or should ensure, survival with dignity.

In my introduction I quoted Rabbi Zeira, "This scroll [of Ruth] tells us nothing either of cleanliness or of uncleanliness, either of prohibition or permission. For what purpose then was it written? To teach how great is the reward of those who do deeds of kindness."[14] That statement is not quite correct, there are many matters that are concerned with the observance of the Law, but it is not the core of the matter. Its concern is, "not in the law, but in the manner of fulfilling the law."[15] By associating the Book of Ruth with Israel's foundational moment and the key beneficiaries of the Law, the poor, the widows and the orphans, its spiritual message is amplified.[16] Ruth has been described as, "rising from the shadows of Moses' unknown grave in Moab"[17] and becomes the interpreter of his Law. Life situations will continue to change and evolve but the message of facing whatever adversity occurs with kindness rather than applying rules has not changed. They can do this as Ruth teaches us that God cherishes those whom society classes as of little value, women, the poor, the foreigner and the convert. Unlike the Law given with fire and trumpets, its fulfilment day by day is through being led by those who hear the "still small voice" and find redemption through imitation of that unique quality of Yahweh, *hesed*.

But even more, The Book of Ruth is the story of the hidden God,[18] whose still small voice cannot be heard nor, for the most part, his hand seen. And people do as they wish. What is seen is his providence, where God uses the smallest accidents but without, "the faintest hint that this total control exercised by the LORD in any way limits the freedom of activity of the people involved."[19] Whereas, in the Book of Judges, God intervenes spasmodically, in Ruth he inhabits, yet hides in every plan and every event. Hals asks if God has drawn dangerously far into hiddenness so that his people risk being able to see him?[20] He answers this question himself when

---

14. Ruth Rabbah: 2:14.
15. Ziegler, *Ruth*, 378.
16. Eskenazi and Frymer-Kensky, *Ruth*, lxiv, lxviii.
17. Eskenazi and Frymer-Kensky, *Ruth*, lxix.
18. Hals, *Theology*, 16.
19. Hals, *Theology*, 18.
20. Hals, *Theology*, 19.

he sees this phenomenon, not as the storyteller's confidence in his skill; but in his confidence in his readers who see God everywhere.[21] Hidden he may be; but not one prayer for blessing has gone unanswered.

The Book of Ruth presents us with a chaotic world, where life can be lived on a knife edge and as a consequence, many, like Naomi and Ruth, are needy. In all of this, they are not shielded from the effects of this chaos but still, in the midst of this, find a powerful ally who rewards Ruth's faithfulness and love. Yet the wealthy are shown also to need the blessing of God and in return are meant to be a blessing to others. The life of love and sacrifice can have blessings that pass beyond the generations. The happy ending of chapter 4 can be attributed to chance in a world where God's face is hidden. His very presence has to be read into the text like the still small voice.

In the comments I have drawn attention to certain words and phrases that reoccur drawing our attention to actions and even creating mirror images between characters and situations. These all point to, "absolute justice—an idea that people are rewarded for their actions."[22] Sadly life is seldom one of "absolute justice" but in the face of this we are introduced to the possibility of this justice transcending two worlds—the dead and the living. As part of Ruth's ambiguity, we are left with the possibility of a God whose *hesed* covers the living and the dead.

The book begins and ends with the writer commenting on the sovereignty of God. He brought food to his people (1:6) and enabled Ruth to conceive (4:16). An appreciation of this sovereignty is seen in the six verses (1:17; 2:4, 20; 3:10, 13), where God's name is used, "to reinforce a blessing, curse or oath."[23] God is thus seen as someone from whom blessings could be asked. Evans asks how much of this response was just automatic and without any understanding. Certainly, a deep understanding of a sovereign God in a covenant relationship with his people should have led them to live out the responsibilities that came with it.[24] While God is seen as the ultimate source of the blessings in this book, the wishes for his intervention are actually fulfilled in God's name by the person asking for his intervention. It is men and women who show God's kindness to each other. Notably, the requests of God are only for those things which can be achieved through others, i.e., marriage and favorable gleaning, but the outcome of the book

21. Hals, *Theology*, 59, 62.
22. Ziegler, *Ruth*, 465.
23. Evans, *Ruth*, 225.
24. Evans, *Ruth*, 225.

is beyond what anyone asks for. Their expectation, and equally ours, and certainly mine can be too small.

One of the promises to God's people was "rest." There was a promise of rest from the wilderness (Ex 33:14) and rest after the conquest (Deut 3:19–20; 12:8–11; 25:19; Josh 1:13–15). But as the people departed from the covenant, rest did not follow until a Judge rose up and vanquished their oppressors. Naomi's hope for her daughters-in-law after all their turmoil was that they would find rest (1:9). Rest for both Naomi and Ruth does come, first through the supply of food in chapter 2 and then more completely in the provision of a husband, child and status in chapter 4.

The idea of a redeemer that makes rest possible is also important. The children of Israel's time in Canaan starts with Moses the redeemer from the slavery of Egypt. Our book starts with a mention of the Judges who redeemed Israel or certain tribes and concludes with redemption on an individual level.

Moore identifies the "wandering Jew" as a "profoundly biblical"[25] theme in Ruth, but not only Ruth, the whole Old Testament and the New Testament as well. The word "Hebrew" probably means "wanderer." Abraham wanders from Ur to Canaan, Jacob from Canaan to Padan Arram and back and then to Egypt. Moses led the Hebrews as they wandered in the wilderness. Judah was exiled to Babylon and returned. Likewise, Christians are meant to be strangers and exiles upon earth (Heb 11:13). And like Israel, who was the one who wrestles with God, Moore likewise identifies any "person, or nation or faith community [as] an organism forever on the move, constantly facing all sorts of spatial, temporal, ethnic, social, political, religious, theological and spiritual boundaries."[26]

I pointed out the repetition of the word "return" in my comments on 1:6 and in part, Ruth does give an answer to the question, "Is it my fate to wander forever? Am I ever going to find my way home again?"[27] Of the wandering Jews of the Bethlehem trilogy, only one does.

Hesed, though only mentioned three times, is also a vital theme in this book and this word, often translated as "kindness," is discussed in detail later in this section. But Ruth's kindness and unswerving devotion to Naomi which make up the basis of the story are arguably not something that all of Israel was to follow. For Ruth, it involved "sabotage[ing] her own

---

25. Moore, *Ruth*, 300.
26. Moore, *Ruth*, 300.
27. Moore, *Ruth*, 300.

personal interests in her acts of kindness."[28] Ziegler asks if, "the excessive nullification of self in deference to the needs of the Other [is] the ideal definition of *hesed*, the one that merits the greatest reward."[29]

A central purpose of the Book of Ruth has been seen as giving a background to the Davidic kingdom, as there is very little in 1 Samuel concerning it; but against this is the potential problem raised by his Moabite ancestry that could exclude him from the Nation of Israel entirely. The Oral Law restricts this exclusion to the men of Moab only, because they were the ones who lacked concern for their fellow man. By describing Ruth as, "a paradigm of kindness"[30] the purity of the line is established. The Book of Ruth is therefore given as a validation of the Oral Law, something which goes against the teaching of Jesus who railed against the heavy burden it imposed (Matt 15:3) and also against the Protestant view of "Scripture Only."

Ziegler says of Ruth that, "The book stretches out towards kingship, elegantly weaving its theology of kingship throughout the narrative."[31] Kingship can provide stable and strong government; but with all the power of the judiciary, military and finance at his disposal, kingship can degenerate into tyrannical corrupt behavior. The Bible set guidelines to guide the king's behavior and the good kings are often portrayed as working with a prophet. Clearly these were not always followed, however in the theme of *hesed* in the Book of Ruth, kings were left with a model of appropriate behavior. She describes it this way:

> It is true that Ruth's type of selflessness is not something Judaism demands from its constituents. *Yet it is an absolute necessity for our leaders*. Not only do we expect it from our leaders, but it is the vital prerequisite for the establishment of the monarchy. Without a Ruth at its helm, without someone with the ability to give unselfishly and totally to the Other, monarchy is not a promise or vision of bounty, but a dangerous threat, a recipe for depravity and despotism."[32]

---

28. Ziegler, *Ruth*, 18.
29. Ziegler, *Ruth*, 18.
30. Ziegler, *Ruth*, 20.
31. Ziegler, *Ruth*, 9.
32. Ziegler, *Ruth*, 25.

Ruth

Ruth's Order in the Canon

In the Christian Bible, Ruth is found after Judges, following the order of the Septuagint, which places the historical books in historical order. This places Ruth among the Former Prophets (Zech 1:4). In the Masoretic text however, it is found in that section called the *Ketubim* (Writings) and is known as one of the five *Megillot* (Scrolls). These scrolls are linked to the Jewish liturgical calendar with Ruth being read on the second day of the Feast of Weeks (Exod 34:22).

Other traditions place Ruth in different positions. The Talmud uses a chronological order based on presumed authors;[33] Ruth by Samuel, Psalms by David and Song of Solomon by Solomon. Alternatively, the Dead Sea Scrolls show its position was fluid.[34] Some, including the oldest versions of the Masoretic text, place Ruth directly after Proverbs with its description of the virtuous woman (Prov 31:10–31) and just before the Song of Solomon. Here it is out of genre, authorship and chronological order.

The order in which we find the Book of Ruth in the various traditions gives us a clue to how people fundamentally understand the story. In our Bible it is an idyllic love story set between the dark days of the Judges and the reign of King Saul. If the book is placed before Psalms, it provides a genealogy and legitimacy to David though that is found elsewhere. The climax of the wisdom book of Proverbs is to marry a good wife, a wife of noble character (31:10, 29) and only Ruth is described this way, so we have the teaching and the illustration.[35] Bill Mounce, comparing Ruth to Proverbs 31 says, "Basically this woman—this paradigm wife—is so good at her work, that her husband can sit and be one of the rulers in the gates. He has got time off to be a gentleman's gentleman, I guess you would say. Here at the end of Ruth, they are praising her in the gates."

All three approaches have merit, but the emphasis of this commentary has been in seeing Ruth as the wife of noble character.

Jewish Traditions about Ruth

Many tales have sprung up about Ruth and Boaz and I summarize some of them here for your interest.

33. Babylonian Talmud, B. Bat. 14b.
34. Moore, *Ruth*, 294.
35. Mounce, "Hebrew Order," para. 55.

It is said that Ruth and Orpah were not just simple Moabite women but members of the royal family, being daughters of King Eglon of Moab.[36] This means that they were not just sisters-in-law but sisters. Eglon was the son of Balak[37] who planned to curse the migrating Israelite community through the prophet Balaam (Numbers 22—24).

Before Ruth appeared on the scene in Bethlehem, Boaz had also been kind toward his kinsmen, Naomi's sons. When he heard of their death, he took care that they had an honorable burial.[38] The reason that it is a crowd who greeted Ruth and Naomi on their return to Bethlehem is because they had come from the funeral of Boaz's wife, who had died that same day.[39] She leaves the scene just as Ruth arrives.

Some rabbis say that Boaz was the judge Ibzan of Bethlehem (Judg 12:8). This judge had sixty children, but it is said that he lost them all during his lifetime because he did not invite Manoah, Samson's father, to any of the marriage festivities in his house. Boaz thought that he need not consider a man who was at that time childless because he could not reciprocate.[40]

When Boaz met Ruth he is alleged to have told her that he had heard from the prophets that she would become the ancestor of kings and prophets; so he blessed her with the words: "May the Lord reward you well in this world for your good work, and may you receive full recompense from the Lord, the God of Israel, in the world to come, because you have come to be a proselyte and to seek shelter under the shadow of His Glorious Presence."[41]

While the Book of Ruth emphasizes her inner qualities she was said to possess great physical beauty: One Rabbi said, "It happened that whoever saw her would have an emission."[42] The urgency of her desire to marry and bear children is explained by saying Ruth was forty years old and not a young woman when Boaz married her.[43] Boaz, for his part, was eighty[44] and

---

36. Ruth Rabbah: 2:9.
37. Babylonian Talmud: Sanh. 105b.
38. Ruth Rabbah: 5:10.
39. Babylonian Talmud: B. Bat. 91a.
40. Babylonian Talmud: B. Bat. 91a.
41. Targum Ruth: 2:10–13.
42. Ruth Rabbah: 4:4. Similar things are said of Rahab, in Babylonian Talmud: Meg. 15a: "She, too, converted, was married to an important person and was blessed with important offspring." See Ruth Rabbah: 2:1 also.
43. Ruth Rabbah: 4:4.
44. Ruth Rabbah: 6:2.

died the day after his wedding.[45] The very birth of the child was said to be a miracle as Boaz was also said to be sterile, but Naomi's prayer and blessing changed that.[46] The Talmud says that Ruth lived a long life, sufficient to see her own great-great-grandson Solomon crowned as King of Israel.[47]

This all makes for a great story but nothing more. David must have had some connection with the king of Moab as he took his parents to him for safety (1 Sam 22:3–5) but that is a long way from saying they were distant relatives. Boaz was certainly old and could well have been eighty and as he was not mentioned at the birth of his son, he was quite possibly dead at that stage.

Messianic Significance of Ruth

As mentioned in the comment, the Jewish association is with Yahweh, the redeemer of Israel who delivered them from slavery in Egypt. Christians consider themselves as people who have been "redeemed" from the slavery of sin, so there is an automatic association with Jesus, the redeemer of the world, the ultimate *goel* and his ancestor, Boaz. Paul quotes Isaiah 59:20 where a *goel* will come from Zion and Jesus' work is clearly called redemption, (e.g., Gal 3:13–14; 4:3–5).

Tempting as this is, the New Testament does not make a connection between the two. It is better to see Boaz as a person who embodies the righteousness that Moses envisaged would be lived by the kings of Israel (Deut 17:14–20). His role is as the honored seventh position in the genealogy of David. His actions in marrying a Gentile, "secure the identification of the Messiah with all humanity."[48] A better case for a type can be made from Obed and Block identifies four similarities:

- Special nature of his birth from a previously barren woman, (c.f., Isaac in Gen 21)
- He is the *goel* who restores life,
- Elevation of his mother after his birth, and

---

45. Ginzburg, *Boaz*, 278.
46. Ruth Rabbah: 6:4.
47. Babylonian Talmud: B. Bat. 91b.
48. Block, *Ruth*, 56.

- His name is "servant".[49]

That is not to say that the book does not have messianic significance. The genealogy takes us to David but not beyond, but there is a connection to his greatest son. In light of Micah's prophecy about the birth of Israel's ruler from Bethlehem Ephrathah, we should see the references to Ephrathah that start and end the story (1:2; 4:11) as significant.

Ruth, a Love Story?

In our modern western experience, it is difficult to find a comparison to the "love story" of Ruth. A visiting pastor to our church spoke about his family connection to our valley in the 1800s. A tragedy occurred and the woman in his ancestry, who had children and a farm, was widowed. Within three months she married a widower. This was a marriage of dire necessity for both parties, yet this does not fit the story as Boaz considers her as someone who did not have to marry an old man out of desperation. At the other end of the scale, the 1960 movie *The Story of Ruth* certainly portrays the story of Ruth and Boaz as a love story but the age of Boaz, though not stated explicitly, prevents us understanding it as a romantic novel as we know it.

We can't even look for a much tamed down version of what we have seen lived out in the media of a young celebrity marrying a very much older man purely for financial security. Such actions would be out of keeping for a woman of exemplary virtue. We need to look to the book itself for an explanation. While it is a love story, it is not love as we know it now. What we see in the story is loyalty and *hesed* shown by Ruth, by Boaz, and by Yahweh.

We sell the story short if we see it only as loyalty and people fulfilling their duty in their cultural setting. The love that Ruth had for Mahlon, though again not explicitly stated, so that she wanted to continue his line, must have been profound and the motivation of her *hesed*. Likewise, the love she had for Naomi was the motivation for her *hesed* to her.

Ruth—A Book of Names

When compared with the Book of Judges, one of the most striking characteristics of Ruth is that people have names. Judges "ends with a profusion of unnamed characters, depicting a society in which people do not regard one

---

49. Block, *Ruth*, 55–56.

another as human beings, worthy of compassion."[50] In contrast, Ruth's primary goal is to establish the name of her dead husband and his inheritance. The only main actor who does not have a name, and deliberately so, is the close relative that refuses to do his duty. The use of names in Ruth lead to some interpretations that see Ruth as an allegory with deeper meanings other than what the story simply says. This builds on choosing one of the possible meanings of the names of the participants. The range of possible meanings are:

Elimelech: The *mlk* ending of the name gives two possibilities. It could be, "The King is my god" based on the name of foreign gods such as Milkom of the Ammonites but an Israelite would understand it as "The King (Yahweh) is my god."[51] Considering the Book of Judges focuses on the troubles in the land coming from the lack of a king, his name is "pregnant with irony."[52] This is the only occurrence in the Bible but is known from the Amarna letters from the fourteenth century BC.[53]

Naomi: The root *n'm* is associated with liveliness or delight. Names with the same root (Elna'am 1 Chron 11:46, and Abino'am Judges 4:6 and 5:1) are compounded with a deity's name so it is possible Naomi is a "nickname."[54]

Mahlon: This name is only found in Ruth and not in any late bronze age languages, so the meaning is less certain. Other names Mahlah (Num 26:33), Mahli (1 Chron 6:19, 29) and Mahalath (Gen 28:8; 2, Chron:11:18) point to a root *mhl* suggesting, "to be sick, sickly or even to be sweet." Campbell thinks this is unlikely and summarizes, "We simply do not yet know what Mahlon and Kilyon mean."[55] Another meaning is claimed, "Mahlon was worthier than Chilion. His name is expounded: "*Mahlon*—an expression of *mehilah* [pardon]," and he therefore deserved to be married to Ruth the Moabite."[56] The name could also be associated with the words *mahol* to dance or even *mehilan* inheritance.[57]

Chilion: This name is known from Ugaritic lists so is contemporary with our story. Suggested meanings are "little vessel" or based on the LXX

---

50. Ziegler, *Ruth*, 31.
51 Campbell, *Ruth*, 52.
52. Moore, *Ruth*, 311.
53. Eskenazi and Frymer-Kensky, *Ruth*, 5.
54. Campbell, *Ruth*, 52–53.
55. Campbell, *Ruth*, 53–54.
56. Meir, *Ruth*, para. 2.
57. Ziegler, *Ruth*, 114.

spelling of *Kilayon* "destruction" A possible positive meaning may be drawn from, "the word that denotes completion, and as a derivative of that word, perfection."[58] Ultimately the meaning is very uncertain. It is unlikely that someone would name their children "sickly" or "destruction."

Orpah: There is no satisfactory explanation for this name. It has been associated with '*orep* meaning "the back of the neck" and associate this with her decision to turn back.[59] Frymer-Kenske suggests "cloud" from the Ugaritic '*rp* as found in Psalm 68:4 and 104:3.[60]

Ruth: Of all the names, the meaning of the name of the main character is the most uncertain. Campbell, based on a similar word on the Mesha inscription,[61] suggests a tentative meaning of "satiation, refreshment." Her name may mean "friendship," "comfort," or "refreshment." It appears to have been Moabite and not Hebrew. A similar word is found in Isaiah 58:11 referring to a "watered" garden opening the possibility that both wives' names have a water connection,[62] which would be striking considering the family left Bethlehem because of drought.

Marah: The meaning of this name is clear and means "bitter" and was also the name of the bitter well in the exodus. There Moses turned the water sweet by throwing in a piece of wood as directed by God.

Boaz: The root b'z does not occur in the OT so the name Boaz is obscure.[63] The LXX spelling of his name "*booz*" suggests the Hebrew "in him is strength" but different vowels give "in the strength of." This would suggest another "nick name" for a longer sentence name such as, "In the strength of Yahweh I will rejoice." One of the pillars of Solomon's temple was called Boaz.[64]

The man with no name: The man who refuses to fulfill his responsibilities so he can protect his own inheritance is not worthy of a name. I have called him Joe Blow and, by being reduced to an idiom the hearer's respect for him is diminished.[65] As mentioned in the comments, the meaning of

---

58. Ziegler, *Ruth*, 114. See Gen 2:1–2.

59. Campbell, *Ruth*, 55–56.

60. Eskenazi and Frymer-Kensky, *Ruth*, 7.

61. The Mesha Inscription, also known as the Moabite stone dates from around 840 BC and tells of how Moab was able to free itself from oppression by Israel.

62. Eskenazi and Frymer-Kensky, *Ruth*, 7.

63. Hubbard, *Ruth*, 134.

64. Campbell, *Ruth*, 90–91.

65. Block, *Ruth*, 249.

the term *peloni almoni* is uncertain and the only other places it is used refer to locations that are military secrets (1 Sam 21:3; 2 Kgs 6:8). It has been suggested that what we have is an onomatopoeic wordplay like helter-skelter.[66]

Obed: The root from which the name is derived is *abad*, to work or serve but is a word that is very vague and Block says of his name, "it is futile to try to imagine the significance they ascribed to it or to the lad by it."[67] He suggests that Obed may be an abbreviation of Obadiah, the servant of Yahweh which is used twelve times in the Old Testament.[68] Still, within its basic meaning of service we can see the Book of Ruth's renunciation of, "Judges self-absorbed narcissism."[69]

While there are a range of meanings possible for the names of the characters, as mentioned, some take one of these possibilities, ignoring the others, to hunt for hidden meanings and deeper truths in the Book of Ruth. People talk with authority about how the family left Bethlehem (house of bread) in Judah (praise) and went to Moab (away from the father) showing Elimelech's mindset of not trusting God. Living in sin there he and his sons paid the penalty with Mahlon meaning sickly and Chilion meaning destruction. As a consequence of their lack of faith pleasant Naomi became Marah (bitter). The problem with such interpretation is that there is no control, and the text can be forced to mean whatever the exegete wants it to mean. It is highly unlikely that Naomi would have given her children names with such negative meanings. In the process it robs the book of its historicity and turns it into an allegory.

Ruth is not an allegory in the sense of being a made-up moral tale like *Pilgrims Progress*, but it is allegory-like in that we are meant to take notice of the names and places, to appreciate the story. Yes, the man who fails in his call to show *hesed* is not worthy of a name but, at the same time, if too much stress is placed on the names the message of the book can be distorted. Campbell says of the names, "it is increasingly clear that the names of the people in the story are not contrived so as to make them especially pertinent to the plot of the story; rather, they appear to be good representatives of the Hebrew (and Moabite?) pool of proper names . . . of the end of

---

66. Moore, *Ruth*, 361.
67. Block, *Ruth*, 249.
68. Block, *Ruth*, 240.
69. Moore, *Ruth*, 370.

the Canaanite period and the beginning of the Israelite period."[70] We are looking instead at, "an eminently plausible story."[71]

Conflicting Timelines

The New Testament gives the genealogy from the conquest to David's kingdom as "Salmon fathered Boaz by Rahab, Boaz fathered Obed by Ruth, and Obed fathered Jesse" (Matt 1:5 [NASB]). The genealogy in Luke 3:31–32 gives the same names but without identifying any of the mothers. The mention of Rahab only has relevance if she is meant to be understood as the prostitute from Jericho. So, according to the Gospels, from Salmon's time during the conquest to David's kingdom covers the space of five generations (see also the genealogy in 1 Chronicles 2).

Judge	Reign	Reference
Othniel	40 years	Judges 3:9–11
Ehud	80 years	Judges 3:15–30
Shamgar	Unknown	Judges 3:31; Judges 5:6
Deborah/Barak	40 years	Judges 4:4—5:31
Gideon	40 years	Judges 6:11—8:32
Abimelech	3 years	Judges 9:1–57; 2 Samuel 11:21
Tola	23 years	Judges 10:1–2
Jair	22 years	Judges 10:3–5
Jephthah	6 years	Judges 11:1—12:7
Ibzan	7 years	Judges 12:8–10

---

70. Campbell, *Ruth*, 10.

71. Campbell, *Ruth*, 10. However, despite being plausible, Campbell believes the story to be fiction.

Ruth

Judge	Reign	Reference
Elon	10 years	Judges 12:11–12
Abdon	8 years	Judges 12:13–15
Samson	20 years	Judges 13:1—16:31
Eli	40 years	1 Sam 1:1—4:18
Samuel until Saul made king	12 years (approx.)	1 Sam 2:18—4:11; Sam 7:2—8:1

Table 6. The Judges of Israel

When Paul preached at the synagogue in Pisidian Antioch, he said, "And after that he gave unto them judges about the space of four hundred and fifty years, until Samuel the prophet" (AV), a period that is longer than five generations. A third timeline consideration is that the day work commenced on the first temple was in the fourth year of Solomon's reign which was c. 966 BC.[72] This is said to be 480 years since leaving Egypt (1 Kgs 6:1). Yet another timeline is introduced when Jephthah started to judge Israel which is said to have been 300 years after the entry into Canaan (Judges 11:26). The genealogy at the end of Ruth and the corresponding list in 1 Chronicles 2:9–12 only have ten generations from Perez to David. Nahshon lived during the exodus leaving only five generations to David, perhaps in as little as 150 years.

Can this short and long timeline be harmonized? Many attempts have been made to bring agreement to these seeming contradictions. Paul's period of 450 years is equal to the 400-year enslavement in Egypt (Gen 15:13–14) combined with the journey to Sinai and subsequent forty years wandering and then say nine years for the conquest. Some translations, (e.g., NIV, NRSV) now read that the 450 years are a summation of Acts 13:17–19 which covers just this period.[73] This leaves the period of time covered by the Judges as undefined and can harmonize with the New Testament. Conversely, it is also equivalent to the rule of the Judges and the periods of oppression up to

---

72. Merrill, "450 Years," 246. This gives a date for the exodus of C. 1446 BC.

73. The AV word order follows the Western and Byzantine texts whereas later translations where there is harmony, follow the Alexandrian texts, the Latin Vulgate and the Armenian Version. Bruce, *Acts*, 268.

the death of Eli. It is expected that some of these judges may have overlapped or been side by side in different parts of the land.

The period mentioned in 1 Kings and Judges is much harder to reconcile if for no other reason than it is hard to imagine a 400 plus year power vacuum that allowed Israel's seeming relative autonomy from Egypt[74] despite not having a national ruler and capital. Matthew's genealogy is said not to contain any gaps as he says there were fourteen generations from Abraham to David (Matt 1:17) so this does not leave room for missing descendants.

I am not going to attempt a reconciliation and there probably is no simple answer at this stage. I have taken the position in the comments that 450 years is an impossibly long period to harmonize with the genealogy and instead have followed the shorter New Testament five generation timespan. With that comes the theological significance of women of faith from nations that incited God's anger being part of the messianic line.

Hesed, a Key Theme in Ruth

A key theme to the Book of Ruth is the Hebrew concept of *hesed*. In the Book of Judges, this word, one of the most important in the Old Testament, is found only twice and both are in an unfavorable context. In Judges 1:24, a Canaanite is asked to show *hesed* to the tribe of Joseph through revealing the entrance to Bethel and so betraying his countrymen, and in 8:35, on Gideon's death, the Israelites had not shown *hesed* to his family. A related word that is used in Judges is *khanan*, "kindness," but even there its use is perverted (21:22). This term is not used in Ruth though its fruit is evident. In Ruth, *hesed* and the acts of kindness are something that comes from, "personal character and integrity."[75]

Ruth is a much smaller book yet *hesed* is mentioned three times and each time it is in a favorable way and is pivotal to the story (1:8; 2:20; 3:10). What does this word which is vital to our understanding of Ruth mean? Morris says that it is, "a term extraordinarily difficult to translate into English, our language has no obvious equivalent."[76] Further, it "exhibits great

---

74. The Mer-ne-Ptah stela dated to c. 1230 BC. which refers to the destruction of Israel mentions them as a people, not a land. "Thus we should seem to have the Children of Israel as in or near Palestine, but not yet a settled people" Pritchard sees the argument as "good but not conclusive." Pritchard, *Ancient*, 231.

75. Moore, *Ruth*, 305.

76 Morris, *Testaments*, 65.

flexibility in usage within the biblical tradition."[77] *Hesed* seems to be a uniquely Hebrew word to describe a concept that probably existed across many cultures. The word is not found in the remnants of Akkadian, Amorite and Ugaritic texts[78] and, though found in Aramaic and Arabic counterparts, "the range of meaning is very different."[79] Understanding this word can only come from a study of the Old Testament where it is used 245 times.

The RSV renders this word as "steadfast love" 178 times but uses fifteen words in all to translate it. The AV uses "mercy" most commonly but also uses ten other different words. The difficulty that reigns when translating this word is illustrated by the following chart:

	AV	RSV	NEB	GNB	NIV
Love words	-	182	149	162	171
Lovingkindness	30	-	-	-	1
Kindness words	43	29	4	19	49
Mercy words	155	2	-	-	7
Loyalty words	-	21	61	20	3
Promise	-	-	-	9	-
Devotion words	-	2	-	-	5
Favor	3	3	-	6	4
Goodness words	14	3	-	-	-
Miscellaneous	-	3	31	29	5

Table 7. Different Translations of Hesed[80]

77. Sakenfeld, *Meaning*, 13.
78. Sakenfeld, *Meaning*, 16–17.
79. Sakenfeld, *Meaning*, 19. In Aramaic the root means to be suspicious.
80. Morris, *Testaments*, 66.

A significant shift in the understanding of the word occurred in 1927 when Nelson Glueck published his study, deducing that *Hesed* is not used to express the feeling between man and his fellowman but "between people who are in close relationship with each other."[81] He believed it to be a, "strong and persistent attitude and is not dissolved by death."[82] This view says that, "*Hesed* was not basically mercy but loyalty to covenant obligations,"[83] meaning there was nothing arbitrary or gracious about it.

Since then, his views on *hesed* have been affirmed, modified or debunked by succeeding scholars. Glueck's view has not received universal acceptance as there are cases that argue against a necessary involvement of obligation. For instance, its use in relation to the defeated Ben Haddad, Laban and, as we have seen, with Ruth. Despite this, it is obvious that there is no covenant without *hesed*. Laird Harris suggests that Glueck's mistake was in not recognizing that relationship and obligations are deeper than the covenant itself.[84]

Hesed appears to be part of the very character of God as indicated by Psalm 62:12, "To Thee, Oh Lord belongs steadfast love," see also Psalm 25:10 and 109:21. As such, "It is not a human achievement but a quality we know from God, a quality man is expected to emulate."[85] God's *hesed* is better than life, (Pss 63:3) and lasts forever, (Pss 136). There is a divine bookkeeping with God's *hesed* where deeds accumulated over 1000 generations are, "sufficient to overwhelm any bad deeds, and thus bring forgiveness instead of punishment" (Num 14:18–19).

The Old Testament consistently presents Israel as failing to meet God's standard and many, perhaps including the AV translators, use this as their basis for translating this word as "mercy." Glueck argued that the term is primarily love and loyalty which produce actions which will be characterized as merciful. Similarly, Harris says "the word 'loving-kindness' of the AV is archaic, but not far from the fullness of the meaning of the word."[86]

This word, more than any other Hebrew term, is closest to the New Testament word grace (Gk. *charis*) described as, "God's redemptive love which is always active to save sinners and maintain them in a proper

---

81. Glueck, *Hesed*, 37.
82. Glueck, *Hesed*, 42.
83. Harris, Ḥsd in *TWOT*, 305.
84. Harris, Ḥsd in *TWOT*, 306.
85. Morris, *Testaments*, 77.
86. Harris, Hesed in *TWOT*, 307.

relationship with him."[87] The New Testament *charis* and the Old Testament *hesed* are both, at least from God's perspective, "entirely free and undeserved," without any obligation. This undeserved aspect is a significant difference between *hesed* and grace. Unlike grace, *hesed* is only active when there is an already existing positive relationship and is not used in settings where forgiveness is needed.[88] *Hesed* is normally rendered as *elos* (pity) in the LXX but Paul who is the main user of the term grace found "pity" inadequate because, "it did not emphasize the long suffering of God and his patience with which he so long forbears to punish sin."[89] From a human perspective however acts of *hesed* can set up an expectation of reciprocal action and this can be the driver for their instigation in the first place.[90] It can also be a benevolent repayment for a previous act (2 Sam 2:5–6; 1 Kgs 2:7). Ruth's acts of *hesed* are the purest because they are done to the dead who cannot repay.

In the pre-exilic period there are generally four features in situations where *hesed* is either sought or given. These are:

- The person who gives *hesed* is recognized as having a responsibility to the recipient,
- The giver is free not to perform *hesed*,
- The act fulfils an important need for the recipient, and
- Only the giver is in the position to help.[91]

The Jewish writers Eskenazi and Frymer-Kensky see in *hesed*, "the greatest act of benevolence God can do for us [in giving] us a sense there is justice in the world, that there is some degree of predictability. That therefore we can control our fate (at least to some extent) by controlling how we treat each other and how we act towards God."[92] Do we always really want justice, as too often our deeds have been unjust and instead need forgiveness and the suspension of justice? Here *hesed* works also as we have seen in Ruth how true benevolence can be contagious and suspends well-earned measure for measure justice. The question is what lesson Ruth has in a

---

87. Richardson, *Grace*, 101.
88. Sakenfeld, *Ruth*, 24.
89. Richardson, *Theological*, 101.
90. Eskenazi and Frymer-Kensky, *Ruth*, xlviii.
91. Sakenfeld, *Meaning*, 24.
92. Eskenazi and Frymer-Kensky, *Ruth*, xlix.

world pervaded by chaos and violence? Ruth shows us what a theology of *hesed* looks like and its power for good, especially when God is hidden. It invites the readers to do likewise.[93]

Structure of the Book of Ruth

Excluding the concluding genealogy, Ruth reads as a continuous narrative and this is the approach taken in my comments. Our chapter divisions date from the medieval period and are not part of the Jewish Masoretic tradition. The only break is after 4:17 as an indication of where the weekly reading ends. The book does divide naturally where we have our chapter breaks with a verb describing the actions of each of the characters.

Chapter 1	Chapter 2	Chapter 3	Chapter 4
Elimelech	Ruth	Naomi	Boaz
Vayelekh	*Vatomer*	*Vatomer*	*Ala*
And it came to pass	And she said	And she said	He went up

Table 8. Natural breaks in the Book of Ruth[94]

Looking at the structure simply, these chapters can be divided two ways. The book can firstly be divided into two halves with the first two chapters dealing with the search for food and the second half dealing with the securing of marriage and children. Both sections start with first Elimelech and then Naomi devising plans, "that mirror those of the decaying social order"[95] but come to nothing. What then follows is the rectification of the situation by virtuous Boaz and Ruth.

A second way of analyzing the book is by understanding this as the work of a storyteller of incredible skill and art which can be appreciated by looking, firstly, at the chiastic nature of the chapters. The story reads so well that it is possible to completely miss the very structured and complex patterns underlying the book. Without looking at the internal chiasms within

---

93. Eskenazi and Frymer-Kensky, *Ruth*, liii.
94. Ziegler, *Ruth*, 366.
95. Ziegler, *Ruth*, 367–68.

the chapters some of which I have highlighted in the comments, the chapters themselves can be chiasms. This is clearest when looking at chapters 2 and 3, where Ruth and Boaz are the focus and mirror each other in their structure and theme. This was mentioned in my comments.

  A Conversation between Ruth and Naomi (2:2)
    B Ruth and Boaz in the field (2:3–17)
      C Conversation between Ruth and Naomi (2:18–22)
  A' Conversation between Ruth and Naomi (3:1–5)
    B' Ruth and Boaz at the threshing floor (3:6–15)
      C' Conversation between Ruth and Naomi (3:16–18)

Also, chapters 1 and 4, with the focus on Naomi, likewise mirror the other in an inverted chiasm, but as opposites where a hopeless situation is resolved.

  A Introduction (1:1–5) covering ten years—The past
    B Naomi and her daughters-in-law (1:6–18)
      C Meeting at the city entrance (1:19–22)
      C' Meeting at city entrance (4:1–12)
    B' Naomi and the townswoman (4:13–17)
  A' Epilogue, covering ten generations—The future (4:18:22)[96]

Looking at chiasms in more detail, we find they are inverted on the chapter level. Instead of moving in a strictly linear pattern the "concentric pattern first moves forward to a certain spot, then backwards again in a regular step by step fashion which corresponds in certain definable respects to its beginning."[97] Inversion of this type tends to treat matters of special importance, as the meat in the sandwich, so as to speak and place it in the central position. Chapter 1 centers around the fact that Naomi was too old to bear children and has a very definite inverted chiastic structure.

---

96. Ziegler, *Ruth*, 363.
97. Wendland, "*Structural Symmetry*," Para. 33.

A Famine (1:1)
  B Emigration from Bethlehem (1:1)
    C Naomi = pleasant (1:2–5)
      D Leaving Moab for Bethlehem (1:6–7)
        E Naomi's speech (1:8)
          F Naomi kisses Orpah and Ruth good-bye (1:9)
            G All weep loudly (1:9)
              H Naomi's inability to conceive (1:11–13)
            G' All weep loudly (1:14)
          F' Orpah kisses Naomi good-bye (1:14–15)
        E' Ruth's speech (1:16–18)
      D' Entering Bethlehem from Moab (1:19)
    C' Naomi = pleasant (1:20–21)
  B' Immigration to Bethlehem (1:22)
A' Barley harvest (1:22)

Chapter 2 which shows how the Moabite Ruth was received in Bethlehem and which focuses on Boaz's conversation with Ruth has its own chiastic structure. It can be shown in a simplified form as:

A Ruth and Naomi (2:2–3)
  B Boaz and the reapers (2:4–7)
    C Boaz and Ruth (2:8–14)
  B' Boaz and the reapers (2:15–16)
A' Naomi and Ruth (2:17–22)

Or expanded:

A Introducing Boaz and the opportunity for grace 2:1–3
  B Gracious greeting by Boaz 2:4
    C Ruth identified and her request for grace 2:5–7
      D Boaz begins to grant favor, Ruth asks why 2:8–10
      D' Boaz answers, God is repaying, Ruth asks for more 2:11–13
    C' Boaz's extraordinary invitation and protection 2:14–16
  B' Ruth recipient of Boaz's generosity 2:17
A' Recounting how she found favor 2:18–23[98]

---

98. Luter, *Chiastic Structure*, 53. Note the table is simplified from the original.

Similarly, in chapter 4.

A Boaz summons the witnesses (4:1–2)
  B Boaz's presentation of his case to Joe Blow (4:3–5)
    C Joe Blow rejects the estate and Ruth (4:6–8)
  B' Boaz's interpretation of the case to the elders (4:9–10)
A' Boaz blessed by the witnesses (4:11–12).

Another way of looking at the structure through its artistry is to consider the word plays which the comments have already drawn attention to. As Campbell says, the author, "seems to have had an utter fascination with words."[99] The book uses many different literary devices such as assonance, e.g., barley, gate and the suggested unit of measure in 3:17. The storyteller takes a word in a particular scene such as "return" and then repeats it through the scene and then takes it up again to link the scene to later scenes. It can also extend beyond words to phrases, e.g.

- 2:2 In whose eyes I find favor,
- 2:10 Why have I found such favor in your eyes, and
- 2:13 May I continue to find favor in your eyes.

Important to the artistic structure of Ruth are the words that mainly only occur twice, but at least infrequently which round out the story where the difficulty in the first reference foreshadows the resolution later in the story. While most are mentioned in the comments, here is a list:

- Lad(s) 1:5; 4:16,
- Hesed 1:8; 2:20; 3:10,
- Security 1:9; 3:1,
- Cleave 1:14; 2:8, 21, 23,
- Lodge 1:16; 3:13,
- Brought back/restorer 1:21; 4:15,
- Empty 1:21; 3:17,
- Covenant brother/Covenant circle 2:1; 3:2,
- Substance/worthy 2:1; 3:11 cf. 4:11,

---

99. Campbell, *Ruth*, 13.

- Take note 2:10; 2:19, and
- Wing(s) 2:12; 3:19.[100]

So, whichever way you look at the book, it is clearly anything but a simple linear story but, "an artistic creation of very high order."[101]

---

100. Campbell, *Ruth*, 13.
101. Rauber, *Literary*, 35.

Bibliography

Alexander, Ralph H. "Yābam." In *Theological Wordbook of the Old Testament*, by Gleason L Archer, Bruce K Waltke R. Lloyd Harris, 359–60. Chicago: Moody, 1980.

Allen, Ronald B. "ʿāmad." In *Theological Wordbook of the Old Testament*, by Gleason L Archer, Bruce K Waltke R. Lloyd Harris, 673–74. Chicago: Moody, 1980.

Angel, Hayyim. "*A Midrashic View of Ruth: Amidst a Sea of Ambiguity.*" http://www.myjli.com/strength/index.php/2016/05/07/a-midrashic-view-of-ruth-amidst-a-sea-of-ambiguity/.

———. "*A Woman of Valour has been Found.*" http://download.yutorah.org/2019/1053/Shavuot_To-Go_-_5779_Rabbi_Angel.pdf.

Australian Government. "*Royal Commission into Institutional Responses to Child Sexual Abuse—Religious Institutions.*" https://www.childabuseroyalcommission.gov.au/religious-institutions.

Barclay, William. *The Plain Man Looks at the Lord's Prayer*. London: Fontana, 1964.

Bauber, D.F. "Literary Values in the Bible: The Book of Ruth." *Journal for Biblical Literature* 89, No. 1 (1970): 27–37.

Blank, Sheldon H. "The Curse, Blasphemy, The Spell, And the Oath." *Hebrew Union College Annual* 23, no. 1 (1950): 73–95.

Block, Daniel I. *Ruth: a discourse analysis of the hebrew bible*. Grand Rapids: Zondervan, 2015.

Bonhoeffer, Dietrich. *The Cost of Discipleship*. London: SCM, 1959.

Borowski, Oded. *Agriculture in Iron Age Israel*. University Park: Eisenbrauns; Reprint edition, 2009.

———. "Agriculture in Iron Age Israel." *A dissertation submitted in partial fulfilment of the requirements for the degree of Doctor of Philosophy (Near eastern Studies)*. University of Michigan, 1979.

Bowling, Andrew. "Ḥārad." In *Theological Wordbook of the Old Testament*, by Gleason L Archer, Bruce K Waltke R. Lloyd Harris, 321–22. Chicago: Moody, 1980.

Bruce, F. F. *The Book of Acts*. London: Marshall, Morgan and Scott, 1954.

Bush, Frederic. *Ruth/Esther*. Dallas: Word, 1996.

Campbell., Edward E. Jr. *Ruth: a new translation with introduction, notes, and commentary*. Edited by David Noel Freedman William Foxwell Albright. Vol. 7. New York: Doubleday and Company, 1975.

Bibliography

Carr, G. Lloyd. "Šālēm." In *Theological Wordbook of the Old Testament.*, by Gleason L Archer, Bruce K Waltke R. Lloyd Harris, 930-932. Chicago: Moody, 1980.

Coppes, Leonard J. "ʿānâ." In *Theological Wordbook of the Old Testament*, by Gleason L Archer, Bruce K Waltke R. Lloyd Harris, 679-84. Chicago: Moody, 1980.

———. "ʿānâin." In *Theological Wordbook of the Old Testament*, by Gleason L Archer, Bruce K Waltke R. Lloyd Harris, 679-84. Chicago: Moody, 1980.

———. "Nāgaʿ." In *Theological Wordbook of the Old Testament*, by Gleason L Archer, Bruce K Waltke R. Lloyd Harris, 551-52. Chicago: Moody, 1980.

———. "Nûaḥ." In *Theological Wordbook of the Old Testament*, by Gleason L Archer, Bruce K Waltke R. Lloyd Harris, 562-63. Chicago: Moody, 1989.

———. "Qārâ." In *Theological Wordbook of the Old Testament*, by Gleason L Archer, Bruce K Waltke R. Lloyd Harris, 813-14. Chicago: Moody, 1980.

———. "Qûm." In *Theological Wordbook of the Old Testament*, by Gleason L Archer, Bruce K Waltke R. Lloyd Harris, 793-4. Chicago: Moody, 1980.

———. "Rāgal." In *Theological Wordbook of the Old Testament*, by Gleason L Archer, Bruce K Waltke R. Lloyd Harris, 829-30. Chicago: Moody, 1980.

David, Hillel ben: "*The Legimimacy of King David.*" https://www.betemunah.org/legitimate.html.

Eskenazi, Tamara Cohn, Tikva Frymer-Kensky. *Ruth*. Philiadelphia: Jewish Publication Society, 2011.

Evans, Mary J. *Judges and Ruth*. London: Inter-Varsity, 2017.

Finberg, Charles L. "ʿāmēṣ." In *Theological Wordbook of the Old Testament*, by Gleason L Archer, Bruce K Waltke R. Lloyd Harris, 53-54. Chicago: Moody, 1980.

FoodBank. *Foodbank Hunger Report 2020*. No publication details.

Gilchrist, Paul R. "Yāṣāʾ." In *Theological Wordbook of the Old Testament*, by Gleason L Archer, Bruce K Waltke R. Lloyd Harris, 394. Chicago: Moody, 1970.

Ginzberg, Louis. *Boaz*. Vol. 3, in *Jewish Encyclopedia*, edited by Isidore Singer, 278. New York: Funk and Wagnells, 1906.

Glueck, Nelson. *Hesed in the Bible*. Translated by Alfred Gottschalk. Eugene: WIPF and Stock, 1967.

Grant, Reg. "Literary Structure in the Book of Ruth." *Bibliotheca Sacra* 148 (1991): 424-41.

Hals, Ronald M. *The Theology of the Book of Ruth*. Philadelphia: Fortress, 1969.

Hamilton, Victor P. "Šadday." In *Theological Wordbook of the Old Testament*, by Gleason L Archer, Bruce K Waltke R. Lloyd Harris, 907. Chicago: Moody, 1980.

———. "Šāḥat." In *Theological Wordbook of the Old Testament*, by Gleason L Archer, Bruce K Waltke R. Lloyd Harris, 917-18. Chicago: Moody, 1980.

———. "Pāgaʿ." In *Theological Wordbook of the Old Twstament*, by Gleason L Archer, Bruce K Waltke R. Lloyd Harris, 714-15. Chicago: Moody, 1980.

———. "Pāqad ." In *Theological Wordbook of the Old Testament*, by Gleeson J Harris, Bruce K Waltke R. Laird Archer. Chicago: Moody, 1986.

Harris, R. Laird. "Gāʾal." In *Theological Wordbook of the Old Testament*, by Gleason L Archer, Bruce K. Waltke Robert Laird Harris, 144-45. Chicago: Moody, 1980.

———. "Ḥsd." In *Theological Wordbook of the Old Testament*, by Gleason L Archer, Bruce K. Waltke R. Laird Harris, 305-7. Chicago: Moody, 1980.

Harrison, R.K. *Introduction to the Old Testament*. London: Tyndale, 1970.

Hartley, John E. "Qāwâ." In *Theological Wordbook of the Old Testament*, by Gleason L. Archer, Bruce K Waltke R. Laird Harris, 791-2. Chicago: Moody, 1980.

Hubbard, Robert L. *The Book of Ruth*. Grand Rapids: William B. Eerdmans, 1988.

Bibliography

Kaiser, Walter C. "Lāpat." In *Theological Wordbook of the Old Testament*, by Gleason L. Archer, Bruce K Waltke R. Laird Harris, 481. Chicago: Moody, 1980.

Kalland, Earl S. "Dā'ēb." In *Theological Wordbook of the Old Testament*, by Gleason L Archer, Bruce K. Waltke R. Laird Harris, 177–78. Chicago: Moody, 1980.

Luter Boyd, Richard O. Rigsby. "The Chaistic Structure of Ruth 2." *Bulletin for Biblical Research* 3 (1993): 49–58.

Martens, Elmer A. "bô'." In *Theological Wordbook of the Old Testament*, by Gleason L Archer, Bruce K Waltke R. Lloyd Harris, 93–95. Chicago: Moody, 1980.

Masterman, E.W.G. "Barley." In *International Standard Bible Dictionary*, edited by Geoffrey W. Bromiley, 431. Grand Rapids: William B. Eerdmans, 1979.

Meir, Tamar. *Ruth: Midrash and Aggadah*. https://jwa.org/encyclopedia/article/ruth-midrash-and-aggadah.

Merrill, Eugene H. "Paul's Use of "About 450 Years" in Acts 13:20." *Bibliotheca sacra*, 1981: 246–57.

Moore, Michael S. "Ruth." In *Joshua, Judges Ruth*, by Cheryl A Brown, Michael S Moore J Gordon Harris, 291–373. Grand Rapids: Baker, 3000.

Morris, Leon. "Ruth." In *Judges, Ruth*, by Leon Morris, Arthur E Cundall, 217–318. London: Tyndale, 1968.

———. *Testaments of Love*. Grand Rapids: Eerdmans, 1981.

Mounce, Bill. *The Hebrew Order Teaches Covenant*. https://www.biblicaltraining.org/library/hebrew-order-teaches-covenant/biblical-theology/van-pelt-blomberg-schreiner.

Oswalt, John N. "Bāḥar." In *Theological Wordbook of the Old Testament*, by Gleason L Archer, Bruce K Waltke R. Lloyd Harris, 100–101. Chicago: Moody, 1980.

———. "Bārak." In *Theological Wordbook of the Old Testament*, by Gleason L Archer, Bruce K Waltke R. Lloyd Harris, 131–32. Chicago: Moody, 1980.

———. "Gābar." In *Theological Wordbook of the Old Testament*, by Gleason L Archer, Bruce K Waltke R. Lloyd Harris, 148–49. Chicago: Moody, 1980.

Pollock, S. "God and a Heretic." In *The Dimensions of Job*, by Nahum N Glatzer. New York: Schocken, 1969.

Pritchard, James B. *The Ancient Near East Volume 1*. Princton: Princeton University Press, 1958.

Rashi. *Commentary on the Chumash. (Bereshit with Targum Onkelos haphtora)*. Translated by Rabbi Silbermann. Jerusalem: Sliberman family, 5745.

Richardson, A. "Grace." In *Theological Wordbook of the Bible*, edited by A Richardson. London: SCM, 1977.

Richardson, A. "Hesed." In *A Theological Wordbook of the Bible*, edited by A. Richardson. London: SCM, 1977.

Sakenfeld, Katherine Doob. *The Meaning of Hesed in the Hebrew Bible, A New Enquiry*. Eugine: Wipf and Stock, 2002..

———. *Ruth*. Louisville: John Knox, 1999

Samson H, Levey, trans. *Targum to Ruth*. n.d.

Stigers, Harold G. "gûr." In *Theological Wordbook of the Old Testament*, by Gleason L Archer, Bruce K Waltke R. Lloyd Harris, 330–31. Chicago: Moody, 1980.

Theology of Work Project. *"Gleaning (Leviticus 19:9–10)"*. https://www.theologyofwork.org/old-testament/leviticus-and-work/holiness-leviticus-1727/gleaning-leviticus-19910.

Trible, Phyllis. *God and the Rhetoric of Sexuality*. Philadelphia: Fortress, 1986.

Bibliography

Ulrich, Dean R. *From Famine to Fullness*. Phillipsburg: P&R, 2007.
Unknown. *Babylonian Talmud, Bava Batra*. https://www.sefaria.org/Bava_Batra?lang=bi
———. *Midrash Rabbah*. Translated by L. Rabinowitz. Vol. Ruth. London: Soncino, 1977.
———. *Midrash Tanchuma*. https://www.sefaria.org/Midrash_Tanchuma?lang=bi.
———. *Mishna Torah*. n.d. https://www.sefaria.org/Mishneh_Torah,_Forbidden_Intercourse?lang=bi&p2=Mishneh_Torah%2C_Forbidden_Intercourse.12.23&lang2=e.
———. *Zohar Chadash, Midrash Rut*. n.d. ttps://www.sefaria.org/Zohar_Chadash%2C_Midrash_Rut?lang=bi.
Weber, Carl. "Ḥayil." In *Theological Wordbook of the Old Testament*, by Gleason L Archer, Bruce K Waltke R. Lloyd Harris, 271–72. Chicago: Moody, 1980.
Weber, Carl. "Hûm." In *Theological Wordbook of the Old Testament*, by Gleason L Archer, Bruce K Waltke R. Lloyd Harris, 212–3. Chicago: Moody, 1980.
Weinstein, Brien. "Naomi's Mission A Commentary on the Book of Ruth." *Jewish Bible Quarterly* 32, no. 1 (2004). 46–50.
Wendland, Ernst B. *"Structural Symmetry and Its Significance in the Book of Ruth."* http://essays.wls.wels.net:8080/bitstream/handle/123456789/777/WendlandRuth.pdf?sequence=1&isAllowed=y.
Wiersbe, Warren W. *Be Committed*. Colorado Springs: David C Cook, 2008.
Williams, Jay G. *Understanding the Old Testament*. Hauppauge: Barron's Educational Series, 1972.
Wiseman, Donald J. "Ḥelqâ." In *Theological Wordbook of the Old Testament*, by Gleason L Archer, Bruce K Waltke R. Lloyd Harris, 292–93. Chicago: Moody, 1980.
Yamauchi, Edwin. "Ḥādal." In *Theological Wordbook of the Old Testament*, by Gleason L Archer, Bruce K Waltke R. Lloyd Harris, 265. Chicago: Moody, 1980.
Yamauchi, Edwin. "Ḥēn." In *Theological Wordbook of the Old Testament*, by Gleason L Archer, Bruce K Waltke R. Lloyd Harris, 302–4. Chicago: Moody, 1980.
Yamauchi, Edwin. "Šāḥâ." In *Theological Wordbook of the Old Testament*, by Gleason L Archer, Bruce K Waltke R. Lloyd Harris, 914–15. Chicago: Moody, 1980.
Ziegler, Yael. *Ruth, From Alienation to Monarchy*. New Milford: Maggid, 2015.

www.ingramcontent.com/pod-product-compliance
Lightning Source LLC
Chambersburg PA
CBHW051056160426
43193CB00010B/1211